Professional Communications
– for a change

Professional Communications
– for a change

Hans Johnsson

Prentice Hall

New York · London · Toronto · Sydney · Tokyo · Singapore

First published 1990 by
Prentice Hall International (UK) Ltd,
66 Wood Lane End, Hemel Hempstead,
Hertfordshire, HP2 4RG
A division of
Simon & Schuster International Group

Data converted by Columns of Reading
Printed and bound in Great Britain by
BPCC Wheatons Ltd, Exeter

Library of Congress Cataloging-in-Publication Data

Johnsson, Hans.
  Professional communications – for a change/by Hans
  Johnsson.
    p. cm.
  Includes bibliographical references.
  ISBN 0–13–728908–1 : $28.95
  1. Business communication.
  2. Communication in management.
I. Title.
HF5718.J57   1990   89–37569
658.4′5 — dc20   CIP

British Library Cataloguing in Publication Data

Johnsson, Hans
  Professional communications – for a change.
  1. Business firms. Management. Communication
  I. Title
  658.4′5

ISBN 0–13–728908–1

---

1 2 3 4 5 94 93 92 91 90

Contents

v

Contents

Contents

Contents

Contents

Preface

Readers will probably get different benefits from this book on communications, especially business-to-business communications. Some will find the checklists and practical advice useful, others may appreciate finding diverse notions about business and professional communications coordinated into one system.

A primary inspiration has been Dr Joseph E. Bachelder of Princeton, NJ who, through his Center for Marketing Communications, put a new degree of professionalism into business-to-business communications. Without his advice and suggestions, spiced with a generous helping of warm humour, this book would never have left the vague concept stage.

'Bad poets borrow', T.S. Eliot has said, 'good poets steal.'

> In what follows I have tried to be, in this respect anyway, a good poet, taking what I have needed from others and made it shamelessly my own. But such thievery is in great part general and undefined, an almost unconscious process of selection, absorption, and reworking, so that after a while one no longer quite knows where one's argument comes from, how much of it is one's own and how much is others. . . . To attach specific names to specific passages would be arbitrary or libelous. (Clifford Geertz, *Islam Observed*, University of Chicago Press, 1971)

Many good friends and colleagues have paved the way and shared their thoughts generously with me. I hope they feel they are recognized in the paragraph above, written by an anthropologist who has entered this book through Mick, my wife and supporter. My thanks go to her and to all known and unknown contributors.

1

A network of
human relations

In this chapter the reader will find a broad presentation of the
main ideas that will be put into practice in the rest of the
book.

The chapter serves as an introduction to the basic concepts
and enables the reader to put all the specifics into a coherent
framework. It will help the reader gain maximum benefit from
the time spent with the applications-oriented chapters later in
the book.

The need for businesses to communicate

Today there is a strong need for businesses to communicate, both ways, to listen to the environment and to make their story known and appreciated. This need has existed for as long as business has existed, but there are aspects that are specific to our time. We find challenges that have never before been faced by business; opportunities that have never been available before.

The tasks may seem to be more complicated today than they used to be. A wider spectrum of issues and subjects is introduced, a broader range of very different audiences is involved, more media and channels can be considered than ever before. How do we handle the situation? How do we structure it? How do we *manage* it?

Communicate – with whom?

An extensive list of groups for business to communicate with has long existed. More recently, new trends have appeared, which have made it clear to business leaders of old and new schools that professional, target-oriented communication is a matter of more than passing interest. It is a condition for strong, successful business enterprises.

Business has always had a strong need to communicate with its *customers*. Much of the traditional literature on business communications concentrates on this contact area, whether book titles refer to advertising, public relations or, more recently, market communications. This need has not diminished. Active customer pressure groups, consumer legislation and new, stricter guidelines and regulations on product responsibility make it more important than ever to stay in close touch with market forces. Indeed, the term 'market forces' itself is taking on a new meaning, that is more significant than ever.

There has always been a need for a company to communicate with its *employees*, beyond the matter-of-fact instructions necessary to get a job done. In today's business climate this is more urgent than ever. Blue-collar and white-collar staff are better trained and educated. There is a demand for other forms of reward than money alone. Staff costs are rising in real terms. This in itself is a reason for business to provide more information about the state of the company and its financial development. Meeting employee demands for more information is not a burden, it is an opportunity. Good

2

employee communications are likely to increase performance and results as well as the individual's sense of self-fulfilment. If properly handled, such programmes can contribute to releasing energy, ambitions and ideas, which might otherwise lie dormant. They will enrich the whole work process to the benefit of all parties involved.

When a company grows to a size that requires professional managers, rather than the owners themselves, there is a need for communication between the company as an entity and its *owners*. In today's big companies, with ownership distributed over thousands of shareholders, this need is growing fast. If the ownership category is defined to include the banks and other bodies with a financial stake in the company, communication with this group becomes an important and ongoing company responsibility.

The *local community* has always, to a certain degree, felt an involvement in the companies within its boundaries. Local companies are valuable to a community. They provide rates and taxes, both as companies and through their employees. They offer additional job opportunities through peripheral services, transportation, catering, etc. They are, in some cases, the reason why a town exists. All in all, towns have been anxious to make businesses feel welcome and make them want to stay. In recent years this largely positive attitude has been mixed with other considerations, such as environmental concerns. The responsibilities put upon local authorities, both from its citizens and from central government, have been heavier and have forced them to take a more stringent stance. Sometimes, demands have been based on poor information or on a poor emotional climate between the company and its local community. When communications are unsatisfactory, the conflicts always turn out worse than if both sides are well informed about the other party.

Business leaders often profess to dislike the power of *central government* over individual companies and over business in general. This is true as a general political stance, but also in more specific cases, for example, in taxation, environmental or product liability areas. In other fields, such as protectionism, some business leaders may well want more government action, not less. Whatever the actual situation is for an individual company, and whether the general political trend is for increasing government influence or for deregulation, the balance of power is never static. With fluctuation as the only constant, there is a need for ongoing, planned communication between business on the one side and various government bodies on the other, and ultimately the general public.

One contact area in the government/quasi-government category is the *educational* world. The business community in many countries complains about the standard of state education. There is a lack of understanding between business and the education system. The specialized training of teachers seldom allows them to gain real-life experience outside their field of study. Most teachers have at best a vague, hearsay idea of what business and industry really are. To complement the theoretical studies of our children, it is vital for business to offer its help to the school systems. Youngsters should be able to take business into account appropriately, in selecting educational courses, in preparing for their careers and, generally, as the future electorate. Active communications programmes with schools in the local area are important to present business in a positive way, showing that business cares. It also applies to those schools and colleges to which a company can contribute specialized expertise.

There are several other important groups with which individual companies should establish good relations. Each company has to analyse for itself what these groups are. One category that practically all companies encounter from time to time, and that may even take precedence for a time over all others, are various kinds of *temporary pressure groups*. They may comprise students, employee groups, women, political or religious groups, racial minority (or majority) groups or concerned local residents. They may have views on employment practices, on working conditions, on the use of chemicals, on advertising or on environmental issues. They may have grievances or complaints against the company or they may wish to solicit company support for various causes. They tend to coalesce at short notice, often at unexpected times and places. Learning to anticipate such reactions or actions, if possible, and handle communications with such short-lived groups is a matter of growing concern to most companies. Failure to do so can have negative repercussions on company life or at least create considerable nuisance.

Communications – a two-way process

The groups we have discussed so far can be called the *contact areas* of the company. Some of them are permanent, some temporary. They can all influence the life and success of the company to varying degrees, at several vital points. It is natural for each company to start its planned communications work with a thorough analysis of which contact areas are of primary importance to it. Such an analysis must at some stage involve active participation from the chief executive of the company.

In some public relations (PR) literature these groups are called the 'publics' of a company. The word you choose may make a difference to the way you view the situation. The word 'public' tends to conjure up the image of a stage on which someone performs in front of an audience. The audience remains largely passive. This is far from the concepts used in this book. We shall use words like *communication* and *contact areas* rather than *information* and *public* to emphasize the goal of a two-way process. 'Man was created with *two* ears and *one* mouth' – the sooner we learn a lesson from this and listen twice as much as we talk, the better will we perform the tasks ahead of us.

In defining the priority contact areas we should therefore not only ask ourselves the obvious question: '*Who* do *we* want to talk with – and *why* – about *what?*', but also the much more difficult and much more searching question: '*Who* wants to talk *with us* – *why* – and about *what?*' The answer to that question could well be a significant factor in the success or failure of your company in the coming years. And yet it is a question very seldom asked – and even more rarely answered. This approach will help focus our attention on critical areas, which, if overlooked, could create serious problems. It also indicates a way to handle another of the key problems in communications today – the information overspill.

Pollution – and a solution

In most Western industrialized countries, especially in the United States, but also in Canada and Western Europe, people are exposed to a flood of messages, through an overwhelming array of media. Yet one of the complaints that many people voice today, whether as workers, consumers, students, travellers or in other roles, is that they 'don't feel informed'.

Professionals in the media and information business have traditionally tried to solve this problem by increasing the amount, the frequency, the volume or the visual impact of their messages. The result is, as could be expected, increased resistance without any measurable change in penetration. Our task must be to find other, more sophisticated ways to achieve the results we want, through selection, professional screening and closer direction of the flow of information.

Noise is sometimes defined as 'unwanted sound'. A concert, beautiful in the right circumstances, may by this definition be called noise, i.e., 'pollution', when it is performed in the wrong place, imposed upon the wrong people, at the wrong time.

Information pollution, by a similar definition, may consist of very well-designed pieces of information, but hitting the wrong targets, at the wrong time. Listening before talking can save a communicator not only money and effort, but can also save substantial amounts of bad will. The world needs communication – not misdirected information overspill.

For a reason . . .

All business communications have a purpose – or at least should have one. This is sometimes set up as a contrast to 'pure' journalism, which is then considered as information for information's sake. In the case of business communications the purpose should be defined as clearly as possible, including considerations of the recipient's needs and interests. This would lead to a true marketing concept in all business communications, not only in communicating with the market. It would be based on finding out and anticipating present and future needs and interests of the other party in a communications process. Communications activities would be screened, designed and directed with these needs in mind. If, as an example, this principle were applied to one of the standard situations of business 'PR', sending out press releases, the number of editorial wastepaper baskets around the world could be halved overnight. And it would be to the benefit of the senders as well as the recipients!

For a change . . .

A vital part of the overall purpose in all business communications is the desire to bring about change. This drive, this urge to bring about change, reflects one of the basic differences between an entre-preneurial mind and the bureaucratic mind. It should be one of the central characteristics of business and industry compared to government-led operations.

In some big business concerns today there is a risk that the flexibility, the preparedness for change, becomes stifled through too much static system thinking. Business has in many cases come to

6

side with the conservative forces of society, the side where bureaucracy should preside. Instead, other short-lived groups have come to be advocates for adaptation, for change.

The market system has always had a capacity to see new needs and to adapt its output of products and services to cater to these needs. This ability of the market system constantly to adapt, to be an advocate for change, to contribute to change, is a direct function of its ability to communicate in both directions.

The need for business to listen, to use both ears, and thus to find opportunities rather than threats in the new ideas, new needs, new ways of thinking is one of the central challenges that faces business today. It is certainly an area where communications specialists, in the deepest sense of the word, have an important role to play, a role to keep the true spirit of business alive.

We have also seen that when inflexible, government-controlled systems realize the need for change, when they look for new solutions, they open up communications as a key element of change.

Managing change – and managing for change

But also in a less general, more day-to-day sense, the purpose of the communications function is to bring about change. Each communications programme, each individual item, is introduced to create change. On a basis of known facts, attitudes, information levels, opinions, awareness patterns, the communications manager works towards the desired pattern. The path from A to B, from the 'benchmark' to the defined target, reflects change, *is* change, desired, planned change. Some of the classic difficulties in making the communications function manageable derive from the generally recognized difficulties in managing change. If there is any function in a company that has to learn the basic task of managing change, it is the communications function.

Communications by objectives – or by mechanics?

A condition for making any company function manageable is to apply management by objectives in a sensible way. The communications function is no exception. But how many PR, advertising, information or communications functions do this, and how many try, instead, to manage and budget by mechanics?

Recognizing this basic condition, the first requirement of the communications manager in making communications manageable is to focus on purpose and contact areas and to disregard channels and media for as long as possible. The important tasks for the communications manager to work with in depth should instead be as follows:

1. To keep his focus on the identification of priorities, including priority groups.
2. To find and register important awareness and attitude factors on both sides.
3. To plan and write down, as specifically as possible, the areas of common interest, and the areas of diverging interests.
4. To define the ideal situation he or she wants to reach.
5. To estimate the resources that will be required to get there – and then get going!

These tasks should be in focus long before questions of press releases or exhibits, advertising or direct mail, films or house magazines come up for consideration. A tendency to jump too fast into media technicalities, to discuss four-colour or black/white, 8 mm or video, trade press or dailies, is one of the weaknesses of communications personnel.

How many communications functions are budgeting or staffing their activities by contact area, by results to be obtained, by changes to be made? How many, instead, take the easy way out and budget by media or channels, putting advertising in one category, printed matter in another, audiovisual aids in a third, etc.?

The personality of a company

One of the recurring roles of the communications function in a company is to build and reflect the true character of the company. In fact, this goes in as an ever-present ingredient in all contact work with which a company is involved, whether or not it is channelled through the communications function as such.

The dominant message of a company is, in the long run, its 'personality', its 'character', its 'profile'. It is based on such factors as the performance of its products, the efficiency and attitudes of its staff, the availability of its services when needed. It is the sum total of its performance and the perceptions others have of its performance. The character of a company is much more than its logotype, its letterhead and its neon signs, although, sometimes, even renowned specialists in 'corporate image' tend to focus on those items.

Sometimes companies try to express their character, their lifestyle, in writing, to the benefit of the company and its many contact groups. A well-designed such description is the 'Vision and Values' of Combustion Engineering Inc., see Figure 1.1. Such codes may be helpful to the individual company as well as to business in general, as long as they do not stifle or discourage necessary change.

Business is people

Universities today are seen as institutions; they are big and static. But the word 'university' originally meant something else, signifying the totality (*universitas*) of students and teachers working together. It was a word for dynamic cooperation rather than for a static institution.

The word 'company' has a similar, deeply personal and human-related sense, originally meaning 'people who earn and share their bread together', in fellowship.

Relations between a company and its several contact groups may become institutionalized, dehumanized. In too many cases today, computers represent the company to the public and colour its image. Mechanization, automation and other '-tions' too often stand as the keynote of modern business life, rather than the simple concept of people who earn and share their bread together, in the service of other people.

Working on the communications side of a company gives us an opportunity or, rather, places a responsibility on us to make the company personal rather than institutional.

The Italian Renaissance period is sometimes defined as the period when humanity was rediscovered and relaunched, after the period of stiff, institutionalized life represented by the Church and the feudal systems of the Middle Ages. The purpose of this book is to present a revitalized communications concept and thus contribute to a renaissance of business life as a person-to-person process. It must be one of the prime concerns of business to ensure that this reality is allowed to penetrate. For an excellent expression of this concern, see Figure 1.2.

Vision and Values

Combustion Engineering, Inc.
Stamford, Connecticut

Combustion Engineering's vision is embodied in the three elements of its mission: a statement that sets the foundation for business strategies and decisions, a set of eight guiding principles by which we intend to conduct business day to day, and a list of factors that help us measure how successful we have been.

Mission Statement

Combustion Engineering's mission is to be a leading provider of engineered products, systems, and services to the worldwide power, process, and public sector markets.

In carrying out its mission, Combustion Engineering will:

- Foster an environment that encourages the professional and personal development of its employees,

- Develop and maintain long-term relationships with its clients,

- Expect management excellence, and

- Fulfill its responsibilities as a good corporate citizen in the countries and communities in which it operates.

In doing so, C-E will achieve its primary financial objective -- to create shareholder value through superior returns on capital.

Guiding Principles: How we intend to do business...

- Integrity
- Client Orientation
- Balanced Risk Taking
- Innovation
- Open Communication
- Teamwork
- Accountability
- Reward Performance

Success Factors: How we Measure Our Performance...

- Create shareholder value through superior returns on capital
- Achieve market leadership
- Provide timely and effective communication with stakeholders
- Be recognized for management excellence
- Maintain cost-effective access to worldwide capital markets
- Increase percentage of C-E's businesses with high value-added content
- Create a culture that attracts and retains quality employees

cont

Figure 1.1 *From Combustion Engineering's 'Vision and values'*
© *Combustion Engineering Inc, reprinted with permission.*

10

cont

Guiding Principles: How we intend to do business...

Integrity

Integrity is the foundation for all of our actions and heads our List of Guiding Principles. It means being honest and trustworthy in all our actions. It means dealing with employees as well as clients with respect and with ethical conduct reflecting high moral standards. It requires sincerity in our communications and actions at all times.

Integrity with clients means consistently offering sound and reliable products and services to meet their needs. It means that we will strive to solve their problems with quality products and services of fair value.

Client Orientation

It is critical for us to understand and anticipate what our clients need so we can provide products and services that solve client problems and increase client profitability. To do this we must build long-term relationships with our clients by knowing their business and listening to their concerns carefully.

Client orientation includes delivering innovative, cost justified products and services in a timely manner to exactly meet our clients' requirements, as we discharge all commitments and fulfill all promises.

Client orientation recognizes and embraces the concept that the long-term success of Combustion Engineering and its employees is directly linked to the long-term success of our clients.

Balanced Risk Taking

Today's market and competitive environment requires that we aggressively develop new products, markets, and technologies. Such opportunities may carry different degrees of risk than those associated with managing the Company in a more traditional environment. We must encourage our people to pursue such opportunities, while always utilizing good business judgement to insure that risks undertaken are balanced by the potential reward.

Innovation

Innovative, non-traditional solutions that fulfill clients' critical needs are important for differentiating us from our competitors. Therefore, we must seek opportunities to expand concepts and take new approaches to how we can improve client operations, our Company functions and individual capabilities.

To ensure that the innovation process provides value to our clients, we must understand their needs by "living in their world," listening carefully to their concerns and engaging each client in the process. The innovation process also should foster for our people an entrepreneurial atmosphere that is open to unique viewpoints, so each of us has the right and responsibility to seek out new ways to solve problems and generate opportunities.

Open Communication

Open communication requires the timely and regular sharing of knowledge that fills "misinformation" voids, builds confidence, enhances credibility, establishes trust and enables people to make decisions and seize opportunities. The process is multi-directional -- up, down, and sideways -- both in its internal and external applications; is done predominately face-to-face in honest and straight-forward fashion, and requires attentive listening and thoughtful responding.

Teamwork

Teamwork is the means for leveraging our diverse resources. Through effective collaboration and cooperation, we can ensure that our products, systems and services effectively solve our clients' problems.

While we encourage individual initiative, we recognize that shared knowledge and creativity will provide us with market opportunities and produce client benefits greater than those created by any one individual.

We must all be willing to work together as leaders, participants and supporters of teams.

Accountability

Individual accountability for commitments is an essential ingredient for business success. Accountability requires that each individual recognize and undertake timely initiatives and interactions with others -- both inside and outside the Company -- which will insure that we meet commitments, solve problems or achieve goals. We must accept accountability for our commitments with clients, business associates within the Company, suppliers, government and community agencies or other stakeholders.

Reward Performance

We reward performance that embodies our operating philosophy, our guiding principles and demonstrates commitment to quantified goals achievement. We encourage peak performance by making clear to all employees the direct linkage between individual accountability, performance and rewards. We acknowledge desired results with fair and timely rewards and recognition

8696-687

Printed in U.S.A.

PUBLIC RESPONSIBILITY

We believe there are three basic categories of possible social impact by business:

1. First is the straightforward pursuit of daily business affairs. This involves the conventional (but often misunderstood) dynamics of private enterprise: developing desired goods and services, providing jobs and training, investing in manufacturing and technical facilities, dealing with suppliers, paying taxes, attracting customers and investors, earning a profit.

2. The second category has to do with conducting business affairs in a *way* that is socially responsible. It isn't enough to successfully offer useful products. A business enterprise should, for example, employ and promote people fairly, see to their job safety and the safety of its products, conserve energy and other valuable resources, and help protect the quality of the environment — including proper handling of hazardous materials and emissions.

   We believe pursuit of environmental quality also includes providing products responsive to the need for lower equipment noise levels, compliance with reasonable emissions standards, and safe operating characteristics. We continually monitor the impact of Caterpillar products on the environment — striving to minimize any potentially harmful aspects.

3. The third category relates to initiatives beyond our operations, such as helping solve community problems. To the extent our resources permit — and if a host country or community wishes — we will participate selectively in such matters. Each corporate facility is an integral part of the community in which it operates. Like individuals, it benefits from character building, health, welfare, educational, and cultural activities. And like individuals, it also has citizen responsibilities to support such activities.

All Caterpillar employees are encouraged to take part in public matters of their individual choice. Further, it is recognized that employee participation in political processes — or in organizations that may be termed "controversial" — can be public service of a high order.

Just as Caterpillar supports the notion of *individual* participation, it may, to the extent legally permissible, support committees aimed at encouraging political contributions — by *individuals*. However, the *company itself* won't make contributions to political parties or candidates — even in municipalities, states, or nations which may permit such practices.

Where its experience can be helpful, Caterpillar will offer recommendations to governments concerning legislation and regulation. Further, the company will selectively analyze and take public positions on *issues*, when our experience can add to the understanding of such issues.

Overall, it's our intention that Caterpillar's business activities make good social sense . . . and that Caterpillar's social activities make good business sense.

Figure 1.2 *From Caterpillar's 'A code of worldwide business conduct and operating principles'*
Caterpillar, Inc, reproduced with permission.

The Japanese company Canon confirms this view in a corporate mission statement published in 1988 in the following words:

In today's world, fragmented by political, economic, religious, cultural, and other borders, private enterprise has a special niche to fill. Private enterprise can reach beyond these divisions, provide a world-wide perspective on issues, and bring people together.

After all, all contacts between a company and its employees, between a company and its customers, between a company and the local authorities, between a company and its bank, between a company and . . . are contacts between people.

- All company contacts are contacts between people.
- All 'public' relations are personal relations.
- All business relations are human relations.

Part I

The primary contact areas

This part will help the reader review the company's contact network and improve it as necessary for the successful growth and development of the company.

2

'It's all in the family':
Staff communications

In this chapter the reader will find advice on why good staff communications are essential, how to define key groups and recommendations and ideas on how to improve communications with the employees.

It will help the reader plan, budget, execute and evaluate result-oriented staff communications programmes.

What is the purpose?

There are many obvious reasons for a company to stay in close touch with its employees, whatever colour their collar.

A president or managing director might start talking about 'keeping the company spirit alive', 'making the employees feel like one happy family', and so on. Such expressions may serve a purpose at centenaries, inaugurations and other solemn occasions (if at all), but they are of no use as targets in designing employee communications programmes or activities.

To get down to useful, workable goals and objectives, a careful analysis of the specific needs in the specific company at a specific time is necessary. No book can do that for anyone – the process has to be based on each situation. But this chapter may help in pointing out a way to work, giving examples and suggesting a few do's and don'ts.

Who are the employees?

In most companies of any size today, all who work there – management, office staff and workers alike – are employees. Only in small companies is it still the rule for the owners to be managers as well. Otherwise management is also a group on the payroll, as are other employees. The question of sender and recipient thus takes on an interesting note. Who is who?

Accepting that all groups of employees have an important contribution to make to the sum total of the company's activities is not a question of 'making concessions', 'being soft' or 'liberal' or 'giving up the rights of the boss'. Management's overriding objective is to coordinate all resources available and ensure that they make maximum contributions to the objectives of the company. Actively listening to the views of the employees and sharing with them the problems and the good news of the company, as seen by management, can release hidden resources and engage employees in the pursuit of common goals.

Without going too deeply into the theoretical aspects of this question, the practical conclusion is that nowhere is the principle of mutuality so essential as in company–employee relations. The two-way communications concept advocated throughout this book is indispensable in this important field.

Talking down to employees from management level is not only inefficient, it is basically wrong. The overall purpose must be to create complete communications systems, where essential information is channelled 'upwards', 'downwards' and 'sideways'. Communications is not a one-way process!

Who are the key groups?

Even in a good company various groups of employees can have separate interests or different opinions on goals or on the means to reach them. Trying to identify such differences between groups and sub-groups within the total category of employees is a basic task of practical communications workmanship.

Which are the main groups to consider in your company? After specifying them clearly, you will probably find that all of them will appear, at least potentially, both as senders and receivers of important messages that can affect the future life of the company.

Management–employee communications

Even if management in most companies is not identical with the owners, it is a group with specific functions, specific interests and specific tasks, compared with other employees, workers or salaried staff. The role of management as representatives of the owners, as responsible for the long-term policies, the hiring and firing, investments and other far-reaching decisions, indicates a strong need for communications between employees and management.

Three lines of communication between management and employees
In most companies there are at least three different lines of communication between management and employees. The formal line of command–report is one, the trade union–management line is another and, in most companies, there are also active committee systems, works committees and other types.

The command/report line
In organization charts of companies, the formal *command/report line* is represented by very straight and very clear lines between very square boxes. Such organization charts have probably never

reflected reality. Today they should be looked upon with a great deal of scepticism.

The straight lines are deceptive. Everyone who has ever worked in a company knows that information – always the basic raw material of decisions and power – only in exceptional cases flows along formal structural lines. In a working communications system it is necessary to take this fact into account and to find and work with the informal patterns, as well as with the recognized formal lines.

Even when the lines do have some meaning, they represent much more discussion and consultation, more two-way flow, than they did only ten or fifteen years ago. Lines that used to signify a traditional military style of undisputed authority should today be seen more as links between members of a working team.

The trade union line

The *trade union* channel is an instrument of widely different impact in various countries and companies. Formal relationships, as discussed above, are certainly not identical from one organization to the other, but the role and importance of trade unions in the total contact system varies even more, even among Western industrial countries, where free trade unions exist. Listening to, say, an American or British manager one day and to a German or Scandinavian manager the next discussing their trade unions makes it hard to believe that they are talking of the same thing – and, indeed, they are not. But no matter how differently management and trade unions look upon each other, there are few cases where the trade union channel, if it exists, cannot be helpful as a means of communication.

Frequent, regular meetings between local union representatives and local management, at times when no immediate conflict is on the table, can help solve practical problems and ease frictions when they arise. Good trade union representatives who know the gut reactions of workers can forward suggestions and recommendations to management on a wide variety of down-to-earth practical matters.

The committee/consultation line

Consultations and cooperation in the form of multi-party *committees* on a permanent or *ad hoc* basis are used to a greater or lesser degree in more and more companies. Many industries have found, for instance, that it pays in hard cash to have the workers who are actually going to use the machines sit in on the meetings when important machine investments, factory layouts, transportation systems, etc., are decided. Listening to their practical experience and taking advice at that stage can prevent costly mistakes later, if only the regular experts and planners are put to action. Again, the principle of 'two ears and one mouth' can lead to communications that pay off – for both parties. Reports of success are mixed with less optimistic judgements of the system. Two factors seem to be crucial in order to reach reasonable results: the willingness of management to present substantial information and to do so in an understandable, clear way; and the procedure set up to pass on the information provided to employees not attending the group meetings.

Blue collar–white collar communications

If management–employees is one grouping, it is certainly not the only one. Workers–salaried employees is another traditional pattern, where increased communications could well be encouraged. While in many companies there are still noticeable differences in interests and background between these groups, in most countries the trend is strongly towards more and more common interests.

The classic differences in educational backgrounds are gradually being reduced through more extensive state education systems. Another traditional difference, job security, is being taken care of by labour market agreements and legislation in one country after the other, limiting the freedom of employers to fire without good cause and without giving notice well in advance. A third difference, the responsibility levels of salaried versus hourly-paid jobs, is being levelled out in many industries by technological development itself. For example, who could say that a salaried typist or clerk has more responsibility than a worker, handling a $20,000 piece of work in a $100,000 machine?

Bridging geographic gaps

In spite of improved telephone and transportation systems, you may well find *geographic* differences to be a factor of growing importance in designing staff communications programmes for today and tomorrow. This is true of one-plant companies, where different departments may not see each other often enough to provide natural face-to-face contacts. Multi-plant companies certainly acknowledge it as a key problem. In companies that are the result of mergers, sometimes of previously competing organizations, suspicion or ill-feeling between plants or departments may play a part for long periods of time. And in large multinational companies there are differences in culture, national traditions, language, trade union practices and wage levels that add to the geographic distance in creating blocks in the interchange of information and opinions.

Some companies have found that geographic differences, even within one country, are so great that little remains as a basis of a common interest in corporate news dissemination. What happens in one part of the structure seems to be of little concern to employees in other parts.

On the other hand, many companies find that such interest can be generated if some simple principles are applied. In Chapter 1 we emphasized that all business relations are human relations. The good communications worker can find touches of human interest in most stories, in most news items, even in most company reports. Unearthing them and giving them life may be the key to interest. And interest is not always something that comes spontaneously. Like love it may sometimes have to be fed and nurtured to yield results.

And, in fact, the bigger and more widely spread the company is, the more important it may be to open up and facilitate the communications through the organization.

Support the 'middlemen'

Groups that deserve much attention in any communications structure are the middlemen. This is true of communications between the company and outside groups. It also applies to communications between groups within the company. Two such in-the-company middleman groups are mentioned here by way of example. Others may well be relevant to your specific situation.

In manufacturing companies a key group is the foremen, the leaders of 20–30 workers. They work on the shop floor; they have immediate access to all the spontaneous reactions and feelings of their people. At the same time, they represent 'management' to their workers. The foremen may be the only management representatives they see regularly.

Several recent studies of information flows in companies indicate that this link in the chain is often weak. Unless actively stimulated, it often performs the information part of their function in a very unsatisfactory way. Both the valuable flow of comments, suggestions, complaints and ideas from the workers to management and the flow of financial, technical and marketing information that is filed down the line from management never reach further than the foreman's box. Active efforts to train foremen in the art of communicating their wealth of information both ways have been shown to be one of the most valuable investments in company communications.

Another key group of intermediaries can be found in multinational companies. As mentioned before, there are many difficulties in creating a feeling of common purpose in these companies. The need to keep in touch with national managers, responsible for the operations in a country or a region of neighbouring countries is usually recognized by headquarters. But the layer immediately below the national managers, who are supposed to carry the ball further, and who are also the base for recruiting the next generation of managers, are often neglected. In addition to specific technical and management training, they need the kind of attitude-building background information that gives them perspective and a feeling for overall corporate objectives, principles and policies.

Other groups

The above programmes are fairly general in their appeal. Several other important groups can and should be selected in each specific company. Are the women or men in your company such categories to be considered? It may be natural in your company to select age groups, groups of similar education, groups with similar jobs or other categories as a basis for temporary or permanent communications efforts.

Here are some suggestions geared to meet less general, but not less important, communications needs. When the groups have been defined, make sure that channels are provided for communications within the various groups, as well as between them, and do your utmost to assure a two-way flow throughout!

Middle management information is often sadly neglected. In small and, even more, in big companies, not least those working internationally, the role of middle management cannot be over-estimated. Keeping them in line with management thinking, philosophies and overall plans not only makes middle managers far more capable of making the right day-to-day decisions in solving big or small tasks, it also helps build confidence in the company and a feeling of being involved, of belonging to the team.

Staying in touch with junior management, listening to their views and opinions, offers a unique opportunity for top management to keep abreast of attitudes of importance to the future development of the company.

Age-related staff programmes, both for the younger members of the company and for the veterans, have a lot to offer. Meetings and other forms of communications with the young, whatever positions they have in the company, make it possible to explain company traditions and background to them. At the same time they create a channel for information in the other direction, perhaps giving management food for thought. Similar programmes with those of long service to the company offer a chance for management to express their appreciation for contributions made. At the same time, management gets a chance to listen to well-considered thoughts and advice from loyal and, with the right of seniority, independent employees.

The foremen are management's representatives on the shopfloor, but also, if they understand their role properly, a channel for letting the workers' opinions be heard in the higher echelons of management. Encouraging this part of the foremen's task and creating opportunities for such a key function in staff communications is vital in any company.

What are the specific goals of a staff communications system?

The analysis and definition of goals and targets of an improved communications system, as remarked at the outset of this chapter, are closely linked to the analysis of groups and sub-groups of prime interest. And, since we wish to obtain specific, preferably measurable results from our efforts, the starting-point must be to find out where relations within the company are not satisfactory.

Asking questions like these may help keep you on the right track:

1. Are the staff well motivated and actively engaged in the company's business? Or are there any sub-groups that do not seem to be aware of, or reasonably supportive of, the aims and long-range objectives of the company?

2. Are there undue tensions between various groups of employees, tensions that create negative effects on job results and performance?

3. Do the employees at various levels know and believe that they have access to management, directly or through a well-

established procedure, when they want to convey ideas, ask questions or make suggestions for change?

4. Is staff turnover higher than desirable in any section, plant, age group or job category?

5. Do grievances or complaints occur in any plant or among any groups of employees without management knowing about it or 'feeling it in the air' well in advance?

6. Do you have a well-established system through which your workers and office staff can suggest improvements in methods or work procedures and get credit for it?

The answers to these and similar questions can be found through relatively simple survey methods or through formal research.

The answers will point to specific areas in which staff communications can be improved. They can help establish 'benchmarks', marking the starting point of a programme, set communications goals, indicate possible improvements and help measure results that have been reached.

The staff communicator is competing for time and interest with other forms of information output, television, newspapers, etc., and with other demands on people's time. This calls for creativity and good communications skills in staff information programmes, just as well as in customer communications. If the average company put a tenth of the creative effort given to customer-directed information, such as advertising, direct mail shots and exhibits, into staff communications, many of the potential problems indicated in the questions above would never occur.

There are some subjects that may require special presentation efforts to generate and maintain interest. The financial situation of the company, the development of markets and production, investments in new facilities, product development and other vital issues are obvious topics. Even if they are or should be of interest to all employees and to their families, they cannot be presented to employees the way they would be presented to bankers or to a government committee. They deserve that extra effort to be appetizing.

Most stories, including the financial development of the company, can be made attractive. Link it to individual persons, pick up interesting, unusual details as a starter, use visuals to illustrate and drive home important points, work from personal consequences and possibilities, connect it to individual work situations – good or bad. In other words, have your communications message well anchored to the interests and situation of the recipient, be it the participant at an information meeting, the reader of the staff magazine or the casual advertising hoarding spectator.

What are the methods available?

The following items are among the projects that should be considered in a company's staff communications programme. Such project budgets may include parts and contributions of various communications methods.

Introduction programmes form an opportunity to create, right from the start, a basis of understanding between a company and its new employees. Such programmes, built up of well-prepared meetings, good audiovisual aids, basic introductory literature, visits to premises and planned personal talks should be timed in small appetizing bits over a period of three to six months, not in big chunks that tend to kill rather than create interest.

To establish the level of the programmes, start out by making a simple survey to check what your present 'six-months-old' employees know and feel about the company and measure that against a reasonable 'ideal' level. Planning this way creates an opportunity to establish a target level and thus to measure, after a while, the degree of success of your introduction programmes.

Staff meetings, lunches or dinners provide a simple way to establish contacts with and within specified priority groups or with the staff in general. They are one of the best if not the only way to create an atmosphere in which requests, desires and suggestions can be made informally and from staff members not actively involved in the more formal trade union or committee systems. If well handled they can be one of the best inputs of information.

Committees, temporary and permanent, make an integral part of company life today. They range from small *ad hoc* groups, set up to solve a specific problem, to permanent company- or factory-based works committees that meet at regular intervals as part of a long-range staff relations programme.

In planning various forms of committee work, it is easy to forget that the sessions as such are only part of the work. Providing committee members with preparatory information and following up decisions and recommendations immediately is a prime responsibility. Another requirement is close contacts between the members of a committee and the 'electorate' they represent. Budgets and plans should include provisions for these aspects.

'Open house' and other family events may contribute more than anything else to making the company human rather than institutional. The style can be both big, amusement park-type events that many tend to associate with the 'open house' and small-scale opportunities for staff and family, perhaps on a department basis, to get to know work situations, work environment, tasks, responsibilities and colleagues of the family members involved. Both styles have their advantages and may reappear on the programme at different intervals.

Staff publications are often the only form of employee communications considered. They certainly have a role to play for any company over, say, 200 employees, or for companies with several locations dispersed over wide areas, or for companies with different employee groups separated from each other by job functions, travelling assignments, racial differences or educational backgrounds.

A well-designed staff publication becomes something more than its master's voice, something more than management propaganda. Editorial policy, style and presentation aspects must be developed to satisfy all reader groups, as far as budgets and editorial capacity allow. Since staff publications are so important, much has been written on the subject.

One principle that is worth considering is frequency. If, for budget reasons, frequency has to be balanced against colour printing, stock quality, number of pages and other factors, frequency should be the favoured factor over and above most others. Anything less than monthly tends to reduce reader interest. Twice a month is even better. Some additional considerations can be found in Chapter 10.

Exhibitions are a communications medium that is often considered only as a 'sales tool'. They can, however, be used for many other types of communication tasks. A good staff communications programme can successfully include exhibitions, fixed or portable, for a variety of purposes. A new investment programme, say in a new factory or in new types of machinery, can probably best be explained through an exhibition, including charts, models, photographs and specific illustrations of 'critical points'.

A new product range on exhibit for the employees can explain competitive advantages, create confidence and also give a background to requirements for precision, delivery time demands and external finish specifications, for example.

Any products, new or old, exhibited to the employees in their 'working life situation' may help create an understanding among employees for customers' demands and for 'service-ability'.

Audiovisual programmes, combining slides and tapes or using internal radio or video, have found increasing uses in staff communications, for introducing new employees to the company, company news, field case histories or presenting the financial results of the work produced.

Contributions, financial or in the form of suitable premises or services, to the leisure-time activities, sports clubs, art circles, stamp collectors' clubs and similar activities are natural, if sometimes haphazardly run, parts of many companies' lives. Integrating these contributions into the staff communications programme makes it easier to create a system that can be respected and understood by the staff in general, expecially if administered with the advice of a staff-elected committee.

Travel programmes are one way of building better staff relations in companies with wide geographic spans. Run on a lottery basis, to avoid suspicions of bias or nepotism, such systems to make contacts between staff groups from various parts of the company empire may be especially worthwhile in international companies. In such companies they can be valuable contributions to understanding colleagues overseas. Also in companies of one country with widely-dispersed facilities they help in establishing a sense of common ground and purpose.

How to budget your staff communications programme

Staff relations have one great advantage from an efficiency point of view, an advantage that can be matched in few other contact areas: it is easy to reach the right people with each specific message. The waste factor, which makes many other communications programmes much less effective, is practically eliminated in staff relations.

The simplest way to budget your staff communications programmes is the same as the simplest way of budgeting your customer information: namely, on a percentage basis. Just as some companies budget their market communications as a percentage of sales, some companies budget their staff communications as a percentage of wage and salary outlay. Most companies could, if necessary, survive an average wage and salary increase of 1 per cent at least if that gave significant improvements in productivity and reduced losses. Test for your own company what a staff communications budget of around 1 per cent of the total sum of total staff costs could achieve and see what results you could anticipate in such areas as reduced staff turnover and absenteeism and increased creative efforts, enthusiasm and loyal work!

While the percentage method is basically unprofessional, it may serve a purpose as a very general guideline on what is reasonable. It must always be followed up by specific target-oriented project budgets, where well-defined objectives, preferably quantifiable, are projected against a background of the present situation.

Whether these programmes are budgeted formally under Communications, Personnel or various line departments is not really important. But the communications manager, working with management colleagues, should make sure that as many aspects as possible are brought up for serious consideration and for decision.

Most companies taking a good look at staff communications will probably find that there are few ways in which they can spend a pound with the same chances to get two, three or more back!

3

'Whose is it, anyway?':
Communicating with shareholders and financial groups

In this chapter the reader will find advice on why good communications with bankers, shareholders, analysts and other financial groups are essential, how to define key groups and how to set goals for financial communications programmes.

It will help the reader plan, budget, execute and evaluate result-oriented financial communications programmes.

What is the purpose?

A strong, clear identity is worth a great deal to any company, in facing any of its many contact areas. It can well be argued, however, that more long-range decisions concerning a company's future are taken in its financial contact area than in most other areas. Consequently, most companies rank their shareholders, bankers and other players in the financial networks among their top communications priorities.

In judging the credit value of an individual client, qualified bankers do not look only at the strictly financial status. They try to evaluate as many sides as possible of the individual – job performance and stability, educational background, family relationships, etc. To get as complete a picture as possible they rely not only on their own assessment of financial criteria, they also take references from people who know the applicant well. The 'image' of an applicant increases or reduces the likelihood of a loan application being granted.

The same, or similar, conditions apply to the judgements on company performance made continuously by bankers, shareholders, potential investors and other categories included in the wider 'financial community'. They are interested in a broad range of aspects of company life and development. Companies that recognize this and regularly provide the financial community with ample information on their development stand a better chance of enjoying the favours that those groups can bestow upon them.

Likewise, any company has a lot to learn by listening attentively to the financial community. Establishing and maintaining close links with it provides the company with a vital source of input from the economic environment, the background of all other activities of the company. Trends in raw material prices, availability of money, industrial development, currency movements, financial legislation and countless other fields are reflected in the discussions and statements of the professionals in the financial world.

Following these trends closely by reading the financial press, listening to public statements and maintaining good personal contacts with 'your friendly neighbourhood banker' provides a basis for decisions that no other source can replace. Anyone responsible for a company's communications programmes, should make sure that the input side of financial relations is well taken care of.

The Securities Exchange Commission and its counterparts in other countries have established strict rules and regulations concerning financial information. A company that wishes to activate its financial communications programmes would do well to familiarize itself with these rules and similar 'codes of practice' at the outset, before going any further. Since the rules change in line with changing opinion trends, make sure to get the latest issues. A consultation with the company's legal adviser may also be worth its while. Remember, however, that lawyers may be well versed in the established do's and don't's. That is their strength. There is room for creative thinking in this field, and there are approaches that are neither compulsory nor prescribed. New ideas are what makes business develop and improve. Good financial communications programmes will be generated when the legal limitations are observed and creative minds are put in motion towards the needs and oppor-tunities of the company and of the specific target groups in the financial field.

Which are the key groups?

Each individual company may, at any given moment, want to put specific stress on certain key groups in the financial field. Yet there is probably no other field where communications managers have so much to learn from the experience of colleagues in other companies. Why not give some of the known or unknown colleagues in neighbouring companies a call and set up a simple get-together for an informal exchange of views on communicating with the financial world? It can often be done, at least to some extent, without the limitations that competition normally imposes.

The group will probably agree on the importance of the following key groups.

The shareholders

Since the shareholders own the company, they ought to be well established as one of the primary contact areas. After all, 'theirs is the kingdom . . . '. But shareholders come in many shapes and sizes – the dynamic business tycoons, the established majority owners, the pension fund, the insurance company, the religious or ethnic pressure group or the legendary 'little old lady'. What are their needs for communicating with their company?

As communications manager, you should periodically take time to go through the company's shareholder register. You may not have the opportunity to get to know all the shareholders individually, but even a cursory glance may give an idea of who they are, why they have invested in your company and what they may want in the way of improved communications. It might even be worthwhile investing in a formal shareholder awareness/attitude survey.

While glancing through the register, check how it is set up for various types of communications use! Remember, it may have been set up by company accountants and lawyers to satisfy the legal minimum requirements of sending the annual report. In that case it may be less suitable for a more active communications programme. Look at it in the same way as you would a customer mailing list, as a valuable direct mail instrument.

Can it be used to make targeted mailings for specific programmes? Can institutional owners or individual owners be selected for separate mailings? Can mailings be made on a geographic basis, for example, to inform of the official opening of a local factory, local management changes or in the case of an important but locally concentrated environmentalist attack? Can mailings be made selectively on the basis of small/big shareholder categories?

The majority owners are normally well represented on the board or even in management. It means that, in most companies, they have access to all the information they need. In fact, many of the programmes you will want to consider aim at giving other interested parties a chance to close in on the advantage that the big owners probably already have. But company management may also feel that it is only fair that those who have made the major contributions and run the biggest risks should also be entitled to more detailed information or more frequent contacts. It is an area that should be entered with much care, however. Business ethics – and the law – do not look kindly on discrimination between shareholders in those matters that influence the value of the stock.

Many companies find that the major information needs are with the minor shareholders. In most publicly traded companies, this group represents a large number of shareholders, and this makes them interesting. While each one of them may exercise limited power in your company, they can, as a group, be essential to the company on critical occasions. They may also have ownership influence in other companies, so they have an opportunity to compare your company with others. Finally, in many other contexts – in daily conversations, in their business and personal lives, as voters – their influence is not measured by their voting capacity as shareholders in the company. They represent an opportunity for the company to gain added support if they become aware of the issues that their company is engaged in, and, if they feel the case deserves it, to become spokesmen of the company.

In recent years, groups of shareholders have taken on a new significance by forming action groups. These groups often represent very small minorities of the total capital invested in the company, sometimes only the minimum to get access to shareholders' meetings. They are not likely to gain a majority in the numbers' game at the annual general meeting, although this has also happened. They may advocate environmental interests, represent church groups, act as consumer spokesmen or speak for women's rights. They may take up racial minority questions or discuss the company's policies in the Third World.

Many company chairmen of the old school may feel that these issues do not belong on the annual general meeting agenda. Whether this attitude is justified or not, the rules of the game do permit the shareholders to take up issues related to the company, to ask for information and to discuss the positions taken by the board and the management of the company. Rather than complain about this, why not prepare for it?

As usual in communications, a grain of pre-action is worth a ton of reaction. Make it part of communications professionalism to anticipate possible reasons for discontent, and try to find remedies before the fire flares up.

- Are your company's policies and actions in order on such issues as racial equality, opportunities for women, fair promotion and hiring/firing practices?
- Have you personally gone through your workshops? And can you say, in all fairness, that the air quality, noise levels and other working conditions are acceptable?
- Do your work processes pollute the air or water around the factory?
- Are your products as safe as they should be?
- Have you examined, and can you vouch for, your company's contributions to the communities where it works?

If the answers to any of these questions are unsatisfactory, maybe you should take on the first task of the true communications person, to make sure that opinions and attitudes, real or potential, are channelled from important outside groups into the planning and decision-making process of the company. You will meet with difficulties in taking this approach. It may take some time before management realizes that it is much better to get such opinions fed into the company through the responsible communications person than to get them from emotional, perhaps strongly biased opinion groups. That way these opinions will be made part of the normal planning procedure, where they can be considered and acted on in the calm meeting rooms of the company, rather than in the highly charged atmosphere of a crowded annual shareholder meeting, with ambitious journalists eager to quote every word that flows from one side or the other.

The best way to handle action groups at AGMs is to try to run the company in a way that gives little reason for emotional shareholder action.

Now, no company is perfect and no company can be expected to please every group that may have an opinion on the company. As long as the company has done its homework and is well prepared, it has a far better chance of coming out of a debate unscathed. It may even be better to take the initiative and raise sensitive issues before others do. If the company has made mistakes, explain the reasons why and outline the measures the company has taken to avoid repeating the same mistakes. If the company is aware of problems, such as the working conditions in some of its workshops, explain why it may take some time to improve them, explain how it will affect the profitability of the company and the plans to invest or modify that you have adopted or have in mind.

If there are valid reasons why some demands cannot be met, or why it would even be wrong to meet them, let them be known. Most of the shareholders will respect the company's firm stand. What is advocated throughout this book is not that a company should be governed by the whims of all kinds of expressed or anticipated opinions. However, it is an important role of the communications function to be aware of attitudes and opinions towards the company among important contact groups and to make sure that they considered and evaluated together with their possible consequences, in the decision-making process.

Potential investors

When studying market communications tasks, we do not limit ourselves to those who are already customers. We also look to potential customers. Sometimes, in fact, one has the feeling that a company is so concerned with gaining new customers that it forgets its existing supporters.

In the financial field it may be as important for a company to make sure that potential investors are given due consideration. This is true not only when the company anticipates future capital requirements but also to earn a general reputation as an honest, open-minded company. A case in point, and a touchstone, could be when problems arise. A note of caution in such a situation will do a company a lot of good in terms of confidence and reliability or, even more important, in avoiding charges of deception or misguided optimism.

In times of anticipated growth, with subsequent needs for new capital, the company may want to take a systematic approach to gain increased recognition among potential investors. When the growth – or at least the financing – is expected to take place in the domestic market, the communications efforts will follow a well-established pattern. Who are the potential investors? What do we have to offer? Which media can be used to reach them?

Provided the communications specialists are involved in the job in time, such programmes can be put together successfully, and with reasonable input of communications creativity, so that full impact can be achieved. The main risk is – as in so many other cases – that the 'technicians', lawyers, financial managers and top management keep their plans secret from the communications manager instead of utilizing his or her contributions and advice from the very first stages.

More demanding is the job of preparing the ground for expansions that are to be financed abroad. Not only are international legal requirements much more complex, but also the communications aspects are infinitely more complicated. Common sense – the communications manager's most important asset – will be invaluable in this situation. But, since his or her common sense has been developed and conditioned under a different set of circumstances, it cannot serve as the sole guideline. Local professional advice is required. The bank involved will probably be able to suggest good financial PR counsel. If not, or to have a choice, the professional PR association of the country can be of service, likewise the advertising agency, or friends in the business press, if they can be consulted without fear of leaks.

Banks and financial institutions

Few companies live on their own financial resources, share capital and generated profits alone. The vast majority of companies are dependent on borrowed capital to a considerable extent. The banks and financial institutions that provide these funds have a substantial interest in being well informed about the companies they support – they carry a risk, on their own behalf and as representatives of their depositors. This interest, as we have already noted, goes beyond the balance sheets and the profit and loss accounts.

Some questions financial experts may want to ask about the company, in addition to the figures, are as follows:

1. Who are the managers, their professional capabilities, their personalities, background and beliefs, their ability to create enthusiasm and cooperation from the staff?

2. What are the ideas and philosophy of the company? How well does it see changes in the continuous flow of events, and how well does it react or, preferably, pre-act to such changes?

3. What is the general 'image' of the company as an employer, as a local citizen, among the customers and among competitors?

These are just a few questions that suggest areas of interest to be considered in the communications flow between a company and its bankers.

If the subject matter is wider than many financial managers of the old school sometimes think, so is the network of contacts within the bank. Although banks, by tradition and regulation, are fairly tightly controlled institutions, with a lot of decision-making concentrated to the top, there is also a lot of very important preparatory work performed by a wide group of staff within the bank. The opinions and views of this wide group of assistants and specialists may considerably affect the development of major and minor facets of bank–client relations.

In building up an improved communications system for a company, it is certainly worthwhile to take some time, together with the company's financial department, to list who in the bank deals with the company's matters.

1. List them by name, if possible. If not, at least by function and department; or combine and create a list that is designed gradually to become increasingly specific and thus to create deeper and wider coverage.

2. Use this list actively for mailing of interesting news, for invitation to 'open house' or informal get-togethers or as a checklist for personal contacts.
3. Establish which information sources they use and appreciate.
4. Find out what areas of the company they know well and what areas are not adequately covered. What do they know about your market, about your product development, about your internal training programmes, about your competition?

Again, do not limit yourselves to informing them – make sure that you establish the right attitude and the proper channels to listen to them as well. They are in contact with many other companies; they have an ocean of information that could substantially help your company make the right decisions or pull in the right directions. They can estimate your achievements compared to other companies and come up with ideas and advice, not only in the field of financing but in such areas as administration, staffing and even marketing. A bank can supply a lot more than money, and a banker is also a human being.

Bank relations, like other business relations, in the last resort are human relations.

Financial analysts, brokers and stock exchange staff

If your company's shares are traded publicly, you will want to establish good contacts with those important middlemen between you and the investing public.

Throughout this book you will find an emphasis on making communications a serious business, far from the standard caricatures of 'PR stunts'. In few areas is this basic thinking so important as in broker/stock exchange communications. You will certainly be interested in creating a favourable view of your company, but nothing can be more damaging to a company's image, in the long run, than trying to deceive the stock market. Attracting investor capital under false or exaggerated 'information' programmes invariably hits back at the company in reduced confidence – or in court action!

The Securities Exchange Commission and corresponding regulatory bodies in other countries have established firm rules, all aiming at protecting the investors. These rules form a minimum level of behaviour, but not necessarily an optimum. They are indispensable as a base, but the wise company tries to do better than the minimum.

One of the critical aspects in much of a company's communications work, and definitely in stock market relations, is timing. Giving information that influences the evaluation of a company's shares to one before another is a cardinal sin that cannot be forgiven, no matter how permissive a society can become in other respects. In international companies it should also be remembered that telecommunications travel faster than the sun. Information released after one stock exchange has closed may hit another in full trading. Maybe companies should take a lesson from the ministers of finance or presidents of central banks who regularly release their changes in credit policy, interest rates and currency de- or revaluations during weekends.

For most companies, the very dramatic moments are few. Most company presidents share with their communications managers the view that the company fares better, the fewer those dramatic moments are. If they occur, they have to be handled professionally. If they can be avoided, so much the better. And the best way to avoid sudden outbursts is to keep in close touch, listen carefully and provide continuous, reliable information on the company's life. Gradual and factual information keeps the stock market continuously aware of changes in the structure, market development and profit situation and provides a basis of understanding that breeds confidence. This confirms again that stock market communications is as far from old-fashioned PR clichés as anything can be.

What are the specific goals of a financial communications programme?

There are cases in a company's life in which financial relations become crucial, where what is said, how it is said and when it is said can be a matter of life and death to the company. In those cases it is vital that there is complete understanding and full confidence between top corporate management and the communications management.

Fortunately, these cases are not frequent in most companies. If they are, something is probably wrong with the company or at least with its communications work. But there are other instances which, while not of the same order of emergency, require complete professional control of methods, media and message. In those instances, it is vital to formulate specific goals that consider all the aspects.

Mergers

A merger (see also Chapter 8) between two companies is one such instance. While mergers are seldom the result of a sudden, unpredicted whim from the company boardroom, they become infinitely more difficult to handle if the information aspects are treated as if they were.

Any merger is a difficult operation, even if the communications process is handled to perfection. If it is not, it may be doomed from the start. Many mergers have become more difficult to handle than they need have been, because of poor communications planning, often because the communications staff have been involved too late.

It is surprising how often lawyers and financial staff work for weeks or months on the legal and financial aspects of a merger. Their consultants, merchant bankers, brokers and legal advisers are allowed to charge exorbitant sums in fees for their no doubt valuable contributions. The communications staff, on the other hand, are often informed at the last moment and their work should preferably be free or at very low cost! At best it can be interpreted as a flattering, although not necessarily well-advised, expression of confidence in the ability and good-will of the communications function.

A conventional way to manage a merger is to keep all contacts secret, to negotiate in closed hide-aways and to deny all rumours until all signatures are on all documents. Then a communiqué is released with the background and all the reasons, such as better utilization of common resources, efficiency advantages of a unified approach, strengthened position on distant or domestic markets, etc.

While this is a very easy way to handle a merger, it is not necessarily one that can always be used. The growing demand for consultation with parties other than the owners, e.g., the local communities concerned, the employees and central government bodies make it especially necessary to plan the communications aspects of a merger with much more penetration and with a much wider outlook than just deciding the right time for the press release.

The communications goals of a merger are based on a number of questions:

41

Question	Effects
How well are the companies known?	Decides the dimensions of the programme.
How will the staffs of the two companies be affected (lay-offs, transfers, immediate/long-range management changes)?	Decides the degree of consultation and the 'temperature' of the communications programme.
How will the markets be affected?	Decides how customers/resellers should be informed.
What financial consequences are expected?	Decides the scope and content of the shareholder, banker, stockmarket communications.
Reallocation of research/ administration/manufacturing resources?	Decides how to inform state and local authorities concerned.
What is the intended result of the merger?	Decides how the corporate identity of the new company should be established.

Asking these questions, and trying to work on them from all possible angles, gives the new company a much better chance to work through the first period after the merger in a satisfactory way.

Other 'special events'

Situations similar to mergers are: rumours of take-over bids, sudden changes in the profit situation, dramatic changes in the market-place such as competitors coming up with new and better products, or a sudden currency change in an important competitor or market country. In all these cases, financial relations are to be handled professionally and with consistency between various sources within the company. The goals and targets as such, while certainly complicated at times, have a tendency, however, to be fairly easy to specify. Also, the communications programme in these cases covers a limited period of time, which makes it relatively easy to measure the degree of success that the programme has had.

Long-range programmes

Setting specific goals may be more difficult in the long-range financial communications programmes. Going back to the defined groups of shareholders, potential investors, banks and financial institutions, financial analysts and brokers, the present levels of awareness and recognition of your company will have to be established, for example, through a 'benchmark' study.

If the shareholders are your key group in the financial field, what are the knowledge and feelings you would want to find towards the company in this group? What do they know about the market situation of the company? How well do they know top management and the ideas and philosophies that they stand for? Are they aware of the product range of the company, and the new trends in product development? What do they know about the company's policies and action in such areas as the external environment, work environment, labour relations and equal opportunity? Or about the company's position on domestic versus international growth and investments?

Basing specific goals on questions like these does not, of course, mean that those are the only subjects to deal with. But they make it possible to find out present levels of interest and knowledge, on important issues, to set up programmes with defined objectives and to measure the progress in awareness and attitudes on these aspects against the communications investment. They also serve as building-blocks for wider, more general goals, such as 'contributing towards a satisfactory supply of capital'. Phrasing communications goals for your financial relations in such general terms alone does not give much guidance for specific action, neither does it give any help in measuring how the programmes have worked out. But if specific steps towards selected long-range objectives are identified, the whole process becomes manageable.

The communication manager's situation in the company, as compared with that of other managers, also becomes more realistic. Nobody expects the production manager to snap his fingers in the air and – voilà – here is a new production line, in full swing, with no running-in problems. But there are corporate managers who, perhaps nurtured by irresponsible PR people, expect immediate results in smiles and happiness. Professional communications work is usually a long drawn-out process, establishing the starting point, defining goals, working step by step, identifying problems, choosing among alternative solutions, allocating sufficient resources – and then getting the satisfaction of measurable gradual progress, with or without the occasional setbacks that are also part of human activities.

What methods are available?

Once the problems and targets are identified, finding the methods to solve the problems and reach the targets becomes a much more tangible task. A range of methods is available.

The annual report

The basic instrument is the annual report. In most countries, the annual report is a legal document and must conform to certain standards. Given this, there is still room for creative communications talent in preparing the annual report. The presentation of many annual reports has improved tremendously in the last ten to fifteen years. A fair number have also improved in real communications value. Unfortunately, in some cases, the communications targets have been overshadowed by glossy paper and four-colour print for its own sake. The responsibility for that development may fall as heavily on company presidents and chairmen as on communications staff and consultants. Rather than getting one's hands dirty in trying to communicate relevant facts in an understandable way, it may be easier to escape into artwork, four-colour print, heavy stock and fancy layouts.

A good annual report should have a lot in common with good financial journalism. In fact, one of the best ways to improve the annual report may be to let one or two qualified economic journalists go through some recent reports and give their assessment. The money spent on this exercise may prove to be one of the best investments in your whole financial relations programme. The journalist will probably come up with one or more of the following suggestions:

1. Make it easy to grasp the essentials. This calls for a page or a spread of easy-to-read key points of the year, as well as communicative charts of sales development, profit development, equity situation, return on capital, dividends and share value, split up in a significant way (by production units, product lines, geographic markets, etc.) and going back at least five years.

2. Give details in areas where significant change has taken place. Select some areas in which the company has altered its course – new products, new markets, investments, research, changes in

profits, markets or organization. Make these areas stand out as important as they appear to the board and management, give them adequate space, illustrate them as they require.

3. Take up one or two important policy issues and explain the position of the board/management on these issues.

4. Make the company human. Explain the development of the company, internal and external, in terms of human background, relating it to people: staff, customers, other important human contributors.

5. Risk making predictions. No one expects a company executive to be infallible, least of all when he talks about the future. Many factors may come in from the cold and make a prognosis obsolete, sometimes before it is printed. Despite this, is there anyone who can foresee a company's future direction better than those who are at the steering wheel? Why conceal from the shareholders and others how you see the course ahead?

Periodic/interim reports

The same basic thinking as is reflected in the annual report should characterize the periodic reports, half-yearly, quarterly of whatever period is chosen. By and large, there is probably no area of shareholder and financial relations where significant results can be achieved more rapidly than in the periodic reports. When well designed, they keep the company image alive to the shareholders, establish a frequent reminder and renew the interest that once led to the investment. Shareholder newsletters have the same function and may be more personal, less formal than the periodic reports.

The business press

The business press is a general, fast and efficient channel for important messages about the company. It includes the specific business and financial publications but also the financial editors of the dailies, for example. In addition to the wide circulation, the most significant advantage from the company's point of view is probably the timing – the immediate distribution of news, giving important facts to all concerned at the same time. As noted above, this aspect is of critical importance in matters that affect the value of publicly traded stock.

In analysing the business press of primary importance to your company, you will find that the number of editors to keep in touch with is usually rather limited. The other side of that coin is that each one of them is worth substantial personal attention by the top staff in your company. And, unless the communications department includes staff members with a thorough economic background, the editors want to be in contact with the financial staff of the company. A brief lunch now and then with the communications manager or consultant will hardly satisfy the financial editor. That does not mean that the role of the communications manager is insignificant. It normally falls to the communications manager to create opportunities for bridging the traditional gap between the journalists and the top company staff, to prepare both sides for the meetings and to make sure that the meetings are followed up afterwards. Preparations on both sides can reduce aggravation and produce tangible results. Such preparations include briefings, so that the journalists are well informed of the general background of the company, its markets, products and earnings records, and so that the financial managers are aware of the editorial direction of the media in question, know what kind of questions they can expect and have prepared themselves with relevant facts and figures. If the financial management is not used to editorial contacts, they also need a background briefing on how to handle interview situations, to avoid unpleasant surprises after the interview. The financial manager who says, 'Yes, of course I said so, but I didn't think he would *write* it' is likely to be very cautious the next time – if, indeed, there is a next time . . . for him!

Stockholders' newsletters

In your stockholder mailing lists, as we have already indicated, you have an asset of tremendous importance to a successful financial communications programme. One of the ways to use it is to establish a stockholder newsletter. The quarterly or half-yearly reports can be integrated into a newsletter series, but you can add a lot more to it. Important orders, changes in management personnel, new products, advertisement programmes, investments (or divestments!) and the reasons for them, new labour contracts and many other company events are or can be made interesting to the shareowners. Like the staff publication, the shareholder newsletter should be characterized much more by its contents and its frequency than by glossy printing or advanced artwork. One page or less, straightforward language, maybe even using your standard letterhead, will do the job, make the shareholders feel that they really have a stake in the company. They will feel this even more if you keep them informed when the company meets with difficulties and problems, which happens to all companies at times. Having established a tradition of open-minded shareholder newsletters in such situations may, more than anything, help maintain shareholder solidarity in times of temporary difficulties.

Investor newsletters

Investor newsletters aimed at stockbrokers, bankers, financial advisers or at those categories among which you would like to encourage investments in your company may be the same as the shareholder newsletters. Both background information and hard facts contribute to give the basis for evaluating your company and create sound, realistic confidence in its development. Integrity and honesty are keywords to any communications programme, but in no aspect of it are these qualities as important as in investor contacts. People may invest their savings based on information they receive. Guiding them in this process is an onerous responsibility. Not only must the facts be right and stand up to any scrutiny, but also the words, the phrasing, the tone, must be beyond criticism. Nobody can blame anyone for unexpected events that happen to the company, but the situation at the moment of publication must be reflected correctly in all information.

Stockholders' meetings

Shareholders' meetings are different today from what they used to be. More shareholders participate in them, even if the percentage in most companies is still hardly worth that designation. Also, a bigger share of those who come take a specific interest in one aspect or another of the company's life. Many shareholder groups who used to see their investment as nothing but an investment now want to use their voting rights and their voices. Contrary to tradition they introduce other elements than purely economic aspects into the questions and discussions, even to the extent that traditionalists among the shareholders feel the newcomers are taking up time for things that 'don't belong'. Be that as it may, the shareholders have a right to ask questions and to be given answers, to communicate with their company and its officers. And there are few ways available to the average or the interested shareholders to get in touch personally with the board and management of their company. The fact that much of the opinions voiced at annual general meetings is organized by more or less established pressure groups does not alter this right or reduce its value. In fact, it is a positive trend in more ways than one, even if it may be embarrassing to those who have to change long-entrenched opinions on what a shareholders' meeting should or should not do. Since many of the questions go beyond strict economic affairs and have at least a bearing or connection with ethics, morals or social development, they create an awareness that the companies are more than economic units, more than statistics, production and legal jargon, that they are, in fact, units of cooperation between human beings, with a responsibility that includes values other than pounds and pence.

Active annual general meetings and other shareholders' meetings should be regarded by management not as a burden but as an opportunity to explain, to present and to analyse their views on big issues that have a relation to the company's life and policies. This opportunity should be used whether or not management is forced to it by minority spokesmen, church groups, environmentalists, feminists, consumerists or other activists of one shade or the other – much more so, as this is often the right thing to do from a purely tactical point of view, too. Allow time for important issues on the agenda, prepare film, slide or other audiovisual presentations, demonstrate what is being done and what remains to be done, what the goals are but also the limitations, costs or otherwise. If questions have been asked one year, come back to them on your own initiative the next year to show that management listens, cares and acts responsibly.

Open house

If shareholders' meetings can be held at or close to the company's premises they offer an excellent opportunity for arranging a shareholders' open house, showing the new investments, what the profits have been used for, new products in actual use, improvements in working conditions, new machinery installed or other changes since the previous meeting. And since in all likelihood those shareholders who attend are a minority of the total number, the others should have an opportunity to receive this information through a simple newsletter, setting out the highlights of the meeting.

Shareholders' clubs

One way to establish closer links between shareholders and the company may be to encourage and support a shareholders' club or association. What one can achieve this way is primarily to get those shareholders who really have a serious interest in the company to stand up and be counted, or at least listed. It is a channel to reach those who have indicated an interest. However, with the advantages that active shareholders' clubs may offer, there is also the risk of biased or one-sided interests gaining a foothold. More importantly, in establishing information programmes with separate groups of shareholders, you must be extremely careful not to present important economic information to some shareholders but not to others, thus creating a situation in which some shareholders are treated unfairly. This, of course, may be illegal as well as unethical.

Financial advertising

If, finally, there is a need to get financial messages across to wide audiences, and if they must come across exactly the way they have been planned, there is one way left – financial advertising. I avoid, on purpose, the conventional terms institutional or corporate advertising, the reason being that these phrases are used so often to cover a convenient way of spending lots of money in no time and with very unspecified aims. Financial advertising, on the other hand, should have defined target groups and closely-defined objectives. It should be used to complement other communications methods, such as newsletters, periodical reports, etc. If one can find newspapers or magazines, alone or in combinations, that cover shareholders, potential investors or lenders at lower cost than direct mail for example, then financial advertising may be a useful tool.

The communications goal must be clear – at least as clear as the goal of a newsletter. And the agency must see this goal in exactly the same way as the company does, before they start producing the advertisements and the insertion plan.

The readers should learn more about the company, as a basis for investment. What does the company know about their attitudes towards the company now? What does the investor knowledge and attitude profile look like? If it is not known, it may be better to use the advertising budget for a survey instead, or there is a risk of making a bad situation worse. Suppose they feel the company's profits are not as good as they should be. Suppose they feel this is due to careless handling of company funds. Now if the company goes on a spree with beautiful four-colour spreads, no matter what the advertisements say, those very advertisements may prove to them that they were right.

When the purpose and the target audience have been defined and advertising has been decided on as the most efficient way to communicate, then again there is no reason why financial advertising should be dull. Even financial readers are human beings. A black frame with charts and figures is not necessarily the only way to present financial advertisements.

What are the messages to get across through financial advertisements? Quarterly, half-yearly or annual results are one type. Organizational or personnel changes, big investments, company mergers, big orders, new products or important research results could be others. Environmental issues, results of court action, controversy with government or consumer bodies may be other reasons for explaining the company's situation and views to the financial public. Financial advertising may be used in an offensive or a defensive situation, to create a positive impression or stop or reduce negative responses. It may be part of a long-range programme or it may be an emergency exit.

Most advertising agencies are happy to produce financial or other types of 'institutional' advertising. Whether or not the reasons for these ambitions are clear, it means that lots of agencies would also like to show the wonderful institutional advertisements they have produced. Why not let them? But insist on going below the surface, to reasons, objectives and results obtained. Going through and carefully analysing the why's and how's of financial advertisements in which one is not directly engaged may be a great money-saver whether the end decision is to advertise or not to advertise this way.

How to budget for tangible results

Since the financial staff of the company will be involved in this aspect of company communications more than in any other, budgeting should be really professional.

If it is the first time, it may become an interesting test case for the communications manager to get to know the reasoning of his financial colleagues, and to show them that the communications manager is a careful steward of the company's resources.

One should take care to go through a full planning process:

1. Establish the 'benchmark' situation in awareness and attitude terms.
2. Define clearly:
   (a) groups that are most relevant to the company;
   (b) key messages to get across or to 'listen in';
   (c) desired changes in attitudes or knowledge;
   (d) advantages of reaching those communications goals.
3. Discuss various alternative methods that can be considered.
4. Make considered recommendations among these alternatives.
5. Agree on acceptable costs in money and staff time.
6. Decide how to measure the results of the programme.

If the planning process is presented in these clear business-like steps, the discussions are sure to be fruitful. The financial management will provide sensible feedback and – as an added benefit – will respect the communications manager as a professional in his field. The process will be a learning experience of great value to all parties concerned, not least the financial management staff.

The financial management will probably find that they are less used to thinking and talking in terms of communications investments than other investments – machinery, buildings and the like. They may also be less used to communications as a business tool than the marketing management, for example, is. This may make them apply their economic expertise more on penny-pinching and details than on discussions on who to reach, with what message and why, leaving more of the 'how' decisions to the communications manager.

Another extreme case may happen – the chairman or chief executive who suddenly finds that 'something has to be done'. That situation is no less difficult to handle for the professional communications manager, since it often involves blank decisions – and blank cheques – without any serious planning. And heaven only knows whether it is more difficult to convince a penny-pinching accountant or a spendthrift chairman that neither approach is good communications management.

The result is likely to be best if financial communications are brought into the overall communications planning of the company, involving both the very top echelons of the company and its financial staff.

4

'There goes the neighbourhood!':

Communicating with the local community

In this chapter the reader will find suggestions on why good 'neighbourhood relations' are essential, how to define key groups and how to set goals for communications programmes geared to the local community.

It will help the reader plan, budget, execute and evaluate result-oriented programmes for improved local community relations.

What is the purpose?

Whether a company is a local service shop or a giant transnational with offices and factories in thirty countries, it is as dependent on its local surroundings as a tree is on the soil in which it grows. Selecting a place where the basic conditions are right and then nurturing a healthy relationship through sound communications programmes are therefore indispensable to a company's well-being. This has always been a basic truth – development in later years has only underlined it and brought it to the forefront of management interest.

The local infrastructure

The local community may be important as a market to many companies; it is the local community that provides the infrastructure to every company in the area. The physical infrastructure, roads and other transportation facilities, power, water and sewage systems, building conditions, etc. is certainly essential and may be one of the first considerations in choosing a site, but in the long run there is also a social infrastructure to consider. What are the attitudes of local government towards the company's type of business? Is the school system adequate to develop workers and office staff with the background the company requires? Do general atmosphere, sports facilities, cultural resources, the tax system, etc. help to attract good people of the kind the company wants and make them happy to stay? If the company is already in business and not satisfied in these respects, how can it contribute to change?

A mutual relationship

But the company is not only entitled to make requests, it has responsibilities towards its local neighbourhood as well. As an individual, nobody would accept a neighbour who dumped his untreated sewage in your backyard. But for a long time this is what companies have done. At long last communities, often through its younger, more active members, have reacted and put pressure on the companies.

If the community is heavily dependent on a company as an employer, how does it deal with a redundancy situation? If it has to

54

make other changes that affect the public or public services, does it provide opportunities for consultation and discussions with authorities and representatives of those concerned?

The need for good local community relations is truly a mutual one. And only very seldom is this an area where the philosophical aspects of company life are involved, as happens sometimes in financial relations or national government relations, among others. More often, local community relations deal with questions of roads and streets, schools, building sites, bus stops, sewage and dumps.

But if these discussions are not based on mutual confidence, respect and awareness of the ambitions and interests of all parties they will take a lot more time for a lot fewer results. And when a crisis comes, a fire or a firing, an exhaust leak or a student protest, what happens to a company that has neglected to build a wide and reliable emotional safety-net while there was still time, and when there was material to build it from?

Who are the key groups?

The essential question of identifying key groups in each contact area is often difficult to answer. In the contact areas of finance, market and national government, it may take much time and research to find adequate answers.

In local community relations the problem is usually easier to solve. Some regular key groups are suggested in this chapter. They are not all equally important to each company, in every situation. There may be additional groups that a company should consider, based on its local situation. An analysis of the key groups is a condition for success, but chances are that it will be possible to reach a workable platform with reasonable effort.

Involve management colleagues

At the start of this process, make sure to ask about the contact networks that management colleagues in other areas have, or feel they should have. Include managers who have responsibility for recruiting staff, hiring them (and firing them) and training them. Those in charge of transportation, buildings, energy systems and supply and other vital support functions should also be approached at this time.

The answers from this stage of consultations will hopefully be specific. As in analysing purchasing influences, where the salesmen are one significant source of input, it must, however, be the responsibility of the communications function to put these specialized answers into a wider pattern of background influences. A local traffic planning engineer is not an island unto himself, as a company logistics engineer may think. His opinions are influenced by a wider network. The communications manager should be prepared to find out where opinions and attitudes come from, how they develop and how they are passed on, in this contact area as in others. It is the communication manager's role to bring views and opinions of the defined key groups to your management's attention – and then to make sure that the company's story comes across both to frontline and background groups.

Involve the company staff

The company's own staff are a key group in your community relations programme. They know the company better than any other group. Most of them are likely to be voters and taxpayers in the community. We have discussed quite extensively the why's and how's of staff relations programmes in Chapter 2. But the role of company staff in the community relations programmes merits some additional attention.

They know the company better than any other group – or at least that is how it should be. And it is what their friends outside the company believe. So in forming opinions about the company their friends consult with company employees they know. Are the employees capable of fulfilling this role in a way that the company will be satisfied with? Surely, they know their own job. But how well are they informed about company aims and objectives, so that they can explain to outsiders in their sports association, church, neighbourhood, political party, family(!), mates in the pub or fellow golfers at the nineteenth hole? As company representatives they have a lot more credibility with their close friends than ever the communications manager or the company chairman has.

Their network of connections provides not only a channel for the company messages. It also creates a source of input, of opinions about the company that can hardly be fed into the decision-making process in a better way. How can that source be made available to company management? The Assyrian kings in ancient times are reported to have cut the throat of the messengers who brought bad tidings. How can one ensure that a company's news input is handled in a more enlightened way? Are the letters to the editor of the company staff newsletter screened so that only 'positive' messages are published? When was the last time a local political leader was interviewed in the staff magazine?

Most companies have suggestion boxes in which the staff are encouraged to put proposals for new nuts and bolts or for different four-angle screwdrivers. This is all very well. Are staff also encouraged to put ideas, criticisms or proposals on how the community feels about the company, how such feelings could be improved or how negative feelings can be reduced in the suggestion box? Eliminating reasons for negative feelings may well be costly, at least in the short run. The cost of setting up systems so that you know about them is probably going to be less than one week's entertainment bills for top management.

Are employees encouraged to be actively involved in community life? Their service on town or city councils, committees or boards, their active membership in service clubs, their involvement in community projects, sports activities and political life may help strengthen the links between the company and its environment.

Create links with local government

How well do you follow the planning process of your community? In town planning, where do they plan for new parks, new roads, modified street crossings, other types of residential areas? How does that affect your company? If your relations with city planning committees or boards are active and smooth, your company's planning input improves. You may also make your own comments known at a stage where changes are easier to negotiate, if necessary.

Get involved in the educational system

In Chapter 6 we shall discuss in more depth the contacts between business and the educational system. Just a reminder here that, since schools are an important facet of local community life, a community relations programme should also take schools into account. Not just the school administrators and teachers, but also the students. They have strong views, sometimes expressed loud and clear, on many subjects that have a bearing on company life. Furthermore, some of them are future employees, stockholders, customers or voters in the community. Helping them form their opinions on a full range of background information is likely to be a sound investment for the future. Some of their present views may well stay with them through the decision-making periods of their lives, so why not learn about them now?

Take the pulse of special interest groups

Not all citizens take the same interest in the community's life and development. But in addition to the groups we have discussed above, who are more or less permanent or even professional community leaders, there are groups that demonstrate their interest in other ways. These groups are not always on the side of business. This is all the more reason to keep in touch with them. There may be a lot of sense in much of what they say, if business learns to listen with a sympathetic ear. And if not, how can you make them see your point of view without staying in contact with them, listening to them and talking with them?

If business is right, but has failed to communicate its side of the story, who is to blame? If, on the other hand, business is wrong on some points, why not listen and take rapid action? The sooner it is taken, the more effective any remedial action is likely to be. The sooner a company changes its ventilation system, the fewer dangerous components will be emitted into the air. But also, the sooner it takes action, preferably before it comes under pressure, from public opinion or legally, the less bad-will it is likely to receive. Pre-action, not reaction, is the essence of good communications programmes, not least in the area of 'interested citizen groups'.

Local environmental groups have, for a period, played an important part in the life of many companies. Many businessmen feel that their demands, at least when they affect their own companies, are unrealistic, premature, ill-considered or based on a destructive desire to get at business and their own company. If this is the case, it certainly proves that one party has made a dangerous mistake – business.

Other such examples are women's groups, parent–teacher associations, church groups, racial groups or action committees, traffic safety committees and many others. Some of these are more permanent institutions, part of the establishment and with business managers among their regular members. Such groups obviously include most of the traditional service clubs – Rotary, Lions, Zontas and the others. Company employees should be encouraged to take up membership in these clubs when the opportunities arise and take an active part in them. In addition to the value they have in developing the individuals who join them, they provide opportunities for contacts with opinion leaders in local business, administration, arts, education and other significant aspects of community life.

Other groups may be more short-term, aimed at a specific target. Keeping track of these groups and establishing relations with them is certainly not easy. Some of them may also, for political or other reasons, prefer not to be known until they go into the arena. But the sensitive communications manager should be able to install some kind of 'early warning system' and be able to advise management of opinion trends, which are more or less organized, while there is still time for the company to pre-act, rather than react.

For obvious reasons, this is an area where standard prescriptions are of less value than in most other cases. Key concepts are *preparedness* to listen, learn and act, and *willingness* to share know-how and attitudes, even with the 'risk' of getting into a real give-and-take discussion. On that basic foundation, a company has to look for threats and opportunities that may be lurking round the next corner of the local street and be ready to deal with them.

What are the specific goals?

As in other communications programmes, there is no way to do a good job without specific goals. In local community relations it is fairly easy to identify such goals, just as it is usually relatively easy to identify the key groups.

In defining the goals, make them clear communications goals. Set them in terms of opinion, attitude or awareness factors, or behaviour/action patterns, and make them mutual, in terms of listening as well as – or even more than – talking.

Start out with an analysis of which points in the company's life and which points in the life and plans of the community immediately affect each other. See the examples on page 60. Each company will no doubt be able to add to the list and adjust it to its specific situation. It is at this stage that the communications manager needs to get the top management and as many as possible of management colleagues in other disciplines involved.

Establish what the present situation is in opinion and awareness

Company	Community
Building plans	Zoning guidelines
Staff recruitment	School systems
Environmental impact	Health and environment authorities
Products	Local consumer reactions
Expansion/retrenchment plans	Employment boards, school systems, building committees, traffic planners
Transportation needs	Traffic and road planning

terms. How well are the community plans known to company or local plant management, and how well respected are they? How well are company plans and intentions known to key groups in the community? What is the emotional climate between community and company? In most cases formal research programmes will not be needed to establish the present situation, but in some cases they would help. Whether or not any kind of formal survey is applied, an effort should be made to define the situation in measurable terms.

Many local government bodies have their own communications staffs or consultants. It is often helpful to both parties to do some of this planning together – after all, it is a mutual interest to create better understanding between business and the local community.

When the goals are set, it might be advisable to set them for a short period of, say, six months. Define expected progress in this period, again in mutual communications terms. With a concentrated effort in this direction, written in specific terms, the methods, the media and even the messages will come almost by themselves.

In all likelihood the cash expenses are going to be quite reasonable. What will be required, however, is will, effort and time from the communications staff and from other managers in the company. Even more important, they may have to face the risk of adjusting some of their own ideas to community requirements.

After the first six months, take out the programme with the short-time goals, run through it and make an evaluation of the results. Make this evaluation as specific as possible, and in the same terms as used when the goals were set.

1. What has been achieved completely?

2. Where have unexpected blocks occurred – on the company side and on the other side?

3. What has been done in part?

4. Where have new aspects come up?

Make this evaluation in writing and discuss it, warts and all, with the management, and draw the conclusions from it. And then, start working on the next six months' programme!

More difficult to measure, even by sophisticated methods, are the long-range results that will be achieved. Those results can be expressed in terms of confidence and mutual respect, awareness of common interests and the need to work jointly, sometimes to make sacrifices on both sides and improved opportunities to plan the future with some accuracy. All of which can contribute to greater security and better economic conditions for the local community, the company and the staff.

What methods are available?

Once the key groups and the specific goals have been defined, the choice of methods will be easy. Some of them will be specific to local community decision-makers. Others will be media used for different contact areas, media that get additional use if the local community aspects are included.

Here are some suggestions as a starting point – make adjustments to suit the individual situation!

Mailings

Is there, in the communications function, a *mailing list* of the chairmen, secretaries and members of local government boards and committees, of the staff of the mayor's office (or similar functions), of local politicians and of various more or less formal interest groups?

Once an up-to-date mailing system for this category is available it will be a resource for many useful applications. And positive reactions will flow back, too. Those reactions, in their turn, will generate additional opportunities to enter into a real dialogue, with active talk and listening on both sides.

Printed information

The company *staff publication*, the *internal newsletter* or the *house magazine* should normally *not* be mailed on a regular basis to other than their target audience. The editor should gear his editorial skill exclusively to the primary target group, not to others. But this general guideline does not prevent the use of occasional issues of the staff paper, for example, for limited distribution to groups that may find a special item of immediate interest to them. It is a simple way to keep local community contacts informed of what is going on in your company, sending them from time to time a marked copy of the staff paper, maybe with the managing director's business card stapled to it.

The same goes for other types of printed information, produced in-house, such as information about a new product, new appointments, organizational changes, etc. The annual report and other periodical financial information should contain interesting material. A speech by one of the officers of the company, glimpses from a marketing report, personnel statistics, information on a new product, news of a significant order, plans for a new materials handling system – all of them can be of interest.

Local news media

The *local news media*, newspapers and radio are obvious channels. Keeping their editors informed of what is going on in your company is a basic requirement in building a community relations programme. But it is also important to follow what is discussed in the local media, in such areas that come close to the company's interests. It is often through the local press, if it is worth its salt, that the company gets the proper input of local opinions or ideas to feed into its planning and decision-making process.

The local news media are also the fastest way to get a message across to the community as a whole. If your message has editorial value it will be used as editorial material; this may be the best bet. However, advertising space is useful to get a message across to what may be the majority of local residents. Using local advertising gives complete control of what to say, and how and when to say it, which may be of prime importance in certain cases. Local advertising billboards give the same opportunity to present a controlled message to the local community, with the advantages and limitations that billboards have.

Local exhibitions

Some companies have tried successfully to set up *local exhibitions* explaining their background, their plans and their part in community life. Public libraries, city halls, banks, schools and other public places are often interested in providing space for such exhibits, if they are made with good sense and taste. Building plans, training and employment opportunities, environmental issues and financial development are subjects that go over well in exhibits, which may of course be made in such a way that they can easily be taken to other sites for additional exposure.

Person-to-person

One of the advantages of the local community as a contact area for a company is that it is just that – local. It means that there are opportunities to communicate in the best possible way: *person-to-person*.

Among the staff there will certainly be some who will take an active part in some of the key groups that have been outlined or who are knowledgeable in the specific interest areas that have been defined. Make sure that you know them so that they can be engaged, to the extent they wish to contribute, in such contact-building programmes. In their own field of interest and among their associates they speak with great authority on behalf of the company, and they are likely to get reliable feed-back.

The company president or local chief executive should certainly also be involved, as well as the company chairman and the whole range of management representatives. In addition to the clubs where they are members, they should be prepared to take on speaker assignments in a wide variety of associations, committees, boards and action groups. Usually, this is not so difficult – it is a natural part of top management's role.

It may be more difficult to get them to take on the role of listener, especially in contexts that may appear very different from their own ideological or political viewpoints, and to get them to report to their management colleagues from such meetings. In some cases it may even be clearly unsuitable to have the company represented by senior officials. Junior managers or other staff may find it easier to establish contacts with groups who have not been used to accept conventional corporate wisdom. And these junior company representatives may also be more apt to listen and to contribute actively to modifying company policies, when required.

The communications manager should certainly be involved together with the others. But the communications function will also help in preparing the others for their presentations, from 'ideological direction' and advice on presentation techniques to the generation of presentation material, slides, overheads, basic fact-sheets, printed matter to go with presentations, questionnaires to be used to take the pulse of interested groups, etc.

Most important of all: the communications manager has the responsibility of seeing to it that the contacts are established with the key groups, that they contribute to reach the specific communications goals and that the company gets feed-back from these contacts.

Going out to other groups is a simple way. When possible, inviting others to come to the company may be even better. Try to create occasions when the company invites community leaders, committees, action groups, boards, associations and other interested parties. Showing on-site what the company does, what it stands for, its problems and opportunities, its worksites and equipment, establishes a more concrete platform for further discussions than any other method. In addition, the company probably has better facilities to stage a film or slide show to give more life to the presentation. Being on one's home ground gives poise and reality to what is said.

Open house

Occasionally, every two to three years say, it might be worthwhile to extend an open invitation to a large group, perhaps to the whole community, to come to see the company. In other words, the company becomes an *open house* for a day or two.

The open house is normally seen as a staff relations project. But the purpose behind it, to show what the company really is and to make it human, applies to the local community as well as to the staff. Remember the definition of the word 'company' in Chapter 1: 'People who earn and share their bread together.'

An employee and family open house can, in fact, often be coordinated with a community open house. Some of the physical preparations may well be used both for staff and family groups and for other interested citizens. Perhaps a Saturday for the families and a Sunday for other groups is adequate, or one weekend for families and the following weekend for other guests. Issue the invitation by advertisements in the local press or by a community-wide mailing. A response of some kind is necessary to ensure that resources, from guides to hot dogs and refreshments, are adequate.

Make it a fun event, but don't forget the purpose, which has to be clearly defined. Be enthusiastic in presenting the open house to the public, but don't make it sound as something it is not. It should not be a carnival or a circus, but an interesting presentation of a slice of real life. Hiding reality behind a screen of Barnum & Bailey is like admitting that real life in industry is boring, and has to be hidden when you let the public in. That way you can easily make things worse, proving to people that their worst suspicions about business have been confirmed – by business itself.

So to sum up: the methods available to keep in touch with the local community include many of the traditional forms of multi-communications, press relations, mailings, advertising and printed matter. But in local community relations one can also benefit from the fact that those one wants to meet and talk *with* (not only *to*) are within close geographic reach. A range of personal communications forms can be used, with the tremendous advantage of providing opportunities for two-way communications – the ultimate goal.

How to budget for tangible results

Since most local community programmes can be clearly defined and seldom involve large amounts of money, the problems are not in budgeting, at least not in traditional, money-centred terms. When the key groups have been defined, the specific interest areas sifted out and the six-months or one-year programme written down and approved, the allocation of money will rarely be the main headache, possibly with the exception of the years of the open house.

The big difficulty, instead, may be to get a commitment on the use of high-level and junior staff time, so make sure that you indicate this in the plan. It should come as no surprise to the top executives that good local community relations require a personal commitment from them, a commitment that goes far beyond a speech in the Rotary Club once a year. It may even go as far as requiring a willing-ness to listen 'with a sympathetic ear' to people they don't agree with and don't like, and after listening, even to admit that there may be some justice in their opinions. When that happens both the communications manager and the company as a whole are to be congratulated! The company's local community relations programme has reached an essential communications goal.

5

'Here, there, everywhere':
Government relations

In this chapter the reader will find ideas on when and why good government relations may be essential, how to define key groups and how to set clear goals for communication with the government.

It will help the reader plan, budget, execute and evaluate result-oriented programmes, for improved government communications work.

What is the purpose?

Much of the principles and practices of good communications are based on simple truths about human thinking, reactions and behaviour. As stated in Chapter 1, a company's communications system is a network of human relations. This is also true of contacts with government bodies, even if it is sometimes hard to believe.

Local–national

The step from local community relations to the loftier area of national government relations is a big one. Community relations are based on local and concrete problems. Different opinions may exist, but it is easier to find common ground. Such common ground can also be found in the relations between a company and the higher hierarchies of government, but the critical issues are often more controversial. While local issues are often practical and down-to-earth, national issues tend to have ideological aspects that make them more difficult to handle for many businessmen.

National, cultural and language differences play a role in all human communications. All ideas presented in this book have to be adapted to national circumstances. This applies to all contact areas and all communications methods, but arguably more so in government relations than in others. If some suggestions in this chapter do not match the set-up in a specific country, the reader is urged to translate the rationale behind the suggestions and adapt them to his or her own conditions.

A matter of credibility

The general decline in public support that business experienced in many countries in the 1960s and 1970s created an opinion-base for control measures, restrictions and public supervisory bodies. This is essential to remember in discussing a company's communications programmes with government in its many shapes. If the problems are at the root of the tree, it is of little use to treat the canopy. If the purpose of company–government communications is to establish a better climate for business, some of the wide, underlying factors must be considered first. The business community in general, and each individual company, must be prepared to work hard to regain the confidence of the general public.

What is required is not superficial 'public relations', but substantial two-way communications, a readiness to listen and to speak, to adapt and to act. This is, indeed, nothing unusual for business. If there is anything that characterizes private enterprise, it is its ability to foresee, adapt to and benefit from change.

Technological change has been promoted and utilized by industry and business when it has had a link to the products and services the companies provide. Awareness of relevant social trends, based on reading and analysing lifestyle changes, should likewise be part of any company's strategy formation process.

A key question is whether the communications function, traditionally, has been strong enough. It may not have had adequate concepts of its own role in creating resources in company-related sociological forecasting or in drawing relevant business conclusions from existing lifestyle research. The result is, as the Conference Board expresses it in one of its reports, that 'Credibility seems to be one of the critical resources in short supply these days.'

The real purpose of government relations

In this chapter we shall discuss some aspects of government relations programmes. It must be clearly understood that any action should be based on the desire to present a clean case, a case that can be presented in good faith.

A government relations programme is not primarily a matter of lobbying but of fair pricing, not about press releases but about sound employment practices, not about glossy leaflets but about reasonable warranties and responsible product development, not about influence peddling but about handling effluence, not about executive air travel to the capital but about the air above the factory.

Who are the key groups?

Since government, at least in democratic countries, is supposed to reflect public opinion, the range of groups for business to communicate with is enormous. In principle it is the whole population of a country. To make a programme manageable, a company's ambitions have to be reduced to its own high-priority groups.

In selecting the high-priority groups, it is necessary to start not only with the company's view of the outer world but also to look at the company from the outside. The selection should be based not only on who the company wants to establish contacts with, but also on who wants to make contacts with the company, to comment on it, to enquire about it, to learn about it or to criticize it.

Some companies have established and promoted 'hot lines' on which people can call in, make comments and ask questions. They have found that they have got access to thoughts and opinions they were never aware of – and it has helped those companies to defuse criticism based on lack of knowledge about a company's real situation. As an example of such issues, several surveys have shown that the public has a grossly exaggerated opinion on the size of the profits companies make. Learning about this helps companies present their profitability in the right terms, hopefully reducing critical comments that are based on factual errors.

E pluribus unum

In other chapters in this part of the book we deal with various priority contact areas, the staff, shareholders and financial groups, the local community, the educational world and the market. It is important to identify a company's contact areas, and smaller groups within the broad contact areas, to make communications work manageable and target-oriented. It is, however, also important to recognize that there are no impermeable walls between these contact areas: they overlap and interrelate in many ways.

While a company must adapt and orient its communications programmes to a variety of audiences, it must also project a unified identity and image. The solution to the conflict is to ensure that every company, no matter how big or how diversified, consistently works from a unified communications policy, preferably with one person or department as the total coordinator.

In this chapter about communications with the government and its roots, public opinion, the problem of overlapping is obvious. For in each of the other contact areas there are people who influence public opinion and thus create a basis for government thinking and government action.

Regional offices of central government

The government bodies closest to a company are probably the regional offices of central government. In addition to representing central government in general they have specialized functions that make them more or less interesting to the company and its business. Some of them may make themselves known at regular or irregular intervals – not always at times or with tidings that are convenient to the company.

Which are these offices? Has the company ever drawn up a list of the regional government offices that it is concerned with, listing their areas of responsibility, the aspects of the company that they may be interested in, the individual persons on their staffs that are of specific concern to the company and any problems that can be anticipated in each area over the next few years? They are certainly listed in the telephone directory, but there is a lot to gain from making a company-adapted list as outlined above.

Such a list, with additions, notes and modifications, will be invaluable as a planning instrument, a checklist, a mailing list and an occasional invitation list. Those responsible for employment and training, building and traffic, taxes and finances, industrial development, environment and ecology are likely to be included, to mention a few.

In drawing up the list, be sure to get proper input from various specialists in the company, building, personnel, transports, finance and others who may have immediate matters on which they should cooperate with regional authorities, or issues on which they have to fight them. Ask them to indicate, as closely as possible, what these matters are, where there are contact blocks, if any, and how they evaluate the emotional climate between these bodies and persons on one side and the company on the other. The number of persons they specify is probably quite limited. Around each one of these names there are certainly other persons, 'above', 'parallel' or 'below', to use hierarchical terms, who influence the relations without being in the limelight.

It may be difficult for line managers in different functions to reach each of these indirect influences personally. There may be more economical ways that a communications specialist can envisage. Some of those methods are indicated below.

71

National government offices

Once the regional boards or bodies of interest to the company have been defined it is a lot easier to follow through with a similar analysis of their counterparts on the central/capital level, if the size or nature of the company warrants such efforts. At central government level there will be specialists that appear only rarely in public, but who gather material, prepare memoranda, form policies and create opinions. Establishing contacts with these people, who often have a thorough knowledge of special aspects of business, may give the company access to plans, intentions, possibilities and threats at very early stages. National industrial organizations, regional government boards and local members of Parliament, Congress, etc. may be helpful in identifying such contacts.

Special committees

Both at the regional and central level there are *ad hoc* committees, study groups, project groups, etc. Getting a list of such groups working in the company's interest areas will provide additional, specific knowledge of the subjects under study and of the persons who work with those subjects. In most cases, they will appreciate being contacted by companies that can help them. A company can offer services in the form of facts, opinions, background material, access to specialists in the company, etc. They will also often appreciate the opportunity of testing preliminary ideas and action lines on people who have an experience from the business angle.

Nationwide organizations

Nationwide organizations of special branches of industry, business in general and of labour are a category that should be of interest to most companies. Although not branches of government, they function in many respects as a channel between individual companies and government offices.

One of their important roles is to do some of the lobbying work for their members, to influence government and public opinion. An individual company can contribute by taking a positive interest in their work and keep them well informed of the company's situation. In their work, they often need basic material, concrete examples of experiments, efforts, problems and solutions from the practical working level of individual companies. A company that stays in touch with them can increase the chances of its priority issues being considered and getting the place they deserve on their action lists.

This is acceptable to many businessmen as far as the industry organizations are concerned. Some businessmen find it more difficult to see that these criteria apply equally to labour organizations. For the individual company, of course, good labour relations begin at home, with its own trade unions. On national policy issues, it may also want to maintain contacts with the national labour organizations. To be able to handle such contacts as required, the company must at least have easy access to names and functions, preferably on a mailing and telephone list, for regular mailings of appropriate material or for occasional contacts.

Political parties

The degree of involvement a company wants to have with the political parties varies considerably, with the size and nature of the company, with national political traditions, whether it is the 'home country' or 'host country' of the company, and with the ambitions and programmes of the political parties.

In most countries it is acceptable to encourage a flow of information in both directions. The political system by necessity engages in economic questions. Companies working in the whirlpool of economic currents can often provide facts, examples and practical views to help political parties towards more realism in building their platforms and action programmes. While, therefore, political parties can often gain from contacts with business, the immediate benefits for individual companies are often more limited. Much of the initiative to establish such contacts should for these and other reasons rest with the political parties rather than with companies. Business in general and individual companies should, however, be prepared to respond in such a way and to the extent that is appropriate.

This somewhat passive approach is certainly correct in the 'host countries' of multinational companies. Examples of corporate political involvement in certain Latin American countries do not encourage companies or politicians to continue on that road. The safest course is to start with local political parties in the home area, ask in what ways they can benefit from the experience and specialist know-how that the company has and take small, cautious steps from there.

International 'government'

A new government tier – international 'government' – is beginning to act with growing force, influencing a still rather small but increasing number of companies.

The United Nations and many of its bureaux and agencies, as well as the European Community, ASEAN, regional international development banks, such as the Inter-American, the African and the Asian Development Banks, international business organizations, such as the ICC, international labour federations and international groups and societies to promote or oppose various causes are assuming increasing roles of international government and international public opinion-making.

The number of companies directly affected by these new structures may seem to be limited to a few very big ones. Those larger companies are, on the other hand, responsible for a significant share of the total turnover of goods and services. Their success or failure therefore is important to great numbers of people – employees, shareholders, customers, sub-suppliers and many others. While most of the big transnational companies are aware of international political development trends, not all have been able, as yet, to plan for them as a normal part of their total communications work, nor to integrate international issues into their everyday routines.

Many of the smaller companies have not even started to consider international 'government' as a key group, although they may have reason to follow actively at least some of the organizations and issues. Many companies, even those of very moderate size, are likely to be affected by international environment recommendations. Development in the European Community (EC) will create new threats and opportunities, not only for big and small companies within the EC, but also for companies from Asia, North America and other regions. Opportunities through international aid programmes may indeed be available even to smaller companies, provided their level of technological or business expertise is of the right kind.

What are the specific goals?

Long-range and short-range goals

Communications goals in the wide government/public opinion fields can be far-reaching or very concise and limited. The overall goal of international business, to maintain its credibility and thus give business a fair chance to develop, is perhaps too wide to be workable in a great majority of companies. Still, this basic concept must be woven into any government relations programme of any company, to allow business as a whole to move in the right direction.

It does not make things easier for the company that government action and public opinion changes may sometimes be incredibly slow, yet sometimes strike with the speed of lightning. The practical consequence of this is that companies have to work with bifocal glasses, half of them designed for long distance vision, the other half focused on short distances and near perspectives. Either type of input, including the long-range type, will be useful only if it can trigger quick responses within the organization. In a communications plan, some long-range objectives should be defined in a five-year perspective, or whatever long-range periods the company is working with, while other goals may be defined in terms of six months or a year.

Planning procedures often suffer from the same mistake: making long-term objectives vague and sweeping, and the short-term goals only slightly less so. There is no reason why long-term objectives should not be specific, just as short-term goals should, but it does require more thinking. A good test on how specific a company's communications thinking is is the degree to which its goals or objectives can be quantified, in percentages, in degrees of awareness, in attitude changes, in quantified reactions, in number of people/among those concerned/who take part, get involved, show interest, etc.

The requirement to be specific is not limited to government relations programmes, but the temptation to escape into generalities may be especially difficult to resist in this area.

Establishing a baseline – a benchmark

Part of the process of analysing the company's key groups in the government relations field is to find out for each key group what the present situation is in such terms as:

- *Awareness*: within the company of what is going on on the other side and within the government unit concerned of the work and ambitions of the company.
- *Emotional climate*: also in both directions.

To make this operational it is necessary to put it down, physically, on a sheet of paper, in as specific terms as possible. A grid or matrix model is probably the most practical way to do it.

When the terminology is vague it is often due to a lack of thinking or facts. If that happens, go back to the sources again, gather more information and specify the present situation in more concrete terms. If the need arises, formal research can be used, either in the form of surveys designed specifically to fill the information gaps or through publicly available studies, perhaps provided by your central business organization or by 'the other side', the various government units.

The government side has the same interest to improve two-way communications – it is their ambition to do their job well – so they may often be helpful in defining the present state of relations. Don't give up until there is a very clear base to work from.

The picture of the present state gives indications of how the situation should be to represent an acceptable, if not ideal, level of communications. The gap between 'what is' and 'what should be' is wider in some squares on your grid than in others. Mark those squares, physically, with a red circle. See the example (p. 77) of a construction company plotting its benchmark situation.

Setting the goals

Now set priority goals for the next six to twelve months (and perhaps for the next five years), and make a specific action plan. Also decide, at this stage, how progress should be measured after six to twelve months to evaluate the degree of success of your programme.

Example: Government relations
Case: A medium-sized construction company. Benchmark evaluation of the emotional climate, awareness and attitudes: in the company; in the key group; towards the key group; towards the company.

Key groups

1. Committee for Fair Employment

2. Federal Highway Commission

3. Project Study Group on the Effects of Studded Tyres on Road Surface

4. Brotherhood of Construction Workers

5. Heavy Equipment Manufacturers Association

6. Regional Energy Savings Committee

Goals/action plan for six-month period

1. Committee for Fair Employment
   (a) *Goal*: Make all those on our staff who are responsible for hiring personnel aware of the existence and ambitions of CFFE.
   (b) *Action plan*:
       (i) Invite the committee to a meeting with our personnel manager.
       (ii) Send all local managers a summary of the CFFE ten-point programme with a memorandum from the president.
       (iii) Send the committee members two to four specially relevant issues of our staff magazine during the six-month period (editor of staff magazine to alert me).

2. Federal Highway Commission. Situation acceptable – no action at present.

3. Project Study Group on the Effects of Studded Tyres
   (a) *Goal*: Make company known to Studded Tyres Study Group as expert on road building and road surfaces.
   (b) *Action plan*:
       (i) Send group members, at intervals, two to three pertinent research reports made by lab.

(ii) Put group members on mailing list of customer magazine for three to four issues.

(iii) [possibly] Offer the committee the services of one of our laboratory engineers as a consultant.

4. Brotherhood of Construction Workers

   (a) *Goals*:

   (i) Improve substantially the understanding among our board and management of the role of the Brotherhood in our industry.

   (ii) Get the leadership of the Brotherhood to understand the effects of inflation on our profit situation.

   (b) *Action plan*:

   (i) Invite our trade union boss (or, if he prefers, a representative of the National Brotherhood) to make an in-depth presentation to our board and management of the Brotherhood, its development and its basic principles.

   (ii) Send the Brotherhood, perhaps through our local trade union boss, explanatory material on the profit development in real (not inflated) terms. To be done in non-negotiation period.

5. Heavy Equipment Manufacturers' Association. Situation OK – no action at present.

6. Regional Energy Savings Committee

   (a) *Goal*: Make the RESC aware of new building methods and materials as energy-saving measures.

   (b) *Action plan*:

   (i) Offer the committee a hearing or a special memorandum on recent development.

   (ii) Include energy saving in new corporate advertising campaign – send pre-prints to committee members.

What methods are available?

In this contact area practically all conceivable communications methods can come into play, in all directions and in all combinations. What follows are therefore just examples: the creativity and imagination in each case will fill the gaps. Besides, if enough attention has been given to the analysis of key groups and specific goals, the methods, more often than not, will become obvious.

Input sources

The most important sources of input are the *general news media* and the *business and political press* in your field.

Make sure that management continuously and without delay is served with cuttings and summaries of articles and statements on important subjects and issues, perhaps even with comments and reflections. Use a clipping service if there is one that is fast and accurate enough for the company's needs, otherwise set up a clipping system within the company.

The selection of material is a particularly demanding operation that requires good judgement and knowledge of what is or may come to be of importance to the company. Too much material spoils the whole idea of saving management time, but it is equally unfortunate if an important issue is omitted or called to management's attention too late.

The clippings should be distributed to the chief executive and to a fairly wide circle of management, as well as to local trade union officers.

House magazines

The *staff magazine*, the *customer publication* and the *annual report* are examples of company-controlled media that should be actively engaged in the big issues. It will make them more relevant and interesting to their readers and it will show that the company is aware of what is going on. It will also help staff and customers see the company's point of view, maybe even to the extent that they, in their turn, carry the message further, in their clubs, associations, political parties or trade unions, where opinions are formed and furthered.

Advertising

Advertising, whether in the form of special 'issue advertising', where the company makes its opinions known, or in the regular institutional, recruitment or market-oriented advertisements, is a strong force in opinion-making, as has been clearly demonstrated by several highly professional, communications-oriented companies in recent years.

Person-to-person

Immediate, mutual communications are never better achieved than in *person-to-person meetings*. The only drawback, but a significant one, is that they are expensive. This, of course, is one reason why other forms of communications are considered at all. In government relations programmes there are many cases in which the high cost of personal communications is warranted. In such cases even top management should be involved, despite the high speed of the taximeter in those occasions.

A way to economize on staff time is to set up group meetings, for example, by inviting groups of specific interest to your premises, with a tailor-made programme for that group and with the proper panel or speaker from the company. In planning such programmes, make sure not to fill the programme from beginning to end. Provide adequate time for questions, for spontaneous remarks and for in-depth explanations, when called for.

A special variety of this approach is inviting committees, citizens' groups, boards or study groups to have their meetings on company premises, with contributions in the form of experts, management representatives, films or other information from the company.

Lobbying

Lobbying as a clearly-defined concept is as American as the hamburger or the apple pie. And like the hamburger or the apple pie, it has spread to other countries as well, even if the shape and seasoning are different.

There has always been a legitimate need for legislators and other political decision-makers to listen to various interest groups in the process of creating or executing policy. Legislators as well as other decision-makers need to have access to facts and opinions from specialists of various kinds to be able to make a balanced judgement.

In the planning process there may have emerged a handful of members of the national legislative assembly whose interests coincide with important areas for the company. If so, it may be a good first step to put them on a very selective mailing list to be used from time to time. Send them only such material that they can really benefit from, knowing their interest profile: speeches by your chairman or president, articles written by some of your specialists in your own publications or in general media, financial reports, research reports, market reports and similar top interest items. Mark the essential parts to make them easy to find. A cover letter from the chief executive or, sometimes, a greeting on his business card will show where the items come from. This kind of mailings, when made with good judgement, will help the legislators and there is little risk that they will see it as undue pressure.

Those from the company's own home area may want to get to know your business a little more closely. Invite them to visit the factory, offer them a presentation and allow plenty of time for questions and answers.

It is when specially 'hot' issues are involved that there is a risk of crossing the border-line between what is acceptable, *bona fide* information and what can be considered undue pressure or influence. If a basis of confidence and credibility has been built up over a long period, be very careful not to spoil it. Before such approaches are made, it is advisable to consult specialists, lawyers or politicians. And, of course, those contacts should always be made, or at least specifically cleared, by the company's chief executive.

Those occasions will hardly be parts of the regular communications programme, but a good communications programme running at the right level creates a positive base for top management should more sensitive contacts ever be required.

Employee involvement

A safe way to increase the number of contacts between a company and the political world of government is a clear company policy to encourage those employees who are interested to take an active part in politics. That, certainly, must never be interpreted as a source of influence from the company on the political process – an employee elected to political office holds it in his own personal capacity, as a citizen, not as an employee of this or that company. But he brings with him his background, his special knowledge about business as he has experienced it in his company. He can for that reason speak with greater authority and expertise on such matters.

In most democratic countries the proportion of legislators and other political office-holders that come from business and industry is far below their share of the total population. Encouraging your staff to take a political interest may in the short run create problems. They will have to take time off for their political work, and they will devote some of their mental energy, used otherwise to the immediate benefit of the company, to their political interests. To compensate, they will widen their horizons, improve their public speaking skills and create another link between the business world and the world of government and politics.

Fact material

Another, less demanding way of contributing company know-how to government at various levels is to offer special *fact material* in areas where the company has specialized know-how. Making a key group analysis and a listing of specific interest areas, a company is likely to find project groups, special study committees or government boards working on subjects that come close to the company's areas of specialization. Why not support such projects by offering contributions from company experts, special studies, research, summaries of past experience, practical test results, financial evaluations, computer programs or even consulting time?

Editorial contacts

Finally, there is, of course, the obvious communications method – working through *editorial contacts* in the general news media. It might be worthwhile to add a selected group of political editors to the usual, perhaps more business-oriented journalist contacts and keep them in mind:

- When the chairman or president of the company has made an important statement.
- When the new energy-saving plan has been put to work.
- When you have made your assessment of the ecological situation of your industry.
- When you find you will have to reduce the employment.
- Whenever issues of public interest come up in the company.

And while these issues fit in well in the range of interests of the political editors, they may also be useful to the editors of the qualified financial or trade press.

How to budget for tangible results

If the key groups and the specific goals have been defined and transformed into an action plan, it will be fairly easy to set a price tag on each one of the items you propose, and to go from there to a cost/value estimate. This, of course, is the professional way to budget communications, as well as any other investments the company makes. Percentages or other more or less sophisticated rules of thumb are always an emergency exit when professional target-oriented budgeting is too difficult.

In government relations, no one could work with the rough yardstick of percentage of sales or other standard figures.

Since staff time, often at high levels, is going to play an important part in many of the actions to be considered, be honest in the budgeting process and take it up as a cost to be balanced against the benefits. In fact, it is only because it does not fit into normal book-keeping systems that this is not standard procedure, counting and estimating staff time for each project, as much as we count the often considerably less important sums of cash that we put into a project.

How should the results of your investments, in time and money, be measured? Suffice it to say that if, in the budgeting and planning process,

1. the key groups have been defined carefully;
2. the benchmark situation has been estimated, if possible in quantifiable terms, as indicated in the rough plan above;
3. specific goals have been set up for each key group;
4. an action plan has been made in specific terms;
5. a price tag has been put on each activity;
6. that price tag, including staff time, has been compared with the specific results you want to achieve;

then in most cases special measurement procedures will hardly be necessary. An evaluation system will have been built into the planning model.

There will be cases where the investment is high and where the results do not show so easily. In those cases it may be advisable to make more formal measurements of results, for example, through an attitude survey.

6

'I know, teacher!':
Communicating with the educational world

In this chapter the reader will find suggestions on why good relations with schools and educational institutions are essential, how to identify the most important 'educational groups' and how to set clear goals for 'educational communications' programmes.

It will help the reader plan, budget, execute and evaluate result-oriented programmes for improved relations with relevant teachers, students and other actors in the field of education.

What is the purpose?

Education and vocational training of the young used to be intimately interwoven with the directly productive sectors of society. Apprenticeship in a trade was the time-honoured way to prepare a young person for responsibilities and service to the community. But increasing specialization in industrialized societies and fast-growing volumes of knowledge to be transmitted from one generation to the next made the school system a world unto itself, separated from the immediately production-oriented world of business and industry. In many countries there is now a clear concern that we have lost something in this process and that there is now a need to build bridges between the two worlds.

In developing countries, where communications with the developed world have created an acute awareness of the vast differences between the very rich and the very poor, the need for training and education is enormous. In addition to basic education, much of the training needs are in vocational, engineering and administrative work, areas where industrialized countries have the background and experience that can be shared in the process of international business. Efforts in this direction are one of the greatest challenges to multinational companies.

Even in the developed world there is deep concern that resources allocated to educational institutions are less than adequate. In a competitive world, education is being recognized as one of the forces of economic, not only human, development and that it deserves more attention, involvement and money than it has traditionally received.

A businesslike purpose

No single company can be expected to solve such massive problems alone. Yet it is part of the attitudes and beliefs deep down in most businessmen that difficulties and challenges must be dealt with and transformed into opportunities. Improvements in the educational system are close to the heart of many businessmen. If big and small companies around the world approached the field of education and training in that spirit, they would find that improved relations with the educational world would match opportunities in many other areas, also in the not too long perspective. They would find opportunities to serve, no doubt, to share their funds of knowledge –

and ideas and knowledge are a kind of asset that does not reduce in value when shared with others.

They would also find direct benefits to participating companies as a result of creating a deeper understanding of business in general and its problems among teachers and young people, of their specific company, of the merits and values of technological development, of the importance of good housekeeping (in business terms, sound returns on investment) and of the challenges and possibilities that a career in business can offer.

No company should start a programme for better contacts with the educational world, in its home area or in far-away places, on philanthropic assumptions. Any company that does, is likely to be disappointed when it does not receive fulsome thanks. Educational communications programmes should be worked out on the same basis as any other business activity, with the clear aim of getting a return on the investment. It is not charity that the world needs from business, it is sound allocations of resources for which the companies will get value in return – immaterial but very real value.

This basic concept was expressed by a seasoned businessman, William S. Vaughn, Chairman of Eastman Kodak, when he closed his speech at an international industrial conference in San Francisco in 1969, in a very matter-of-fact way, with the words: 'The corporation that is not in the business of human development may not be in any business. At least not for long.'

Who are the key groups?

In industrialized countries, the educational systems offer an array of levels, lines, disciplines and alternatives, which, to complicate things further, have little or no resemblance to the schools that top management were in touch with in their salad days. Driving with the rear mirror through the school system is therefore less practical than in most other areas of life. In evaluating where to put in effort – for a selection must be made – it is easier to work from two specific criteria: geographic affinity and subject matter. Geographic areas at home or abroad where the company has important factories or offices are certainly a possible priority. Schools that specialize in such lines of technology or other fields of know-how as the company is active in are another natural priority. In addition, teachers and publishers of educational material are groups to consider.

Local school systems

Local elementary schools probably discuss some of the more important companies in their area when they study the local community. A company would do well to check if it is on the curriculum, and if the teachers in the local schools are aware of their existence, their main field of activity, some of the products or services they provide, and the approximate size of the company.

Local and regional school boards have substantial influence on the direction and contents of the educational process in the area. Does the company have a listing of those who serve on these boards? What do they discuss at their meetings? What are the plans and projections they work with? To what extent is local business represented on the boards or given opportunities to listen and take part in the regional planning of elementary and secondary education systems?

Within the framework of the ambitions and traditions of the national school system, individual teachers have great responsibility and freedom to plan their courses and modify them to suit local needs as well as the personal interests of the students. They also welcome opportunities to widen their own horizons, knowing only too well that their training and education have often prevented them from getting first-hand contact with what is going on in the world outside of schools and colleges. Teachers' unions, the faculties of the schools in the vicinity and groups of specialized teachers are among the key educational groups for a company to work with.

Specialized schools

Among specialized schools, those in various kinds of engineering and business administration come closest to the hearts of most companies. The more specialized they are in subjects of interest to a company, the greater, obviously, is the mutual interest to get together. Development in business and various fields of know-how is fast, and it is often difficult for students and teachers to keep up with the latest news. Contacts with experienced companies offer an opportunity for them to stay in touch. In most cases, therefore, the climate for contacts with teachers and students is favourable.

At university level specialization has gone a long way. If a company can make contact with the right ones, and the right teachers, the waste factor should be very low. This is a field where top-level technicians and administrative staff should be encouraged to participate, to their own and the company's benefit as well as the benefit of students and teachers. Contacts will go far beyond an occasional visit or standard educational material to include examination papers, undergraduate or graduate research projects, special studies, lectures by company staff, in-depth visits and study tours to company labs, offices, workshops or worksites. If such contacts are allowed to develop and deepen over a longer period of time, both sides are likely to get a good return on their investment – students and faculty in terms of awareness of what goes on in 'real life' and companies in terms of new perspectives on their work and progress.

Textbooks

All companies should take an interest in what is said about them or their field of specialized know-how in the textbooks, films and other educational material used in schools. Incidentally, finding out about this could well be a task a company could commission – for a fee – to a teacher or advanced student, perhaps as a vacation job.

A systematic analysis may reveal inconceivable depths of ignorance on the part of the authors. It may show that a competitor has been able to provide material on a scale that the company never thought possible, that new knowledge has been overlooked, that there is a lack of practical examples and applications or that authors and publishers look at things differently from the company. It may well be that development has been so fast that even the most ambitious and knowledgeable authors cannot keep abreast of it.

If a company finds that any of this is true, publishers of educational material may well rank among its key groups.

International aspects

Companies active in other countries, especially in developing countries, will come across radically different educational systems.

In developing countries, instead of abundant learning opportunities there will be a stunning lack of basic resources. Instead of trained teachers, sophisticated programmes, well-stocked libraries and well-equipped laboratories, there will perhaps be nothing, or next to nothing. A company's contributions to education in these areas may only be drops in the ocean. But again, of the resources that a company already has, perhaps produced for internal or customer training, much can be used in vocational schools or can help other teachers create more varied programmes with direct ties to real-life situations.

Working with the school authorities in those countries is one way to make sure that efforts are in line with local and national ambitions and plans. Also, contacts with organizations such as UNESCO can provide data for planning educational material in a company's field of expertise.

Starting with the company's own staff in developing countries will give a good feel for the needs in the community for more and better training resources and will give ideas for active contributions, to the benefit of the host country and the company's own work there.

What are the specific goals?

Specific goals should be set for the educational communications programme for each of the key priority groups selected. It may be easier to define such specific goals by establishing, in a grid or matrix form, intersection points between those key groups and some of the following four types of goals.

Helping management understand

Middle management left school ten to twenty years ago, top executives perhaps twenty to thirty years ago. They could probably use some up-to-date information on the school world today. It would help them in establishing personnel policies, staff training programmes, recruitment guidelines, customer training systems, making donations to their alma maters, etc. Providing for an adequate inward stream of such information is a good starting point.

Be specific in defining what is reasonable to convey from and to the various groups, for example: 'To make all those responsible for hiring personnel aware of present courses in maths in grades 10–12', or 'To make our management aware of what is said in textbooks about ecology and the chemical industry', or 'To get our research personnel to realize how cryogenics is taught at universities today' or 'To inform our board and top management about teacher attitudes towards business'.

Explaining the industry

The second intersection point may fall in the area of explaining to teachers and students important facts about the company and the industry, perhaps including a few basic facts about the role of business in general.

These goals may be expressed specifically in such terms as: 'To give the elementary school teachers in our community a feeling for the contributions our company makes to Middletown', or 'To explain what types of job mechanical engineering companies – ours as one of them – can offer graduates from the vocational lines of high school', or 'To convey our opinions regarding female managers to the teachers of the nearby College of Business Administration'.

Sharing expertise

The third area in which to find fruitful fields of specific company contributions to key educational groups is sharing expertise and know-how with students, teachers and other educational experts.

Specific goals in this field would include: 'To discuss with teachers concerned how various methods of inflation accounting would affect our results', or 'To make high school teachers understand the reasons why a company like ours invests in developing countries', or 'To offer our contributions for the next editions of the two most used text books in steam engineering'.

Sharing material

Finally, another area in which much is done and much more could be done to the benefit of education as well as business is to provide teaching and learning aids. Industry and business have a lot of material that has been produced for marketing and sales, for internal training, for recruitment, for shareholder information, etc. Much of this material, in the forms of slides, printed matter, memos, videos, films, charts, speeches, forms, etc. can be used as it is, or with slight adjustments, perhaps with an introduction or some additional background, as excellent, realistic educational material. The costs for the company are limited, since the material has already been produced, often in large quantities, and the marginal numbers required for educational purposes have little or no significance compared with the positive value it has to the schools. Analysis of how your key educational groups can benefit from such material should be a goal in itself, of course followed up with action.

Specific goals may be, 'To establish with the teachers concerned which of our technical publications can be useful to engineering students/teachers in the area', or 'To find out which of our slide presentations and films are suitable to high school or college audiences among our key groups', or 'To examine how business schools teach annual reports analysis – can ours be used as an example?'.

What methods are available?

The definition of goals, as suggested above, can be made in many different ways. No matter how the goals are defined, they will give an indication of the methods available to reach the goals.

Visits to the company

One of the standard methods used – and misused – in school-company relations is the group visit to the company. There is little doubt that such visits can create interest and provide excellent opportunities for real understanding among young people of what a company is and does. Unfortunately many of us have also experienced the opposite. Dull walks through noisy factories, while a retired guide tries in vain to make himself heard to more than the two or three closest to him, at best topped off with a fruit drink and a biscuit in the company canteen. No wonder that business has a very limited attraction to many students. To most of the students in the class, that visit may be the only direct contact they will ever have with that company. Their opinions of the company, its products, its ambitions, its employees and of business in general may be affected for their lifetime.

So, when you plan school visits, try to make each school group feel that their visit in unique: it *is*, for them. Discuss with the teacher in advance what he or she hopes to get out of the visit, if there is anything in their recent courses that you can tie in to, if there is something they would like to know more about or be briefed on. Prepare sets of worksheets with a brief background, adapted to the schools that make regular visits, and send them to the teacher a week or two before the visit, with some additional material for the teacher or for students who take an additional interest. Give examples of four or five questions to keep in mind during the visit and plan the visit so those questions get answers. If you arrange a question and answer session at the end of the visit, throw some challenges so that questioning really gets off the ground! If your factory is noisy, explain why, and also what you do to reduce the noise. Avoid lengthy explanations *in* the factory – give a short briefing *before* you enter, possibly with reminder cards for the most important points. Loudspeakers are seldom a good solution, they tend to do nothing but add to the noise. Presentation systems exist, based on a microphone and ear plugs for each group member. If you can afford such a system, it is much better. Discuss with the teacher how the visit can be followed up, maybe through a written report, a presentation in the class, a discussion about certain aspects of what has been shown, some of the students making a special study of some problems that have connections to the company or the industry. If the teacher feels it is appropriate, offer some token gifts as prizes to be awarded by the teacher to those students who do the best follow-up work. The whole idea is: make the visit a useful programme, integrated into the curriculum, not just an interruption of it. Handled that way, school visits to your company can be more than a day's break, they can involve students and teachers in fruitful cooperation with the company for long-lasting results.

An alternative that may be applicable in some cases is a visit to a place where your company's products are being used. If you are an engineering company making construction equipment, it might be of great interest for an engineering school to get your help in seeing a tunnel or a road project where your machinery is at work. Or if you are in the agricultural chemical products industry, set up a visit to a big farm to show how modern chemistry is an important part of modern farming. Give the idea some thought and the chances are you will be able to come up with an application that suits your company and its line of business.

The company goes to the school

Sometimes it is difficult or unnecessary to move a whole school class. In such cases it may be in the interests of the school and the company to arrange for a company representative to go to the school and make a presentation. It sounds easy enough and it does not have to be too difficult – after all, the experts in the company know its work, its products and its processes better than anyone. However, just as much as in school visits to the company, or perhaps even more, make sure that the preparations have been made in very close cooperation between the company representative and the teachers involved. The duration of the presentation, films or other audiovisual aids to be used, the scope and contents of the speech, collateral material, such as leaflets, worksheets, question-naires, product samples, etc., should all be thoroughly discussed between the teacher and the guest speaker. A successful presentation by a guest speaker can make a tremendous contribution to the school situation and can leave a good impression for a long time – but a flop will be remembered even longer! So do everything possible to make the guest presentation in the school a success!

Get to know the school situation

It is not so often that the reverse situation can be arranged – a school representative making a presentation to company staff. However, in view of the need for better contacts between business and the educational world, that possibility is worth considering. A bank, an insurance company or an engineering company could invite a maths teacher to explain to its managers how maths is taught in schools today. A headmaster or other school representative could be invited to explain to the staff of the personnel department how the new system of credits or marks is supposed to work, or why the schools are so anxious to help provide practice opportunities for their students. Such invitations may result in better understanding in the companies of what is happening in the school world, and often end up in very useful talks to the benefit of both parties.

Teacher briefings

Teachers are one of the few groups of adults who are given a chance to continuous short or long briefing sessions and formal courses – maybe not as much as they would like, but still . . . The subjects of such training courses are often decided by central school boards. Whoever arranges them may appreciate getting an invitation from a company to discuss how it could contribute in some form to such training courses – hosting one of them, wholly or partly, providing demonstration facilities, speakers, educational aids or other assistance.

School administrators and teachers are aware of the frequent gaps in contacts between business and the educational system, so the chances are they will be interested in exploring what can be done to improve teacher training.

Teachers in engineering or business administration may come first to mind, but why not also include teachers in other subjects, such as social sciences, biology (or other school subjects that include ecology matters), psychology or languages. If it can be arranged, they will appreciate knowing about practical applications of their subjects in companies, to increase the motivation and real-life connection of the courses they teach, and the company representatives will have a chance to discuss what they think is important for the students to become familiar with.

In many cases such training sessions can develop to include deeper discussions about the role of business and how it relates to other sectors of the society, about industrial development and about the specific company, how it works, its markets, the problems and opportunities it faces.

The company's own literature

As a follow-up or as a separate effort, schools among your key groups can be offered your customer magazine or other items to be sent to the staffrooms or to the libraries as a regular service.

Work experience

One of the follow-up questions teachers may ask is whether the company can provide opportunities for shorter or longer periods of work experience, for students or for teachers.

If properly planned, work experience may be of great use, but a company should not go into it unless it is prepared to take it seriously. No teacher, college or school student is likely to benefit from just being put into the company machine for a period and then going back to school. To the contrary, poorly planned work experience is more likely to destroy whatever feelings the person has about business, except the very negative ones. So if such opportunities are offered, make sure that they are well planned, well supervised and well followed up.

Summer jobs

Summer jobs are another matter, although a company does well in giving temporary student employees a briefing on the company and its work on one of the first days, with a short leaflet and an indication of where they can get more background if they want it. One never knows – quite a few of them may want to come back on a more permanent basis, so give them a chance to know the company, and vice versa!

Bursaries and scholarships

More advanced and deeper types of personal student–company relationships include bursary arrangements. They can be devised in many forms and represent a wide range of involvement from the company, from providing students or a student a full period at university to offering students a programme of real-life contact with the company. Companies active in developing countries could do well in setting up facilities for gifted college or university-level students from such countries to come to a developed country for a period, to go deeper into a subject or a process or a technique that will add to their future capacity in their own land. Such programmes could include a period in the company's home laboratory, engineering offices, financial/administrative departments, production management, etc., or it could cover a period as a guest student at a university in a developed country, or, again, it could involve work/practice programmes in other areas close to the company's own. Obviously, such programmes have to be developed in close cooperation with the national educational boards or the universities concerned so that they are of real use to the student and the country.

If such a programme is started, it is advisable to begin on a small scale. Not because of the direct costs, they are not so frightening, but because it is important that the programmes are planned for longer periods. A low-level programme that is guaranteed for several years is more valuable than ambitious schemes that start with a bang and then have to be discontinued. Also, administrative and other unforeseen difficulties may occur that make it better to start in low key. If the programme is worthwhile and gets a good reception it can be stepped up gradually.

Educational material

Both in developed and developing countries, schools and universities can use good educational material. Much company material is or can be adapted to serve as good training material. Ask a teacher or other educational expert to go through company films, slide presentations and film strips, sales and technical literature, annual reports, periodical publications, engineering graphs and charts, etc., and advise how to proceed.

Some of it can perhaps be used as it is, other items may be more useful if provided with a 'frame', an illustrative case story, an introduction, a context story, a questionnaire, a reference to regular textbooks, etc., and some may improve if adjusted in one way or another – adjustments which may be made in subsequent editions.

Publishers of educational material may also want to discuss the company's specialist know-how and whether it could be in the company's interest to transform some of it into regular educational books, audiovisual presentations or other educational aids. The advantages to the company may be considerable. Even if they are not, in the short run, the company could do the whole industry a good service at no cost.

Even wider circulation could be given to selected aspects of the company's know-how, to the benefit of the company's image as specialists, if published as 'sponsored books' used in formal education but also sold in book shops.

Exhibits

If there are certain schools that know far less about the company than they should, or if there are specific problem areas connected with the industry or the company, a way to redress that situation may be to produce and show a programmed exhibit.

All schools have libraries, entrances or other areas where they could set up a screen exhibit, if the subject and the presentation fit into their plans. Of course, this must be done only after consultation with the schools concerned. They should be given a strong voice in the choice of matter, presentation and timing of such an exhibit.

To be really useful, the exhibit should be the backbone of a total communications programme on the chosen theme, that is accompanied by films or other audiovisual material, printed material, interview or personal presentations, posters, worksheets and perhaps special programmes for students who take an active interest, for example practice programmes. Such a special exhibit, accompanied with all or some of these ancillaries, should remain for a three- to four-week period in one school at a time.

Since the budget and effort required is higher than most companies put into their educational contacts as a routine, the subjects chosen should be so important, to both the students and the company, that the project is really worthwhile.

How to budget for tangible results

The immediate or long-range effects of improved school contacts concern so many different fields of the company's life that it is hard to relate costs to benefits in one single area. Obviously, recruitment aspects come into play, both in terms of the company's attractiveness to possible job applicants and in the quality of the students that leave our schools. Additionally, some of the students we get in touch with through a more active educational communications programme may end up as customers of our products. Finally, all of them will play a role, as voters and citizens, in forming future policies and opinions towards industry and business.

But the change created through better communications between a company and the educational world is not limited to 'the other side'. Changes within the company as a result of better understanding of the schools and their problems and development may be an equally significant consequence, one that companies should count on, plan for and welcome as one of the advantages to make up for costs and effort.

Only very seldom do educational contacts add up to any significant shares of a company's total communications programme. Nevertheless, they should be planned and budgeted as carefully as any other programmes that involve company money. It means going through the analysis of key groups, establishing present levels of awareness and attitudes, on both sides of the fence, setting priorities, defining goals, listing possible actions and comparing costs with the value of reaching the goals.

Only in exceptional cases can that evaluation end up in an exact cost/value relation. Going through this process, however, makes it possible to discuss intelligently each step that is considered, and, allowing for judgement and approximations, as in other areas of company activities, one will arrive at a budget that is a lot better than guesswork.

An American advertiser says about his pizza: 'Try it, you'll like it!' Top management will like the communications work with the educational world, once they have tried it!

7

'Where the buck starts':
Market communications

In this chapter the reader will find a broad discussion on the old and new needs for active market communications, with specific advice and suggestions on how to reach the obvious and not so obvious groups that constitute the 'market forces', and on the goals for *market* communications – not only *marketing* communications!

It will help the reader plan, budget, execute and evaluate result-oriented programmes for keeping in touch with the market and for successfully and effectively communicating the right messages to the market.

Old and new needs

There has always been a strong need for business to communicate with its customers, its market. It becomes even clearer, expressed in negative terms: If buyers and sellers do not know of each other, there can be no business.

The old need for business to tell customers about their products and services has got new implications today. Maintaining an active dialogue with customers and other market influences is not only a way to sell more, in a short-range perspective, it is one of the strategic ways for business to adapt to a changing climate, to make business more responsive.

Listening more actively to customers, getting to know them and their decision-making process better, is a function that can be upgraded in many companies. It is not enough for buyers and sellers to *know of* each other. They must *know* each other. More than ever, it is necessary to establish two-way communications with the market. One-way advertising is not enough.

Market communications is a field where more resources are used, both in terms of human effort and cash, than in any other kind of business communication, probably more than all other kinds together. In literature on communications, in education at business colleges, in research programmes, etc., it is market communications that tops the lists, often with the focus on the consumer marketing process. The cost-effectiveness of business-to-business market communications is not very well known. Even worse, much of the knowledge that exists is not always applied in day-to-day work.

Selling costs are rising dramatically per sales call. At the same time, salesman productivity, measured in number of calls required to close a sale, seems to go down. Buying influences 'behind the scenes' are stronger and harder to identify. Salesmen, on average, meet only a fraction of the real influences on a sale. How do the others get their information? What is the role of non-personal market communications in this process? How can the productivity of the total market communications process be improved?

Attention has often been focused on the 'fun' parts of market communications, the creative and execution phases. What can be done to improve the planning and follow-up phases? Can waste be reduced and results improved through more professional management of market communications?

Communications theory and research have focused more on market communications, since that is where the big money is, than on other fields. In reality, much of the resulting knowledge is not limited to market communications. It applies to certain communications methods and to the media in their function as carriers of messages, not necessarily to the audience. Can communications in other areas, where the same resources have not been available, benefit more than they have so far in applying theories and research to their fields, even when they have originated in market communications?

What is the purpose?

Market communications – a two-way process

The chapter on market communications is based on the same philosophy as staff communications, government communications, financial communications and the others. It has three simple elements:

1. Communication is a two-way process where 'listening' is as important as 'speaking'.
2. Business communication is made for purposes that can be defined.
3. If the purpose is well defined before programmes are executed, the results can be measured afterwards.

Market communication includes all forms, methods and techniques, new and old, personal and non-personal, used to increase the customers' awareness and acceptance of our company, its products and services. It also includes the systematic feedback into the company from customers and other influences in the market-place, applied to help the company's decision-makers understand and feel what is going on in the market.

The distinction between contact areas on the one hand, and communications methods on the other, is as helpful in market communications as it is in communicating with other contact areas.

We shall first discuss the various influence groups, some new, some old, some obvious, some not so obvious, that together make up the contact area 'the market'. It will refer primarily, but not exclusively, to business-to-business market situations.

Some of the main methods traditionally used in market communications, but also for other contact areas, are covered in more detail in Part II, Communication channels and methods. This chapter will, however, discuss some specific methods more exclusively used in market communications, again primarily with reference to business-to-business.

Who are the key groups?

More than you think!

If a customer enters a shop to buy a scarf, say, the salesperson behind the counter can be reasonably sure that the customer is also the main decision-maker on that purchase. There may be additional hidden influences on the purchase, such as the customer's wife or husband, but by and large the visible client is the main decision-maker.

For a business-to-business salesperson, the situation is more complicated. The purchasing agent who signs the contract may, in fact, have had very limited power to bear on the purchase. Hidden influences, hardly ever seen or considered by the salesperson, may have made all the important decisions leading up to the signature on the order form.

All research available on this subject confirms that the number of persons who have a say in business buying decisions is staggering. For a major purchasing decision, the number of buying influences is not five or ten, it is twenty-five, or fifty – or more! And we are still talking about influences that, at least in recent marketing literature, are recognized as important contributors to specific decisions. Who are the other influences, those that are hardly even discussed? How can one reach them, listen to them and influence them? How does one communicate with them – in both directions?

To start, let us list some categories of key market influences for business to communicate with:

1. The identified purchasing influences in customer and prospect companies, i.e., those who see the salesmen, negotiate, sign contracts and take delivery.
2. The unidentified purchasing influences in customer and prospect companies, i.e., those who identify needs, make specifications,

104

 rank or recommend suppliers, grant funds, approve investment
decisions and perform other behind-the-scene functions.

3.   The operators, users, service mechanics and others who are in
direct practical contact with the product or service, in customer
and prospect companies. They may be considered as a
subdivision of 2 above, but since their characteristics differ in so
many respects, it is more practical to see them as a separate
group.

4.   Government or quasi-government offices or agencies and other
political or quasi-political influence groups, openly active or
opinion-makers behind the scene.

That does not represent a complete list – trade media, business
organizations and consultants are examples of other groups that
should be added.

It may be a good exercise to try to identify, in specific categories,
by market segment, the four groups above, for the most important
markets and product categories.

The obvious influences . . .

Most companies can easily define one key group of purchasing
decision-makers, those who place the order, those who say the
magic yes to the salesman, who send in the contract, who call on the
phone to order those spare parts, who accept the company's bid
over seven others after three years of negotiations. They are an
obvious key group. They are listed in the golden mailing lists of the
companies, they get Christmas greetings or gifts, regular sales calls
and all the new literature. Chances are high that they will be
reached by ads and direct mail. They are well cared for, and they
should be.

If you are not completely sure of who the direct buying influences
are it might be a useful exercise to go through, together with some
of the sales staff, a few 'typical' business transactions. Look at them
from the selling side or from the buying side – or both.

Why look at the transaction from the buying end? One reason is
that it is a natural approach in communications always to try to see a
situation from the other side, whether it is a question of staff,
government, financial or any other contact area. Another, more
specific reason is that much research, confirmed by practical
experience, shows that, especially in business-to-business dealing,

the initiative is often taken by the buyer, not by the seller. Most products are bought, not sold.

Worksheet 7.1, p. 122, may be helpful in this process, both to identify who the immediate buying influences are and to get to know the customer's frame of mind in relation to the offer.

. . . And the not-so-obvious ones

What about all the other influences? Usually there are more purchasing influences for each purchasing decision than most salesmen think, let alone meet. Research and experience tell us that in professional purchasing cases it is a rule rather than an exception that a majority of the purchasing influences never meet a salesman or even appear on the mailing lists.

If all those hidden influences, thus, are not talked to by the seller, would anyone believe that they are listened to? How could they?

Still it may be the reactions of one of these hidden influences that will cost the company the next order and nobody will ever know – until, perhaps, it appears that the competitor has just got a terrific order . . . So, trying to find and identify the influences behind the scene, perhaps in the following categories, may be a worthwhile exercise:

Who in the buyer company identifies the need or writes the specification? If he does not know of your elegant solution, he may describe his problem in a different way, so you will never even be considered.

Who services the products of your kind, that are already installed in the customer's plant? If the maintenance engineer has heard stories about your bad service from colleagues in the pub, he may take you off the bidders' list. You will never know why you did not even get the inquiry.

Who is the person who authorizes the funds or requests estimates? If he has an opinion of your company as a 'highway robber', you will not even have a chance to present your new low-price alternative.

And what about the customer's employees? In many companies today, employee participation affects purchasing decisions. Few European companies would introduce new production machinery or methods, new plant equipment, new formulas for paint spray, new automation devices or new control measures without consulting those who are going to use the equipment, work with it or be exposed to it.

If the shop floor operator knows that a new model of chisel hammer takes away 90 per cent of the dangerous vibrations in the arm of the user, do you think he will accept another model, even if it is half the price?

What are the implications on market communications of these new types of buyer influence? The consequences are likely to go far beyond who to talk to or advertise to – although that is important. They also mean listening to other persons more than before, and then adapting the sales approach, packaging, instructions, sales literature, supply patterns – and the product itself.

Are there any political influences that come into the pattern, short- or long-range? What about consumer protection or worker-safety legislation? Government and quasi-government agencies of various kinds are in themselves proof that business has been so busy using its mouth that it has forgotten to use its ears. Now that they are here, business had better start listening to them, for they have the power, if not the glory.

What are the specific goals?

There are two kinds of goals:

1. The company should get to know all the actors in the market better, who they are and what they think and feel.
2. The actors in the market, known and unknown, should get to know the company and its products and services better.

Each of these general goals, when we have defined the WHO, can be broken down in specific operational elements on the basis of WHAT, WHEN and WHY. And when that is done, we can tackle the question HOW, which will be discussed in the methods section.

First, some simple questions:

1. What do they know, think and feel about our company and its product range?
2. What do we know about their needs and interests?
3. In which situations is it important for us to know this?
4. What are the consequences, what difference does it make, if we know or not?

Which methods are available for the company to learn more?

A company that can answer those questions satisfactorily, with appropriate breakdowns, is in a strong position. The company that cannot, can find out. There are several techniques for improving the knowledge of customer awareness and attitude levels.

Much information may already be available in the company, but scattered in different departments. Finding it and putting it together may be a good start.

Customer panels may be one way, formal surveys another.

The marketing department can help. They will provide fact-sheets, graphs, sales trends and statistics. Their prime concern is share of market. The communications task is share of mind (as a way to reach share of market).

Internal analysis within the company

Much of the inflow of information can be obtained through the people in the company who have personal contacts with customers. Salesmen and other staff routinely report back on customer reactions, what they think and feel. Reports can be complemented with personal interviews by company staff or outside specialists. Just keep in mind all those purchasing influences that the company salesmen never meet, speak to or listen to.

Some of the information on hidden influences may exist in other departments than sales, marketing or communications. A goldmine of information could be available in the company, unknown and under-utilized. An internal customer reaction audit may be a way to discover it. Here are some examples:

1. The supervisor of the user's field department told the supply manager, in no uncertain terms, that he was furious about the delay of those spare parts.

2. The customer's market for square widgets has been going down for a long time, so the customer has decided to close that line. No more use for your good old square widget boxes. Somebody in the company read about it in a trade magazine, but forgot to tell marketing.

3. One of the company's good friends in the purchasing department left to go to another company, so he is not going to handle

purchases from you any more. Your personnel manager heard about it, but never made the connection.

A systematic analysis may reveal vital facts about customer attitudes and opinions to the company, its service levels and its product performance.

Ask the sales staff. Try to get the real reasons behind lost sales, beyond the standard reaction: 'Our price was too high.'

Ask the service staff about recurring customer reactions to product reliability, maintenance, operating conditions, etc. Go beyond standard service reports and statistics.

Check with the accounting and credit management staff. What are the reasons behind late payments, poor collection results and other 'financial reactions' from the customers? They may be based on negative attitudes to the company's performance in one way or another.

Ask the switchboard and reception area staff. They may know more about reactions to the company's performance than anyone thinks. Happy or unhappy comments from customers, accessibility of managers or service staff, frequency of complaints, etc.

Customer panels

Panels have long been an accepted way in consumer companies to listen to their buyers. Complaints, suggestions, requests come up easily in a panel environment.

Few business-to-business companies use this method in a meaningful and systematic way. If the company feels it has excellent two-way contacts with its buyers – fine. It may be true – at least about those customers that the sales staff regularly meet. But what about the others, those who contribute indirectly to decisions that affect purchasing or those down the line who use the company's products? Customer panels may be worth a try.

If you are an industrial paint manufacturer, how many times have you met the workers who use your paints in the finishing end of the tractor plant, the computer company, the furniture manufacturer or the toy factory? Letting them have a say, on an informal panel, directly to your product development staff might be a great way to get new ideas. Or why not get the marketing staff of those companies to tell you about the demands *their* customers have on surface treatment, paint quality and development in the user branches?

Or what about the design engineers in the customer companies? That group is one of the hidden influences behind many purchasing decisions, affecting such parameters as quantity (maybe they consider alternative designs using materials that do not need paint), quality (they may have a de luxe line in the works, for which other paint qualities would be needed) or timing.

Getting these groups together, in small panels, at their plant or yours gives immediate feedback on customer attitudes and awareness levels and explains action or non-action. It also makes the customer understand that you mean what you say when your advertisements declare that you are a customer-oriented company.

After going through some important customer companies, you may find out why some companies are not your clients. If not, arranging similar panels from prospect companies could be a challenging step.

And, as a final step – or perhaps a start – invite some of the key people in the government agencies that you are or should be in touch with to a similar hearing. There is no law that says that only agencies should take initiatives to hearings, so why not be a pioneer and invite them to a hearing or a panel?

Start on a small scale – and don't make a publicity gimmick of it. Be serious about it, and you will get serious feedback, to be fed into your decision-making process.

A special method to find out about future customers needs so one can prepare for them in time is applications of the *Delphi method*. In short, it means asking experts in the field, customer specialists, university researchers, qualified writers and other specialists what they think of future trends in a defined field.

Setting up a Delphi project requires a great deal of thorough preparations. The method cannot be covered in detail here, but if the idea appeals, then get some material from your favourite librarian and work from there.

Customer surveys

When direct personal contacts are not possible or economical, or when a company wants honest reactions from customers without embarrassing them, customer or market surveys can be used. Surveys on awareness and attitudes are the communications manager's best way to measure where he stands and what he accomplishes with the other tools in his tool-box. They should be as natural to the communications manager as a yardstick is to the carpenter.

Surveys can be made on a large scale or with small samples. They can be general or very specific. They can rank from nationwide polls to routine follow-up of customer attitudes after delivery.

The aid of professional attitude survey specialists (see also Part III, Chapter 17) is probably required. Costs can usually be kept within reasonable limits, in relation to the benefits, but it is advisable to encourage competition between suppliers of research services. Give a survey project reasonable time, but don't necessarily set academic standards. What you need is a platform for intelligent action, not a treatise.

It may be enough to consider, at this stage, three ground-rules:

1. Make sure the anonymity of respondents is respected. Leaks must not even be suspected.

2. Avoid making just one survey of any kind. The results are likely to be much more useful if two or three or more surveys are made, and compared as a basis for action. Make similar surveys on different customer categories or on similar customer categories in different locations, or make consecutive surveys with reasonable time intervals.

3. For communications purposes, make attitude or awareness studies. Market surveys are something else, although sometimes similar methods are being used. Avoid mixing the two.

Following the trade press

Following the trade press is a natural way of taking the pulse on attitude and opinion trends in your field. A lot can be fed into the organization through careful reading of the specialized press, both articles and competitor advertising, with appropriate summaries and conclusions.

How has systematic feedback from the trade press into your company been organized? Through traditional circulation lists of ten to twenty names, in the corporate pecking order? How old is the information when it reaches the levels in the company where somebody takes action? Have you considered not only 'your own' trade press but also that of your main customer industries?

It could be wise to restrict the number of magazines circulating past everybody's desk, but be generous about increasing the number of subscriptions to each magazine. Some companies work by the 5/5 rule, meaning that no employee is allowed to put his name on more than five circulation lists, and no circulation list should have more than five names on it.

The person who tops the circulation list does not necessarily have to be the highest in rank. There is a price to pay for the advantage of being first on the list. The price is the responsibility immediately to alert anyone in the company who should be informed of a certain item mentioned in the magazine, be it in the ad pages or in the editorial copy.

Which methods are available to get your message across?

In most companies the market communications budget is still made conventionally, by traditions, percentages and rule of thumb.

Are there better ways?

The first obvious choice is to decide what can be done through personal and what has to be left to non-personal methods.

How do 'they' form their opinions?

In the process of getting to know your customers better, it is useful to find clues on how they establish their knowledge, attitudes and opinions. Where do they get new ideas and how are the old ideas confirmed or modified?

What are their readership habits in terms of trade and general press? Do they show common patterns in visiting trade shows, being members of associations or going to conferences? What is their position in the companies? Do they have any common denominators in educational background, age, lifestyle or demographic aspects? Do they tend to be conservative or open to new thoughts, risk-takers or safe players?

If any common patterns emerge, they can give clues to how to reach them and influence them.

The role of the salesman

Of the four influence categories discussed earlier in this chapter, only the first category, the 'obvious' group, can be reached at all through personal sales calls by salesmen, and even that category probably only to a limited degree. The other groups are never reached by salesmen.

A salesman, like most other employees, works around 1,500–2,000 hours per year. A great deal of that time is spent in paperwork, travelling, administration and other duties than direct eye-to-eye contact with the customers.

McGraw-Hill reported in 1988 that the average cost of a business-to-business sales call in 1987 was more than $250. What is more: the same survey reported that, on average, it took 4.6 sales calls to close a sale, resulting in a salesman cost of $1,160 to close a sale. The average order amount was reported to be $125,000.

What are the corresponding figures for your company? Whatever they are, it is imperative to get the maximum value out of them.

Most business selling requires competent contributions from high-quality salesmen, so let us use the salesman himself as the first basis.

How do your own salesmen evaluate how they use their time? Would you be willing to use ten minutes at the next sales conference to get a better idea of how much of the total resources should go into personal selling and how much into 'multi-communications'?

The Center for Marketing Communications in Princeton, N.J. (now integrated in the ARF Business Advertising Research Council) has developed a form, reprinted here as Figure 7.1. The idea is to let the salesmen themselves estimate how their time is used for different tasks and how it can be used most productively. Adapt the form to your own needs and ask your salesmen, or a selection of them, to fill it out. (Show them the headlines of one column at a time and ask them to fill it out before they go to the next headline.)

'How much personal selling can we afford?'

There are two things for which personal contacts are very well suited:

1. Working out, with the buyer, specific solutions to his problems (making special varieties, presenting customer-adapted ideas, answering his direct questions, helping to reach individual decisions on type, speed, quantity, formula, output, etc.).
2. Negotiating the conditions and closing the sale.

Breakdown of personal selling responsibilities for:

Product	Market		
Column 1 Salesman's jobs	**Column 2** Percent of total sales work	**Column 3** Percentage that can be carried out using mass communication	**Column 4** Multiplication of Col. 2 x Col. 3

Daily routine work

1. Locate and contact new companies for prospect list   ( ) ( )   ( )

2. Develop and maintain company's image among customers   ( ) ( )   ( )

3. Make customer and prospects more familiar with additional details of the product range   ( ) ( )   ( )

4. Inform customers and prospects on new products and areas of application   ( ) ( )   ( )

5. Keep the customer happy after the sale is made   ( ) ( )   ( )

Specific sales work

6. Develop customer interest in specific products or services   ( ) ( )   ( )

7. Contact additional buying influences within the customer company   ( ) ( )   ( )

8. Influence the prospective customer to specify your product   ( ) ( )   ( )

9. Prepare proposals/tenders   ( ) ( )   ( )

10. Follow up technical matters   ( ) ( )   ( )

11. Negotiate   ( ) ( )   ( )

12. Close the sale   ( ) ( )   ( )

Additional tasks involved in selling this product:

_____   ( ) ( )   ( )

_____   ( ) ( )   ( )

_____   ( ) ( )   ( )

                  TOTAL: 100%

Questionnaire completed by:

_____	_____
Name	Title
_____	_____
Department	Company

Figure 7.1 *Charting the salesman's tasks*
The Advertising Research Foundation, reprinted with permission.

114

Ideally, the salesmen should use most of his time for those two things, and get as much as possible of other tasks done through non-personal market communications.

How can this be expressed in budget terms?

Obviously, the traditional way of counting percentages of sales is completely useless. A slightly better method is to compare the shares of total market communications cost of non-personal versus personal methods. Try it out through the formula:

$$\frac{\text{non-personal market communications}}{\text{personal selling} + \text{sales administration}}$$

A 20/80 ratio is not unusual in business-to-business. That does not mean that this ratio is right in all companies, at all times, not even for the different product ranges or different customer categories of one company. There is really no way to escape from a serious analysis based on the present situation, your own objectives and the specifics of each market segments. Experience, confirmed by research, indicates that more business-to-business companies could improve total communications effectiveness by increasing the share of non-personal communications.

Four profit-oriented objectives

Remember the old expression, 'If you are not in business for fun or for profits, what the hell are you doing here?' Advertising, direct mail, trade shows and other similar activities can certainly be fun. But the only reason for them is their contribution to company profits. Yet many managers find it difficult to define the profit objectives of market communications. The standard answer is often: 'To sell more'.

Let us consider four profit-oriented objectives:

1. Increased salesman productivity (= more sales per sales call).
2. Stronger price position (= ability to defend a desirable or necessary price level).
3. Improved motivation of the sales staff.
4. Higher sales volume.

The ranking may or may not reflect the relative importance of the four factors. This obviously varies in different situations. My personal experience is that the first parameter, increasing salesman productivity, is the most important of the four in the overwhelming majority of all cases.

There are two basic ways to optimize the use of the expensive time the salesman spends with the customer:

1. Preparing the salesman, through intensive training.

2. Preparing the customer, through non-personal communications.

In defining how much of the total market communications efforts that should be made by personal and how much through non-personal methods, the only criterion that can be used professionally is the same criterion as business uses in all other investment decisions – profitability, in the long and short range perspectives.

Worksheet 7.2, p. 124, offers ten questions that can give additional help in reviewing your own priorities and in balancing the resources to be allocated for personal – non-personal communications.

Experience and tradition set upper and lower limits. The company feels it must have some salesmen, and it must 'do some advertising'.

Most companies would profit from a more careful analysis of the balance between 'manual' selling – with its very special advantages – and 'mechanized' selling – with its ability to carry similar messages to bigger numbers at, normally, lower costs. The balance can and should be examined at regular intervals.

The company that relies too much on its salesforce to do a difficult job without enough support from multi-communications acts like a general who sends in the infantry without enough artillery or air support. The company puts the salesman and his expensive time into the wrong stages of the total process, without considering more economical alternatives.

Going back to our earlier discussion of the 'not-so-obvious' influences: to reach those who exercise an influence behind the scenes, who authorize funds, identify needs, write specifications, recommend or select suppliers, use or service the products or excercise influence in the political spectrum, there is hardly any other way than multi-communications. Fortunately, there is a wide range of methods.

A wide range of communications methods

Having analysed the tasks and roles of personal selling versus multi-communications, the company can proceed with the choice of weapon in the arsenal of communications methods.*

Some of the methods can be so widely applied for different communications areas – not only marketing – that they are treated in the next part of this book. Advertising, using paid space in general media, direct mail, printed matter, editorial work, exhibits and audiovisual aids are among those methods. This section, therefore, is limited to some other less considered methods to be used in the communications process between a company and its markets. While some of them are 'personal' they basically build either on group relations rather than one-to-one meetings or they are a mixture of personal and non-personal methods.

Customer seminars and training programmes

Every company has a lot of expertise in its research laboratory, engineering department, production department and other areas. Could any of this expertise be useful to specialists in customer companies? Not that competitive secrets should be given away. Even so, there may well be enough material in your files to fill several valuable *customer seminars*, courses or training sessions.

A marine turbine company arranged high-level customer seminars for many years, to the benefit of shipbuilding engineers and naval architects/designers. Since customer seminars naturally include time for questions and answers, they got in return a very good feel for what the market was looking for in marine propulsion. The seminars were not run by the salesmen for the clients' buyers. Participants on both sides were highly qualified groups of market and engineering experts. Papers presented were filled with diagrams, charts, tables and facts. After the seminars they were compiled into binders that were used for years as working manuals for naval architects and marine engineers. Guess which company managed to come out first with a new type of machinery that met the demands of the market? And guess what that did to its market share?

A similar form of customer relations is important to many industrial companies, but could be used by many more: planned *training programmes* for users of their equipment. Such training programmes can cover the whole range from extensive instruction

---

* The reader will recall that in this book the term 'advertising' is used only to denote a specific method, a technique of conveying a message, using paid space or time in general media. Other forms of conveying a message are called what they are: audiovisual aids, direct mail, printed matter, exhibitions, etc. When they need to be dealt with together, they are called 'communications methods'.

books, through programmed training with self-instruction, with or without audiovisual aids, to full-fledged training periods on customer sites or on the premises of the selling company. They can be finished with formal examination with diplomas, which could even be a condition for user guarantees. Such training, in the interest of the buyer as well as the seller company, will ensure proper handling of the equipment to avoid damages, costly breakdowns or repairs and to increase worker safety. An additional benefit to the seller company is the loyalty that the training generates among the users, who feel familiar with the product and can handle minor problems immediately should they occur.

Active contact work with the trade press

Working with the trade press actively, keeping it informed of what is going on in the company, is a natural role of the communications department. It means a lot more than sending out press releases on new products. It should involve complete responsibility for all contacts with the market-oriented press.

It is a fundamental rule in all press relations that advertising and editorial contacts should not influence each other. Still, the intended readers are the same for market-oriented advertising and editorial material. If advertising and editorial work are not handled by the same person, or in the same department (see more about these aspects in Chapter 18), at least the two should have very open lines between them. They should reflect coordinated company views in such regards as media priorities, basic philosophies, central messages, etc. Details about editorial work are outlined in Chapter 10 and about advertising in Chapter 11.

Suffice it to say here that in countries that have a qualified business press, companies should realize that they have a strong interest in supporting its sound development. In countries where it does not exist, organized business and individual companies should do their best to create favourable conditions for it. There are few channels that are more helpful and effective, in a cost/value analysis, than professional, independent business and trade magazines.

A special kind of market-oriented editorial work is the company-sponsored customer magazine. Some aspects on this medium will be discussed in Chapter 10. While these magazines sometimes appear to work in competition with the commercial trade press, it is often possible to have the two support each other. And in countries where adequate trade press has not yet emerged, the customer magazine offers a unique opportunity to maintain wide customer contacts with acceptable frequency.

How to budget for tangible results

Even among market communications managers one sometimes hears, with a mixture of pride and complaint, that it is not possible to measure the results of communications work.

Admittedly, it is not always easy. However, the problem in most cases is not one of measurement. It is rather a question of not having defined the objective. It would be equally difficult for a production manager to make an investment plan or a production budget, if he did not know what to produce, in what quantities and to what quality specifications.

'Tossing a coin' is one way of doing it

What is the budgeting process for market communications in your company? Do you recognize some of these expressions:

- 'Same as last year' (perhaps with the addition of x per cent more or y per cent less).
- 'X per cent of sales last year.'
- 'Business is tough this year. Let's cut the market communications budget.'
- 'What are our competitors doing?'
- 'Let's see what we can afford when we have budgeted everything else.'

Are there better ways?

Well, there certainly are more businesslike ways to decide on company expenses. Expressions like those above would hardly be acceptable in other areas of business life.

The money invested in market communications, both in consumer-oriented companies and in business-to-business is big enough to deserve full attention. Amounts for business-to-business communications in the United States have been estimated to be in the range of $100 billion. The amounts are likely to be somewhere in that order, as a percentage of GNP, in other industrialized countries. More professional planning should be able to contribute to a better return on this investment.

If this is true in the national macro-perspective, it is equally true at

119

the company level. A better budgeting and planning process could save money or produce better results for the money spent, or both.

Planning for measurable results starts with a definition of the objectives to be reached. There is no way to avoid the question: 'What is the exact job to be done?'

It is perhaps in this field that confusion traditionally plagues market communications. Too little time and effort are spent on really analysing the goals and objectives in clear communications terms.

Four profit-related objectives for market communications have been suggested above (see p. 115). They can only be reached via changes in attitudes, awareness and preference. The changes should ultimately result in action.

While it is true that no sales are ever accomplished without communications, in most cases communications do not play the whole game. Other factors, price, business cycles, special requirements, delivery times, etc., may well outplay the best situation in terms of awareness, attitudes and preference. And those are the main areas that can be influenced by communications.

Start by looking at some present communications programmes. Which areas do they aim at – and in which direction? Are they more geared to knowledge (awareness), to emotions (attitudes) or to action (preference)? Then set goals for planned projects in those terms, in market communications as well as in other contact areas. It does not make them less specific, but it may make them harder to define, at least before one is used to the technique.

Try tentative, but specific, communications goals like these:

1. Increase awareness of the new products in the target audience from 23 per cent to 40 per cent before the end of this year.

2. Change the positive attitudes to ergonomic nutrunners among foremen in the automotive industry from 20 per cent to 50 per cent.

3. Move our preference ranking in the chemical industry from six to three in two years.

4. Make 150 valuable leads from this advertising campaign.

5. Get ten customer executives to attend the next seminar.

In the planning process of the next market communications project, try to get everyone committed by agreeing to a sentence like this:

'This project will be considered successful, if

. . . .

as verified by

. . . .'

A step-by-step budgeting process

This chapter has already offered some suggestions on how to establish benchmarks, how to define objectives and how to measure results. Additional thoughts are provided in Chapter 17, measuring results. A company's step-by-step budgeting process could look like this:

Make the budgeting *specific*:

- Break down the budgeting by business lines, customer segments and/or geographic markets. Look at sales and profit goals, long-range and short-range, in the same terms.
- Calculate total marketing costs (personal selling, sales administration, capital requirement and other marketing costs) broken down in the same way.
- Discuss and rank the importance of possible profit objectives for your market communications work, such as:

Make salesman time more productive
(Calculate costs/sales call, sales calls required for closing, average sales amount/call, average profit contribution/call, etc.)
Defend a price level
(Calculate 'our' price level compared to competition, profits if price level could be maintained or increased, etc.)
Motivate sales and other staff
(Present motivation and attitude levels, potential profits if workers and staff made 'that little extra effort')
Sell more/gain market share
(Potential sales to new customers, in new areas, in new market segments, etc.)

- What are the hurdles that can be broken, eliminated or lowered through better communications? Discuss this by the same breakdown.
- How much would it be worth to reach those goals in reduced costs or increased income? How far in the right direction can you get in the next budget period?
- Allow enough funds and time to establish benchmarks and measure results, in other words, for appropriate research. How much? As a guideline, if needed, 'it should be worth a nickel to know what you achieve with every dollar'.

After this, look at the *overall market communications needs*, through the same steps, so that you allow enough funds for common activities and programmes aimed at making the company as such more attractive as a business partner.

Starting with specifics and then going to overall needs tends to make the whole budgeting process more professional than starting with generalities and then breaking it down.

Get the time perspective right! In most companies, budgeting is made on an annual basis. While this is practical, from an accountant's point of view, it may be completely wrong from a professional market communications perspective. A seasonal campaign may have to straddle two accounting periods. A product launch may be tied to the new product being ready. A programme may have a time perspective of several years, especially if funds are limited.

Try to keep the process focused for as long as possible on 'who' and 'what', rather than on 'how'. In other words, link the budget to target audiences and desired changes in these audiences. Who do we want to influence, with what messages, to achieve what changes compared to now?

After setting price tags on this basis, with amounts that, at this stage, are felt reasonable, it may be time to talk in terms of various communications methods that can be used to achieve the goals indicated. Don't make decisions too early in the budgeting process on media and methods, on advertising or brochures, on direct mail or audiovisuals!

A process of this kind will help any company, big or small, to make a goal-oriented market communications budget, and a programme in which each part, in principle, is measurable and accountable.

Worksheet 7.1   The buying process

The purpose of this worksheet is to help you get a better grasp of how purchasing decisions are made in specific business-to-business buying situations.

Product/product group: _____

1. Who are the customer *industries*? (In SIC codes or equivalent)

2. What is the contribution of this product/service to the customer's operations?

    ☐ Save production costs
    ☐ Reduce other costs. Which?
    ☐ Reduce risks. Which?
    ☐ Improve productivity
    ☐ Improve product quality
    ☐ Improve work conditions
    ☐ Other _____

3. What are the alternatives to our proposal?

    ☐ Different method
    ☐ Modified system
    ☐ Alternative technique
    ☐ Same, but other brand
    ☐ No purchase at all
    ☐ Other _____

4. What is the frequency of these decisions?

    ☐ Ongoing need
    ☐ Periodic renewal
    ☐ Seasonal
    ☐ Budget cycle
    ☐ Replacement of old
    ☐ Expansion
    ☐ New application/process
    ☐ Other (even 'irrational'): _____

5. What is the customer's time-frame/'urgency factor'?

    ☐ Immediate need. Time: _____
    ☐ Planned need. Time: _____
    ☐ Need perceived but no immediate hurry
    ☐ No need perceived

6. Customer locations?

    ☐ Decisions
    ☐ Use/installation

7. Buying influences in a typical deal? (In job classifications)

   ☐ Immediately perceived
   ☐   Well known
   ☐   Not known
   ☐ Behind the scene
   ☐   Well known
   ☐   Not known
   ☐ Irrational influences
   ☐   Well known
   ☐   Not known

8. What is the 'value package' that a customer is looking for and appreciates?

9. Describe a typical purchase from start to finish, including who takes the initiative, typical amounts, time-frame, customer staff involved, negotiation and closing procedures, delivery, payment, warranties, installation, after sales, etc.

Worksheet 7.2   Personal–non-personal communications

Before making decisions on methods and money, try the following ten questions. If you wish, put a number value from 1 to 5 on each answer, where one end would indicate a preference for personal and the other would show a need for non-personal communications. Add the total and see which way your budgeting should go.

1. **What is your untapped market potential?**

   Low_____High
   1   2   3   4   5

If you cover your market very well, that is, you have a small, untapped market potential, chances are that you are well known and highly regarded in the market. It should be possible to let the field salesforce do a higher proportion of the total communications job. On the other hand, if your remaining market potential is big, it will probably be too expensive for you to cover it by personal salesmen, so you will want to use multi-communications more.

2. **What is the average order amount?**

High_____Low
1   2   3   4   5

If the average amount of each order is high, and if you have a decent profit margin, it may be right for you to put a big share of the total job on personal selling. If, on the other hand, the average order amount is low, you would probably want to 'mechanize' a bigger share of the total communications task to have the customer 'pre-sold' to a higher degree.

3. **What is the ratio of new products and applications?**

Low_____High
1   2   3   4   5

If your range of products and services is well established, and few new aspects or items have entered the range, you may rely more on the salesmen to 'keep the ball rolling'. But if your company is an innovative one, it would be a heavy burden, and an expensive one, to have your salesmen present these new ideas, products, services, applications and methods. A great deal of that work could presumably be made more effectively through various forms of multi-communications.

4. **How well known is your company?**

Well_____Not well
1   2   3   4   5

If your company, generally, is well known, even if it is through other means than market dominance, your salesman's job is a good deal easier, and he can expect to get a fair hearing when he makes his sales calls. In those cases, it may well be right to have the salesmen do a great share of the total job. If your company is not well known, all experience indicates that it is a worthwhile investment to make it known through multi-communications to make the salesmen's time more productive.

5. **How well have you identified your customers?**

Well_____Not well
1   2   3   4   5

If your customers are well identified, it is easy for your salesmen to make the right appointments and to get to see the right people with a minimum of waste. If you are uncertain about who your customers really are, it should pay off to use well-planned multi-communications programmes to get your customers to identify themselves, then get them to meet your salesmen. Sending the salesmen out in the field to try to find customers haphazardly is an expensive game of 'hide-and-seek'.

6. **What are your growth ambitions?**

Low_____High
1   2   3   4   5

Your growth ambitions may be higher in some areas than in others. If you are in low-growth areas, why not let the salesmen 'keep the pot boiling'. It is probably favourable to use salesmen to a higher degree in such cases. In product or market areas where you want to grow fast, you will want to get maximum efficiency out of your salesmen. A stronger effort in multi-communications helps make the customers ready for the salesman when he comes.

7. **What is the mobility of your customer staff?**

Low_____High
1   2   3   4   5

Individual customer companies have different mobility rates and so have various categories of industry. If you work with stable customers with low mobility, for example, mining and banking, the investment your salesmen make in building personal relations with customers is sound and reasonable – provided, of course, that your salesmen stay on the job long enough. If much of your selling is to companies with high mobility, for example, construction projects or seasonal work, chances are that your salesmen will meet new faces every time they visit the customer. In such cases, put less effort into personal selling and more into other forms of communication, for example, trade press advertising or direct mail programmes, geared to function rather than names.

8. How big is the number of purchasing influences?

Low _____High
1   2   3   4   5

No matter how well you have defined them, if the number of persons involved in the customer's decision process is big, it is more difficult, or at least more expensive, for your salesmen to meet them all. They may also be on levels, 'above' or 'below', where your salesman has little opportunity to see them. If the purchasing decisions are made by one or a few people, they are more easily accessible to your salesman. Few buying influences = bigger share of total job for the salesman, big number of influences = bigger share for multi-communications.

9. How strong is the position of your products on the markets?

Strong _____Weak
1   2   3   4   5

If your products are well established as the ★★★ product in its class, through sheer performance data or through lack of competition, it may be satisfactory to work mainly through salesmen. If not, put a bigger share of the total effort into multi-communications.

10. How high are your salesmen's costs?

Low _____High
1   2   3   4   5

If your salesmen's salaries are low, travelling distances between customers short and if the need for your salesmen to make preparations before each sales call are not too cumbersome, it is reasonable to use salesmen to a greater extent. If, on the other hand, you have to use high-level, well-paid salesmen whose time with the customer is very expensive, then there is reason for you to consider other forms of communication to increase the return on SHC (cost of one salesman hour in direct contact with the customer).

8

'Broadside':
Communications across the board

In this chapter the reader will find a presentation of some critical situations in which the company should be able to relate successfully to many contact areas and audiences simultaneously – situations that are or develop into 'tests of mastership' in business communications.

It will help the reader plan, budget, execute and evaluate result-oriented communications programmes to develop corporate identity, to support mergers and acquisitions, investments and disinvestments, crises and emergencies, anniversaries, inaugurations and other major events in a company's life.

The tests of mastership

Most of the communications tasks we have discussed so far have been geared to improve a company's relations with one specific contact area. While it is practical to see communications work in this perspective, for planning, budgeting and follow-up purposes, there is a touch of self-deception in it. All communications programmes have an overspill, can reach other than the primary groups and can have other effects than those intended.

The fact that there is an overspill between contact areas does not mean that the contact area principle is wrong. The 'overspill factor' does mean, however, that there has to be consistency in a company's total communications efforts, an overall consistency in the key messages, goals and media. Market communications are not only the marketing manager's responsibility, staff relations not only the responsibility of the personnel manager, local community relations not only a job for the local plant manager. They all interlock, they are all aspects of the same company, facets of the same unity.

This chapter will discuss cases that are very different. They have actually only one factor in common: the company's relations with a wide spectrum of contact areas is at stake.

The time factor goes from long-range projects to cases where the time factor is measured in minutes. The cases include disasters and anniversaries, projects originating in the company and actions inflicted on the company by outside forces. The common denominator is the need for strong coordination of a company's contact work.

As different as they are in origin, time or subject-matter, as big is the tool-box to be used in handling them. The press corps is one media group to be considered in most of these cases, but it is by no means the only one. These cases, in other words, call for a high degree of skill on the part of the communications manager. They are among the mastership tests of a communications professionals.

The identity of a company – a strategic issue

The centre of the communications activities of a company is the company itself. Every action a company takes, or does not take, not only every communications activity, tells the story of a company, reveals its identity and affects its identity. In a time of change like ours, it is more necessary than ever to anchor a company's identity more deeply than in name and graphics. Graphic fashions change, leadership and ownership of companies change, products, markets and business trends change. These are basic facts that a communications manager has to consider and discuss thoroughly with his management and others concerned.

What the identity really is

The identity of a company is something other and much more than its image. The image of a company is what people think about it – the identity of a company is what the company really is. Since honest business communications is not a superficial veneer job, putting a glossy finish on any base, the responsibility of the communications manager goes beyond the image, into the identity of the corporation. And the identity cannot be isolated from the strategy of a company.

The real identity questions of a company are the kind and quality of the products and services it provides, the relations it builds with its customers, the way it deals with its staff, with the communities where it is located and with the shareholders and financiers who put their money and trust in the company; in sum, the way it meets the expectations of its environment. A company that tries to create an image without first having defined its strategy, what it is and what it is aiming for, will find that it loses one quality no company can be without: its credibility.

The identity programme is a typical example of a communications activity that concerns all the contact areas of a company, its own staff, the local community, national government, the shareholders, the schools, the market and all other groups the company feels are important. And although variations in presentation are acceptable and even advisable in many cases, the core of the identity programme must be one unified set of principles and practices. A company can never survive as a split personality, showing itself as a low-price company to its customers and a high-margin company to its shareholders, neither can it expect to be believed if it makes a lot of noise about its research programmes to academic and professional audiences while its own staff know that the research budgets are cut every time there is a temporary downturn in the business cycle.

The identity of a company is not the letterheads, the packaging or the neon signs, it is not even the name. The name itself, and the ways of displaying that name, are reflections of the identity. An individual person's name, or style of dress reflects the personality, but character goes deeper than these outer signs.

A company has taken important steps towards an identity, a character, when it has a consistent business philosophy, a direction and a way of doing business that reflect a consensus of what management, employees, customers and other groups think of the company. An identity programme must be rooted in the strategy of the company. An identity programme that concerns itself only with logos, letterheads and advertisement layouts is doomed to fail.

This approach reflects a different view from that expressed in many articles and manuals on corporate identity. Most such articles concentrate entirely on the name and graphics aspects. While these aspects are certainly important, and those articles and books definitely ought to be read by a communications manager in a situation of identity considerations, they often start at the end rather than at the beginning. To restrict the role of the communications manager to the situation when a change has already been decided, and the 'only' job that remains is to jazz up the façade, is or should be a misuse of talent.

Discovering the need for an identity review

Although Freud said that a child only marginally changes its personality after two years of age, most of us feel that we have to work on our own personal development continuously, throughout our lifetime. Similarly, a corporate identity programme is not a temporary action taken during a limited period and then forgotten in the form of an identity manual gathering dust on a shelf. Building an identity is an ongoing process, requiring constant inspiration, supervision and revitalization. It is a process that has to feed on both internal ambitions and plans and on systematically gathered and analysed reactions from key contact groups.

If the task of building a corporate identity never ends, nor does it have a beginning. The need for a conscious identity effort can arise suddenly, from one obvious reason, or in a more incipient way, through the increment of many small incidents until there is no option but to do something about it.

Sudden reasons include:

- Changes in the board, in the ownership, in top management or in communications management, making it desirable for the new team to plot a new, clear course.

- Changes in product mix, marketing policy, production resources or financing, creating enough waves to make management think of strategic issues.

- Mergers, acquisitions or divestments, changing the direction of a company.

- Internationalization of a company, perhaps moving into areas where government demands call for new kinds of policy commitment.

Other reasons for an identity review may be more difficult to discern. A vigilant communications manager should look out for such signs as:

- Sales figures going down 'for no specific reason'.

- Difficulties for salesmen to maintain a reasonable price level.

- Share prices going below where they 'should' be.

- High turnover and/or absenteeism among the staff.

- Low returns in recognition and attitude changes on corporate advertising programmes.

- Difficulties in raising capital on the money markets.

When these problems arise, the board and top management may search for other, more superficial reasons than failures in identity. One reason may be that a failure in identity matters, taken as seriously as they are here, reflects on corporate leadership, that is, on themselves. In such cases, much diplomacy and a lot of courage are required from the communications manager attempting to influence management to take a strategic view of the key problems, not the symptoms.

When the need has been established

A thorough strategy review is the first step towards an identity programme. Even for a communications manager with a qualified background, carrying through a strategic identity programme is an unusual challenge. Listen to colleagues and learn from their experience. There are specialized books on the subject and good magazine articles. Check with library staff and solicit their active help in finding background material.

The discussion on positioning has a lot to offer the corporate communications executive in search of a company identity. The task is very much one of defining the character of a company in relation to other companies on the market. Not only the competitors, although this may be the first dimension. It is also a matter of defining the company in relation to other companies in the same community, other companies on the same stock exchange list, other companies of the same size, or other companies hiring the same types of people.

Any identity project of significance will require support from qualified consultants in communications. The company's advertising agency, if it is good enough, is a natural first choice, but it is advisable to check with one or two more, to get a wider outlook and new aspects.

Where do we stand? – Establishing a benchmark

One of the first steps should be an in-depth analysis of:

1. What the board and management would like to see as 'ideal' public reactions towards the company.
2. What the public really thinks, knows and feels about the company.

The differences between 1 and 2 should provide material for the identity programme.

What do the primary contact areas think about the company on such aspects as the durability and quality of its products? Is the company considered to be progressive, conservative, research-minded, international, accessible? How well are the staff recruited and trained? Are the employees proud to work for the company – or not? What are the company's service facilities? Which price level does the company set in comparison with its competitors? How are guarantees, complaints, product deficiencies handled?

A benchmark study of this kind is normally made with the help of a qualified attitude research agency. Since it is the basis of a project that can be very significant to the company, this is not the time in which small savings are the primary consideration.

There are two simple guidelines to consider, before commissioning the benchmark survey:

1. Don't include any questions that do not have a very good reason and can contribute to specific decisions.
2. Decide now to rerun the survey within a specified time-frame, as a follow-up.

Internal analysis
As a separate item, but coordinated with the outside benchmark study, make a careful internal analysis of opinions and attitudes within the company. Management, sales staff, local plant managers and the board are to be scrutinized as closely as the external contact areas. Include other staff categories that can add views on how the company is seen and considered, such as service staff, general employee representatives, whether or not they are union officials and the editor of your staff magazine.

Skeleton programme
The internal and external surveys and ideas from other sources provide the platform for a skeleton programme to be written down in preliminary terms. Consider its consequences on staff development, customer relations, government and financial relations and other aspects, and submit it for discussion to a number of key influences, obviously including top management. Keep it tentative at this stage, and stress that modifications and contributions are invited. Don't rush this procedure but keep it moving. If the company is diversified, make sure the various business lines are represented in these discussions. If the company is international, make sure that different countries are involved. Invite comments of a practical nature as well as on basic principles.

Remember, it is not a question of creating an image – the task is to create an identity, to crystallize what the company really is and stands for.

Where do we go? – Turning the programme into reality
Finally, there is a consensus on the basic characteristics of the company, the essence of what it is or should be and an agreed platform on targets and identity features. This is when the real work starts, transforming the outline into reality.

Before any outward action is initiated, it is wise to locate what should be changed within the company. If the company has a reputation for poor service, improve it. If the switchboard is not perceived as polite and competent, change it. If the environmental image is bad, maybe there is a reason for it. Do something about it!

The tools available
Then it is time to do the internal and external communications job. Part II includes ideas and suggestions related to the different communications methods. All of them, print media, audiovisuals, space advertising, editorial work, conferences, etc., will be considered

in a successful identity programme, based on a thorough awareness of the company's aims and present situation.

Here are some of the tools available in the process:

Instructions, guidelines
These can be instrumental in carrying out the essentials of the identity in a short time, throughout the organization. Normally, however, instructions alone achieve very little in the way of changed attitude or behaviour, should this be required as part of your new identity programme.

Training
Special meetings and conferences to present the new identity programme are necessary if the changes are considerable. Even more important are constant supervision and encouragement so that regular training programmes within the company, from the introduction of new employees, through typing and lathe-work courses to management development programmes are revised to reflect the new policies.

Staff reviews and organizational changes
A new identity, if it has lots of new aspects to it, may call for direct or gradual changes in the organizational set-up of the company and/or staff changes in key positions. Resources have to be transferred from, say, research to after-sales service, or from central headquarters to local management, or from production to marketing. Such changes may have to be made before the new character of the company is transmitted to the public, or they may be made step by step in a longer transformation process, redistributing priorities to correspond with external and internal demand.

Graphic guidelines
In much of the literature on the subject, the graphic aspects of an identity programme are sometimes treated as the programme itself. While this, certainly, is putting the cart before the horse, a carefully designed graphic programme can and should be used to promote the corporate identity. It would be too superficial, however, to see this as the goal in itself. Clothes do not make the man – nor does the exterior make the company. But, when the inner identity has been established, it should be confirmed through a consistent appearance. This is where the graphic manual has its role.

Graphic identity manuals have sometimes been described as the cure of all company ailments and also as something more complicated than building a space ship or composing a Beethoven concerto. They are not.

Important elements of the identity guide are the company logotype – the seal of all the values the company stands for – graphic systems and standards, colour principles, letterhead, business cards, space advertisements, product packaging, product design, company vehicles, exterior signs, exhibition and trade show design, company uniforms and, perhaps, building design and interior decoration.

How strict should the graphic manual be? In the 1960s, the general rule was for detailed regulations of all elements of outer identity. Big companies today, especially if they are international or have ambitions to become international, prefer to limit the absolute rules to the most essential elements, such as the company name and logo, giving recommendations only on other factors.

Internal communication
Obviously all internal communications media must be used to carry through a high level of internal awareness of the new identity, its principles and practical consequences. In addition to meetings and conferences, the message must come across through line managers, memoranda, internal staff magazines, trade union officials and other internal channels.

External communication
The whole battery of external media should be considered. As soon as possible, all external communication, advertisements (sales and recruitment), leaflets, direct mail, annual reports, audiovisual presentations, exhibits, house magazines, etc., will be mobilized to explain and reflect the new identity of the company.

The name itself
Changing the name of a company is a major operation. Much has been written about the procedures, legal aspects and identity aspects. No one in his right mind goes into that process without good reason. But it would be just as wrong to shirk the issue simply because it is difficult. If the analysis shows that the present name hampers the efforts to establish a desirable company identity then consider a new name. If the company enters new geographic areas, new product ranges or new customer categories and the old name is restricted to old fields of interest then keeping the old name could be a burden, unduly restricting the chances of success. If the course of the company has changed considerably, a new name can become

a natural element in the change of direction, to help and support the new role of the company.

International aspects

The requirement for unity and consistency also includes the international identity.

While a company is certainly 'allowed' to modify its actions and programmes to suit the specific conditions of the individual countries in which it works, there has to be a framework that ties it together from country to country. An increasing number of highly respectable companies have codified these principles in some degree, and international business and government organizations, such as the ICC and the United Nations, have encouraged the establishment of such 'codes of conduct'.

Most international companies would benefit from starting their identity work from a firm basis of such codes. They are invaluable when defined and adopted throughout an organization. Even more, the very process of their creation puts management on many levels and in many functions to the task of expressing their beliefs and hopes for company policies, for a code of conduct, while it certainly has to be endorsed fully by the board and top management, can never do its job if it has not been created in thorough consultations with wide groups of company management and personnel, representing a spectrum of varied company specialists and divisions.

As for the graphic identity, a graphic manual may be important in the small company as a help towards planned growth. In the multifaceted, multidirectional and perhaps multinational company it is a necessity, even if it has to allow for cultural and language differences. What would an Arabic, a Chinese or a Japanese version of the company logotype look like?

Big business events

In every business there are certain events that stand out from the everyday flow. Such events include big orders, new investment programmes, acquisitions and mergers, the launching of new products, plant closures and new board appointments. They should be preceded by, linked to and followed up by communications programmes across the board, geared to all or most of the contact areas of the company or companies concerned.

Wide impact range

Even events that are primarily the concern of one specific area may have side-effects that merit consideration beyond the immediately affected group of interest. The launching of a new product may be considered a market communications job. But if it involves changes in the production programme, it is also of interest to the staff. It may involve new production resources, so it is of interest to local labour market authorities or agencies. It may involve purchasing of new raw material or semi-manufactured products, so it is of interest to the suppliers of the company. It will, hopefully, involve new profit opportunities – and, usually, risks too, so it is of importance to shareholders, banks and other financial groups. It may have positive or negative implications for environmental, racial or political groups.

In most cases though, one contact area remains the main focus. The timing, much of the contents and presentation methods are dictated by that contact area. The communications manager should manage the process of bringing the other areas into action as appropriate in each case. He or she should take responsibility for the overall aspects and for the consistency of the message to the various groups, anticipating the positive and negative reactions the same information may generate in different groups and advising the specialists in the company accordingly. A few examples of major business events will show how such projects concern several of the company's contact areas. They represent opportunities for the company to communicate with a wide spectrum of contact areas.

Know-how – and know-when

Timing may be a very important element in communicating major events. And again, it is not only what the company wants that counts. Other interested parties may well have an influence, not only on what to say or how to say it, but also on when.

A key element with regards to timing is the changing decision-making process in business. Decision-making in business, at least on big issues, used to be a matter for a few who belonged to a closely-knit group of 'decision-makers', as it still is in some countries and in some cases. Once the decision was made and hammered out in detail, time was ripe to make an announcement. A press conference chaired by the chairman or president was the natural solution.

In most industrialized countries today, and probably increasingly so in the future, the whole process is different. Some of the parties that used to be at the listening end are now involved in the preparation of the decision or the event itself. They may now very well be on the speaking side – with and without the company's consent and control!

A 'new' type of decision-making?

Mergers are a case in point. Decisions to merge two companies used to be made in mahogany-panelled boardrooms. When the deal was closed, often after lengthy negotiations between a very limited number of directors, and perhaps only the chairmen, the news of the merger was announced to the public.

Today in most countries there are stock exchange rules or laws that oblige a company to announce, without delay, a merger offer or a takeover bid, before the negotiations have even started. In many countries there must be representation from the employees or at least consultation with them, in the process of negotiating a merger. Public authorities, labour market agencies, community planning boards may also be part of the process at the preparatory stages. The pros and cons of the merger may be openly discussed in public. The communications process is not an after-the-fact shot but an active ingredient in the whole work towards the deal, a dialogue leading up to the result.

What is true about mergers today applies increasingly to such events as new investment decisions or conversely, cutbacks or pull-outs, where labour and community representatives are more and more involved from very early stages of the planning procedure.

The change in procedures, with increasing stress on early, two-way communications, is often experienced as an added burden on top of the already onerous job of being a manager. And there is no doubt that in most cases the 'new' ways of doing business complicate life for the business executive. They have, in fact, led to non-action in more cases than one. Whether such aborted events are a result of the open discussions as such or of lacking experience and expertise in handling communications in a new situation is hard to tell.

The contribution of a communications manager, in cooperation with other parties concerned, is developing systems and principles that are in line with the wider participation models – the alternative may very well be a risk of stagnation. A still-life may be a beautiful picture to look at in a gallery; in business it is a contradiction in itself. And communications staff are used to the role of being agents for sensible change with due consideration to all parties involved.

Even after a consultation process . . .

Part of the problem may rest with the word and concept of

'decision'. In terms of 'purchasing decision', 'investment decision' and other 'decisions' in business, the phrase has the ring of an order, given by an old-fashioned field-marshal. In reality, of course, important decisions, even those made by dictators, have been preceded and followed by communications phases in both directions. 'Decision-makers' have listened to advisers and experts, gathered information and held consultations. After the 'decision', he informed those concerned and studied the results in the form of feedback from those affected.

The difference in today's system is that consultations play a more active role, that more people are involved in them. It may, therefore, sometimes be more difficult to discern clearly the specific contributions that each party makes towards the final course of action. It also means that much of the 'selling' required to create the desired action is being done at various preparatory stages, rather than after the decision point.

Many unnecessary controversies, resulting from getting decisions – even objectively good ones – pushed down one's throat, may be avoided through good communications, before and after the 'decision'. Seen in this light, the role of the communications staff is certainly more than just 'mailing a press release' – after the fact.

... News is still news

Taking all this into account, there is still a legitimate need to publicize certain big business events. Some events are news to a great number of interested parties, other events may have been in the public light for shorter or longer consultation periods. Yet sooner or later it is time for a decision.

A big order may still be news, affecting employment, investment programmes and financial results even after a lengthy negotiation period. It may mean entering into a new customer category.

Launching a new product may represent new technological advance, give opportunity to put a staff member or team into well-deserved limelight, create interest in the market-place or increase the company's status with the investing community.

Appointing a new executive is a matter of interest to all those who are to work for her or him, to the financial community, to local authorities, to the customers and suppliers of the company, and none have been participants in the appointment process.

An investment decision, a cut-back, a joint-venture, an acquisition, although thoroughly discussed, even publicly or semi-publicly, have an interest value when they have reached an important decision stage.

A wide range of media

Preparing for the announcement includes an analysis of who could be interested, who should be entitled to special attention in announcing the event and then choosing a suitable array of communications methods.

To traditional PR thinkers, the immediate answer is that these events call for press releases or press conferences.

Press contacts are certainly one way of spreading information about events in business. Based on the analysis of priority interest groups in each case, one may well find that other media are as suitable or better. How about letting the staff publication make a scoop for once? Or, if the shareholders are a priority group, prepare a direct mailing for them. Or if the customers are the key group – and the 'timely disclosure' is not a significant issue – prepare the salesmen and let *them* bring the tidings of comfort and joy – or the opposite, when necessary. It confirms their role as knowledgeable company spokesmen and the only personal contact with the company for many customers. To sum up, in preparing information programmes on big business events, set the priorities in terms of contact areas, then look creatively at the various possibilities for choosing channels of communication.

Person-to-person information and press information are two frequent ingredients, but there are others as well. If time is important, use telex or telefax to reach distant plant locations, news media and 'special persons', such as board members, banker relations or union officials. Back it up, when necessary, with background material, printed matter, photos, slides, overhead charts, etc. If a meeting is called, for the press or for the staff, make sure that all those involved in the event are there to answer questions and give their comments. If various staff or community groups have played a role in preparing the event, don't put the chairman on the rostrum alone. If dissenting views have been heard and considered in the preparatory phases, explain fairly why they have had to give way for other points. Concentrate on the facts and the consequences, but be prepared to give background if required. If at all possible, take the opportunity to relate the specific event to corporate strategies and long-range objectives.

Mergers between two companies

The communications aspects are widely different for a merger made between two approximately equal companies and one where a big and powerful company buys a small company or one in difficulties. In the latter case, the differences are enormous depending on which side of the deal one stands.

Successful mergers – and unsuccessful

When planned mergers go wrong the reasons can frequently be traced back to mistakes in the information planning. For too often, top management and their legal and financial advisers concentrate their discussions on balance-sheets, inventories, manufacturing resources and, at best, marketing opportunities, without considering, until it is too late, the human aspects.

Successful mergers are based on the same concepts as this book – all business relations are human relations! In the old days there may have been reasons for planning mergers without looking to the human aspects – although it was probably never the best way. Today, and even more so tomorrow, it is no longer possible. The sooner business leaders realize this, the better and smoother they will be able to put into effect the continuous adaption and change in our business system that the merger process as such signifies.

'Can you keep a secret?'

Mergers may still, although perhaps more and more rarely, be planned in secret and sprung on the public. There may even be cases when this is the more human approach, cases when long negotiations in public would damage job opportunities, product development and the profits of both companies concerned.

In such cases it is of great importance that qualified communications expertise is brought to bear at least as early as bankers, lawyers and other specialists, and that the advice of the communications person is heeded as much as that of the accountants. The reactions of the stock market, customers, employees of the two companies, local and national authorities and others concerned may have more influence on the final success of the merger transaction than the figures of the balance-sheets. If there is no public discussion in advance of the merger as such, it is part of a well-considered merger to prepare the opinions of various key groups, to make sure that an announcement, when released, falls on soil that is as ready as possible to receive the message. That process requires a light hand and much skill in communications strategy and practice.

If a merger is prepared behind closed doors, a very strict and tight information plan must be an integrated part of the project. Those who have the responsibility for the total merger project may prefer to leave the information planning to the last stages of a preparation period. If they do, they take great risks. They may know that they have good information staff or consultants available. They may trust their professional skill to the extent that they believe they need no preparation time at all. The risks are obvious. They miss professional advice at early stages, which means that important issues may be overlooked. And walking on a tight-rope as far as time is concerned may jeopardize the whole communications process. Just imagine if something were to happen to the communications expert they need without enough time to get somebody else at short notice!

If the cat gets out of the bag

Even more serious, though, as witness lots of unsuccessful merger attempts: negotiations prepared in secret are always subject to risks of unplanned leaks with unexpected, sometimes disastrous results. Getting a qualified communications manager into the process at a very early stage may not in itself eliminate all risks of leaks. Communications experts will not leak – they know enough about their jobs not to let that happen – but there are still others who may find it hard to keep a secret. If a good communications person is involved, he may help prevent leaks by stressing to the others the consequences of indiscretions. The real value of having the communications specialist on board, however, is that he is prepared if there is a leak, despite all precautions. In fact, it must be part of his brief always to have an emergency plan in these situations, as in others.

From a secret project to a public process

Secretly prepared mergers are likely to vanish from the business scene. This is probably advantageous to all parties concerned.

The reasons why business mergers are going to be, more probably, the results of long periods of more or less active public debate are fairly clear. Government agencies are taking an increasingly keen interest in the life and work of business in all industrialized countries. Trade unions, local councils, various citizen groups and political parties are observing, commenting on and influencing what happens in business with an equally growing interest. In many European countries today it is almost impossible to merge two companies without consultations with the employees and without the consent of public bodies or agencies. Discussions may take place in newspapers, pamphlets, advertising or at public meetings, arranged by one party or the other.

The new role of the communications manager

If the communications manager plays an important part in secretly prepared mergers, his role is still more significant when mergers are the end-result of a five-act drama played before the public. The communications specialist, in those circumstances, is moved from the prompter's box to the centre of the stage or even to the director's chair, so important is the continuous interplay between the actors on stage and the various publics. If the public as a whole, segments of it or representatives of it are the final judges, the whole procedure must be set up accordingly. Who can be better qualified as a catalyst of public opinions than the communications manager?

A growing number of leaders in all business functions today – legal staff, financial managers, personnel managers, plant managers and other management personnel – are capable of making these considerations and taking them into account in a complete merger project. Yet, in most cases it is the communications manager who has these aspects closest to heart, and who should therefore be closely involved in the planning and execution programmes. He is the one who is professionally trained to have his 'antennae' tuned to the whole horizon, and who has or can get rapid access to all groups, big or small, that may influence the process.

The communications manager, in this situation, should contribute his professionalism, not only on the 'how's' of a merger, but also on the key questions of 'when' and even 'whether'.

As one proceeds along the long and increasingly tortuous path of a merger negotiation, the communications manager must be so thoroughly involved in the whole process that he is able to predict opinion obstacles that may be waiting round the next bend, or recommend a path that avoids some of the roughest parts.

In most cases, even the best merger creates problems and has adverse effects on some of the parties involved. Those aspects should be brought to light as well, preferably at an early stage, and openly admitted, combined with an account of the efforts made to minimize the drawbacks: offers to transfer personnel or production, reasonable time-tables to allow successive adaption to the new situation and other considerations made to the various angles of public interest that may play a part.

New investment programmes

Unlike a merger, a new investment programme traditionally has an undisturbed note of progress, optimism and other positive connotations about it. New investments create job opportunities, offer improved return on investments, express the confidence of corporate management, provide a higher tax basis, new opportunities to suppliers, increase the values of property, etc. An easy task for the communications function of the company? Yes, in most cases it is. But this should not prevent the communications manager from giving it due time and thought when an investment is being planned.

In the first place, new investments are among the business events that a company should get maximum benefit from. They give tangible proof of the company's capacity to grow, of the strength of private business in promoting growth, employment and new business opportunities. These benefits should be made clear to the staff, to customers, to the investing public, to government agencies, to local and national business and consumer organizations, to trade unions and to others who participate in the development of an area or a branch of business.

Secondly, not even an investment should be handled without some additional thought. With all the twists and turns of progress there may be other considerations that should not be overlooked. Every investment made in one area means the same investment not being made in another. Was an alternative considered or even discussed? What are the reactions there? Even a new factory, although practically always an improvement over older plant, may have adverse or dubious effects on the air, the water or the land around it. The products made may, to some people, be questionable as contributions to society. While it increases employment in the area, it may be so highly automated that its employment effect is insignificant. It may even mean a cut in employment elsewhere. One supplier may benefit from the new process, another may be the loser. What are his reactions?

Thirdly, every new investment, not least in today's volatile world, carries a great deal of risk. At the time of announcing the investment, it is natural for every businessman to back up his investment wholeheartedly. He has weighed up the pro's and con's, and come to a positive conclusion. He is enthusiastic – rightly so! No matter how attractive the role may seem at the time of announcing the big plans, the communications manager should make sure that the messages are expressed and phrased in a way that protects the company if, against the odds, unforeseen difficulties arise. A note of caution at the moment of joy! See it as the inherent role of the communications manager always to see things from at least two angles: 'On the one hand . . . but on the other . . .'

Launching a new product

As mentioned briefly, launching a new product may seem like a marketing communications job and only a marketing communications task. No doubt, in marketing communications there are few single items that offer so much of a challenge as this one, especially to the manufacturing industry, the process industry or to companies of other kinds selling to professional buyers. The making or breaking of a new product may depend on the speed and accuracy by which the message of a new product reaches and convinces the right people in the market, domestic or international. But with all the marketing importance that the launching of a new product undisputably has, that is only one aspect of it.

Launching a new product with only the market in mind is like announcing a new investment only to those who are going to work in the new plant, an essential group, but only one out of a much wider spectrum.

In a business marketing situation, one may be tempted to think of the market only in terms of those who buy the product. It may be prudent to give opportunities for much wider recognition if the market communications programme is planned to include the customer's customers too – those who are ultimately going to benefit from the new product in terms of safer, more reliable gadgets, lower costs, higher outputs, better finish, more reliable guarantees or whatever benefits the new product helps create for the customer's customers.

The launching of a new product can be something much bigger than a marketing event. It is of fundamental interest to many other groups. A new product, which the company believes in, has a value that goes beyond its market value. Sometimes those additional aspects mean more in hard cash than the market success.

The *company staff*, if well informed about the new product, may feel justified pride in their contribution to producing the new item. Some of them will have contributed more directly in developing, designing, testing and producing it, but the others will have played an indirect part. Giving them an opportunity to feel solidarity with the company through the contribution they have made to a new product is one of the small positive factors that engenders company loyalty and that makes modern business life more human. They will also realize that, if successful, the new product will increase their job security and other benefits of working for your company. Explaining the important facts about the new product to the staff puts them in a position to answer – with pride and knowledge – questions that may be asked at home, in clubs or other private circles in which they are the authority on company matters.

Local authorities like to know about the successes of the companies in their area. Rightly or wrongly, they may feel that they have contributed and thus the company moves up a few steps on their interest ladder. Besides, on another occasion the company may have to contact them on matters of which it is less proud and happy, matters in which it may have to solicit their support. Why not invite them to share the pleasure of the company's optimism, when there is reason for it?

A new product, representing new technology or new applications, is often of interest to *teachers*, at least those in specialized schools. Information on new products and services helps the teachers to keep their teaching up to date, adding to the established facts and procedures described in the standard literature of the classes they teach. So if the company wishes to be known as a progressive, creative company to young students in its special fields of expertise, give schools and teachers a chance to find out about the new products.

Bankers and other *financial supporters*, including the shareholders, like to know that their money is being invested in such areas that are of interest for the future. When a new product is developed and launched, they should know that their resources are being put to good use. As with the company staff, giving the shareholders a chance to know more about a new product tends to create a feeling of solidarity, of belonging.

Working one's way like this through other contact areas of the company, it will appear that there are links that can be strengthened – and a new product is an opportunity to do this. It can help be the vehicle that personalizes the company, makes it different, memorable, enjoyable. Why not take those opportunities across the board? Obviously, the same cautions apply as in announcing new investments. Each new product is an opportunity, but it is also a risk. Let the enthusiasm come through – it is needed today, as always. But in the midst of all the enthusiasm, make sure you avoid exaggeration and show respect for the difficulties that always accompany new product launches.

Closures

A product that becomes obsolete can in most cases be phased out without too many problems, although the communications aspects of such a change also deserve attention.

Phasing out a factory or an office is a lot more demanding. Human aspects, economic considerations and public interest are all part of the process, often with seemingly conflicting interests.

Accepting change is easy . . .
The very existence of closures and other disinvestments is a fact that must be accepted. In a dynamic business situation it is impossible to avoid change. Change means upward and downward swings. This must be at the base of the difficult task of explaining the closure of a plant. An essential conclusion for every company, not least in periods of success, is to emphasize this risk and to make it part of all the communications work of the company. If this is done in good times, it is easier to explain when less successful incidents happen. In individual cases, there always seem to be more specific reasons. Those reasons may not appear to have the same value to the various groups affected. The trade union may feel that a closure is caused by bad management, while management is convinced that the cost situation, due to unreasonable union demands, is the real culprit. Tough business trends, obsolescence due to new technology (yours or the competition's), unaccommodating bankers, government interference, ecological complaints, zoning disagreements are other reasons that with or without good cause are blamed for a closure. These reasons or combinations of them will certainly be analysed. Once a decision to close a plant has been made, they have often been penetrated to the bone, with no better alternative in sight.

The basic reason is always that available resources, buildings, machinery, manpower, etc., cannot be satisfactorily deployed on that site, at that time. Given an adequate safety net for transition difficulties, every society must accept and even encourage optimum allocation of its resources, which in a changing world means changes in the structure and use of resources, from one area to another, from one technology to another, from one type of products to another, from one production system or marketing method to another.

. . . as long as one is not personally affected
These facts of life are easy to accept as intellectual generalities. In an emotionally loaded situation, when a person's complete existence is about to be upset, they are nevertheless hard to accept. Even if a company has been wise enough to prepare its staff and others in good times that change is a necessity of life, there is still a need for the company to make its presentation of cutback plans very gently and very professionally, in the best sense of the word.

149

As in the question of mergers, there are basically two different approaches, one which was all-dominant some years ago, another which is gradually becoming more generally adopted. The old method is the secretly prepared, suddenly announced decision, the other is the more gradual, step-by-step approach, in which the opinions of the various publics are taken into account, and in more advanced companies consulted, before the axe falls.

Sudden change is difficult to accept, sudden negative change that affects a person directly is, in most cases, an almost unbearable shock. Presenting a decision to close a plant at short notice, without advance warning, is a method that can hardly ever be defended, no matter how big the advantages in figures may seem to be.

Advantages and disadvantages
On the surface there are advantages in making sudden announcements. Production can be kept running with little or no disturbances, until the machinery is stopped completely. People, suppliers and the whole production process are intact.

If, instead, the production is slowly grinding to a halt, all kinds of problems are created in the slow-down period. The best people quit, suppliers lose interest, a general feeling of disorder and the breakdown of discipline takes over. What is gained is that staff and other groups understand that the company cares and that it knows what it is doing – big decisions don't come at the snap of a finger. So which should you choose, when facing two difficult alternatives?

Each situation has to be judged on its own merits. Each case deserves to be considered from these aspects. And if the communications function is engaged at an early stage, its contributions can influence and improve the final decision, at least as far as timing goes. Since many of the so-called economic considerations are often based to a great extent on poor communications, even the need to close down may be reconsidered. Better market communications, staff communications, local government communications or financial communications may improve the marketing results, the motivation of employees, the regulation difficulties and the supply of funds. Such results do require plenty of time, and if a closure is seriously considered, that time is probably not available. The only thing left is to influence the timing of the announcement and the realization of the decision.

Contrary to traditional policies, companies that have been in the situation find that it is hard to make a sudden announcement work. There are always leaks and the secrecy itself tends to create suspicions and lack of confidence – and rightly so. In practice as well as in policy, the lesser of two evils is to disclose early.

Building a basis of confidence

Keeping the regular communications lines open through company committees, staff meetings, staff publications and good relations with the trade unions, it is only natural to discuss difficulties and negative trends before they reach the crisis proportions. On that basis, your staff and others concerned will be prepared for good or bad news as it comes.

This is not a policy that can be instituted at the last minute before the grapes turn sour. It has to be founded on long-term confidence and mutual respect, which is why the best time to ease communications problems in hard times is to begin in good times. Only very seldom does a company move from profit to serious loss in a matter of weeks. More often it is a question of months or even years, if the signs are read and interpreted correctly. In a situation of good cooperation, telling the bad news as well as the good news becomes more than a joke – it becomes a way of life. It takes guts on the part of management to stick to its principles when the winds go against the company, but if the situation comes to a crisis, namely the threat of a closure, the staff will be warned. They will be prepared and that makes it somewhat easier to accept the situation.

Give it time

Once the decision is final, give enough time for the decision to take effect.

In one country after another, legislation and/or union-management contracts call for certain periods of formal notice from management. Often there are also detailed rules governing the reasons that can be accepted for cutting back on the activities of a plant. It is obvious that rules and practice of that kind have to be strictly observed, but that is only a minimum, stiff as the rules may seem to a company in difficulties. Giving more time than the minimum should be the aim of the company, as well as providing ample opportunities for real consultations on timetables and procedures to ease the hardship that the closure will bring to the employees.

The same applies, of course, to all others who are affected by a cessation in the company's activities – the local community, suppliers, customers and others. Early consultations, ample time for reorganizations and taking alternative courses, enough time once notice is definite can help make the last days of the factory's existence less bitter than it would otherwise be, for these groups.

To sum up: closing a factory is never an easy operation:

- If communications were good to begin with, the closure could perhaps have been avoided.
- Keeping communication lines open reduces the shock, if the ultimate decision is inevitable.
- Listening attentively to comments and suggestions and heeding the advice of those directly affected tend to mitigate the reactions and the damages.
- Giving enough time from decision to realization eases the difficulties further.
- Closures are inevitable in times of changing technologies and business trends, but there is no excuse for making them unnecessarily brutal. It is the task of the communications manager to contribute his experience, his feelings and his judgement in this demanding job.

New management

A business event that requires skilful communication to all groups that a company deals with is the 'accession to the throne' of a new chief executive officer. Whether or not it is part of a total reshuffle, maybe even a change in ownership, the appointment of a new company chairman or managing director is an event that means a great deal to all contact areas of a company.

The formal announcement is the easiest part of the process – a short press release and a quick word round the company are what it takes, to begin with.

As is so often the case, timing is the key issue and requires maximum consideration from many angles. Who are the parties that feel, with more or less justification, that they are entitled to be notified in advance of 'the others'? Assuming the board makes the decision, are there any absentee members who should be informed, out of courtesy or to avoid backfires? Or are there other candidates who should be spared the shock of reading about the appointment in the morning newspaper? The company's bankers or major investors? The trade union leaders who will have a new person to work with – unless, of course, they have been consulted in advance.

Chances of a smoother transition of power increase considerably if the chairman of the board, or other engineers of change, give the communications manager an opportunity to advise in time on communications aspects of a change in the top position of the company. The plan that should be a result of that confidence will include aspects that may not come to the chairman's mind. It will also include a detailed timetable of pre-notifications as well as the formal announcement, with the appropriate media considerations. Incidentally, why should – as so often happens – the staff magazine be the last one to carry the news?

The plan should preferably also include thoughts on the introduction period after the announcement: the persons and groups of people who should have a chance to meet the new chief executive as early as possible. Various staff categories, managers at near and far locations, trade unions, local government staff, competitors and colleagues, managers of neighbouring companies, leaders of various industry associations, local newsmen, etc., are to be given their opportunities to get acquainted with the new man or woman, especially if the choice was in any way unexpected.

The path of a new chief executive is rough, with or without a well-considered introduction. Why make it more difficult than it has to be just because the introduction is not given full attention by those who can ease the way – among them the communications manager?

To sum up

Big business events present opportunities and, in fact, requirements for the company to appear in public, to state its case, to call attention to its present and future development, in short, to create understanding and interest. This is true of all big events, whether conventionally 'positive' or 'negative'.

Handling the communications aspects of big business events are a challenge to every communications manager and to any manager involved in it, more so the more people and parties that are taking part in the process of preparing the event, making the final decision and seeing the whole thing through.

Special events

The previous section dealt with big business events in which communications as such play an important and often growing role. The events, however, had significance and substance as such, consequences for employment, business development, economic success or failure, etc. The events to be discussed briefly in this section are of a different nature. That does not mean they are unimportant – but their value is mainly, or entirely, of a communications nature.

Anniversaries, demonstrations of products or facilities, inaugurations, etc., are designed for a communications purpose. Their roles are to change awareness levels and attitudes. They are, in other words, a communications tool as much as an advertising campaign or a direct mail shot. From a strictly professional point of view, they should therefore be included in Part II of this book, rather than under this section. Since they have some similarities with the big business events dicussed above, I have found it more practical to deal with them here, thus also clarifying the differences.

Anniversaries

Anniversaries may have had their golden age in the early twentieth century – brass bands playing, the flags waving in the wind, the governor making his speech, decorations to the veterans of the company, memories – 'the modest start – the difficulties – our present position as one of the leaders in the field . . .' You may laugh at it – or at least smile.

The smile may be understandable – but still not entirely justified. In our personal lives we feel a legitimate need once in a while to stop the overwhelming flow of events around us, to look back and take stock of what we have achieved, to gather strength and take our bearing for the next stretch. An anniversary, if well handled, can play that role in a company's life. It can serve as a pretext for a company to recharge its batteries.

In Chapter 1 I put forward the idea that a basic task of the communications work in a company is to 'de-institutionalize' the company, to make the company personal, human. Not only to present that image, but to change the company to become more human. An anniversary can be a step in that direction.

When should an anniversary be celebrated? The answer may seem obvious – an anniversary as well as a person's birthday is more fixed to a specific date than any other event. To some extent this is true, of course. But there may be more leeway than one thinks. I would venture the proposition that within a three to five-year period, any company could find a date in its history that could be used as a reason to celebrate an anniversary. I am not proposing that a company should do as my old student organization once did when they found it was time for a good party – we celebrated the 'coming of age' – a 21-year anniversary – of the student building! But you can go a little way along those lines: decide the right time for an anniversary, approximately, and you will probably be able to find some important event in the past that could merit an anniversary.

Once the date has been decided - and be sure to have enough time for preparations – get people involved! Remember, one does not get people involved in order to celebrate an anniversary properly, one decides to celebrate an anniversary in order to get people involved. Getting people engaged is not the means, it is the end!

Employees at all levels are always a key group. Get committees working on part-projects, especially developing ideas around staff and family participation. An anniversary is a good opportunity to tie in the *family members* with the company. Make sure the programme includes attractive events for the children! Such programmes should not divert interest from the company as standard circus or playground activities do, but be linked as closely as possible to the company and its range of work. Using regular factory or office equipment is a thrill to most youngsters! If you can make a corner of the workshop available to them where they can try their hand at using the tools and machinery that is a part of the company's normal life they will never forget it. Let them ride forklifts, trucks – obviously with strict safety regulations! Give them a chance to see the work-site where their father or mother spends so much time. Prepare a game, maybe to take home, which ties in with the company.

The *customers* are an essential contact area for all companies. An anniversary creates a reason to invite representatives from customer companies, both those with whom the sales staff have regular contacts and those higher up in the hierarchy – the technical, financial, marketing and executive management. Product shows and workshop tours may come first to mind. They may be valuable parts of a programme, as well as other more conventional forms of entertainment. But stretch the imagination a little further. Arrange qualified seminars in the company's area of proficiency, with high-level technical and market experts present. Involve customers – make them realize that the company wants to listen to them, learn from them, gear the future to their needs. Demonstrate the company's leadership, show the latest results of development work, let them see laboratories and R & D centres. Let them try products and services, activate them, make them see themselves as partners in progress.

The *local community*, its political, educational and business leaders and the general public, often know amazingly little about the everyday life of companies that have been working in the area over the years. An anniversary is an occasion to bridge such communication gaps. Invite the neighbours to visit the company! Show in charts and exhibits what the company means to the community in employment, rates, taxes, etc. Make, if possible, a 'social audit' balance-sheet, showing the flows of services and contributions both ways between the company and the community. Include environmental factors, educational needs, requirements for transportation and public services, giving as accurate a picture as possible of the interdependence. Also, show the workshops and offices and let your neighbours participate. Prepare and carry through presentations in the local councils and public boards, in the service clubs, in the women's clubs, in the schools, in the youth organizations. Make a donation to a good cause, perhaps directed to the training and education of young people, a bursary, an international exchange programme, a college scholarship or similar activities. Sponsor a seminar on the future problems and development trends of the community as part of your anniversary programme!

The majority of the *shareholders* may have made their investment only as an investment. Try to find ways to use the anniversary to create stronger links between the shareholders and their company. Make the anniversary general meeting an event that attracts more shareholders than usual, and prepare a programme that makes their attendance worthwhile. The usual speeches by the chairman and the president can be given extra attention, a longer perspective, a deeper analysis, more facts and opinions.

Use audiovisual material, maybe short film sequences, to add life and reality to the presentations. Encourage the participants to send in questions in advance and set up a knowledgeable panel to answer them, maybe with an experienced outsider as moderator. Let the shareholders take part and feel welcome in as many as possible of the programmes set up for other categories – involve them!

Examples of this kind could be poured out for the categories mentioned above, as well as for other groups important for your company.

The purpose here is not to provide a checklist of all possible ideas for an anniversary. The aim is to illustrate the main point, that a 'created event', like an anniversary, can be used as an important tool to communicate the idea of your company as a personality, as a living entity, with human features, to the various categories that make up its natural habitat. Involvement, both ways, is the passport to success in this case, as in many others!

Inaugurations

The anniversary has its roots in the past, although the programme can be very much anchored to the present and the future. Many of the suggestions above can be applied to any communications programme, without linking it to an historic date. Open house, speakers' programmes, educational contacts, etc., stand on their own feet whenever the company desires to use them.

A good reason for an event, if needed, and a reason with a more forward-looking perspective is the *inauguration*. A new factory, a new office building, new facilities for the staff, a new leisure-time project, those are all milestones in a company's life. They can well be compared with important events in an individual's life, such as weddings or the move to a new home, events that an individual person normally wants to celebrate. So why not let the company take the opportunity to be human, to show that happy events should be shared with friends?

Inaugurating a new facility is a demonstration of confidence, an expression of optimism and the will to improve, to grow. Whereas an anniversary can include programmes, covering a long period, maybe a full year, an inauguration is a concentrated effort, an event of a day or possibly a weekend, so it is much more important to plan it well, especially the invitation list. Those forgotten cannot be invited to 'the next round'. Each detail in the programme has to be considered and prepared, some of it even rehearsed, until everything will work to full satisfaction. (Even so, there is always one more thing that you have not anticipated.)

The advantage of special events in a communications programme is that, within fairly wide limits, one can control their timing, scope and direction to fit in with other aspects of the company's planning. You are on top of the situation. Incidentally, that also means that you have the full responsibility. The success or failure is on *your* shoulders.

Emergencies

The opposite to special events, in all respects, is emergencies. There are no flags or fanfares, no way to control them once they have happened, no way to fit them into a planning system. They just happen. Yet, or perhaps for that very reason, they are of great significance in the life of a company, as are accidents to a human individual. The way they are handled from a communications point of view reveal a great deal of a company's character, its real identity. An emergency badly handled can spoil years of goodwill-building and millions of dollars spent on advertising and other attitude building efforts. By the same token, an emergency well handled can give more credit to a company than most artificial events.

Emergencies cannot be predicted – so how can they be prepared for? How can you prepare the company to handle a fire, a major accident, a flood, a poison leak, a wild-cat strike or a product fault?

A colleague of mine, whose company had suffered three major disasters in a relatively short time, summed up his experience from the communications side in seven points:

1. The requirements on the communications function are acute when an emergency hits the company.

2. There must be a firmly established communications function in the company if a disaster is to be handled well.

3. The communications function must know the company thoroughly – not least the technical aspects. The emergency situation leaves no time for extensive consultations.

4. The communications function can take a big load off the back of other managers who are badly needed elsewhere, when the emergency strikes.

5. The media, despite their general request to meet top management in a difficult situation, appreciate the opportunity to get professional assistance on a collegial basis, as an alternative to a stress-stricken top executive.

6. Photo service is of utmost importance and should be secured immediately.

7. An attitude of trust and openness towards journalists is a must and pays off in the long run. Tell the truth, even if it hurts. The journalist is going to find out anyway!

The important conclusion is that it is too late to prepare oneself and the organization to handle an emergency, when it has already happened. What can be done *now* to prepare for action when necessary?

Discuss with the management team the need to be prepared for emergencies. Qualified PR consultants are able to run full-day seminars for company managements on 'crisis management'. An investment in such a seminar may well pay for itself many times over. A first step is training management in general media relations.

Some of the items that are handled in depth at crisis management seminars are listed below, not as a checklist or a substitute for a seminar, but to indicate the kind of subjects that need to be considered.

In an emergency, more often than not, it is the 'instant' media that demand your attention. The daily press, radio, television and their service agencies, the photo agencies, the news wire services will make demands on you to the limits of your capacity – or beyond it. In the contingency plans it is wise to prepare for some things that may otherwise be lost when the heat is on.

Check:

- That the staff publication is fully informed.
- That photographs and other documentation are secured for the future.
- That records of all action are being kept (audio- and video-tape recordings are easy methods).
- That the customers and sales staff are being adequately informed.
- That competitors receive accurate information to avoid inflated rumours.
- That absent staff members, board members, etc., are considered.

If possible, assign 'crisis' responsibilities to staff members in advance of any emergency. Envisage various possible crisis scenarios with the staff and draft action plans accordingly, with responsibilities assigned for different areas. In an emergency, the communications manager's capacity will be heavily taxed by matters calling for immediate attention. Other members of management will also be busy with urgent business. The support lines should ideally function without direct supervision, which is only possible, when responsibilities have been assigned, and preferably trained, in a cooler climate.

Do your utmost to make sure that accurate and consistent information is given to the public through newspapers, radio and television, that the top staff are available if possible, that access is given to those who can provide the best background and impressions, and that the communications manager is on top of the situation as it develops.

Openness, frankness and honesty are more important in an emergency than on any other occasion, but they must also be tempered with consideration for the rights of others. It is obvious that, in the case of a fatal accident, for example, relatives should be informed before the newsmen. In exceptional cases, police may have the right to withhold information and expect full cooperation from company officials.

In all press relations, and in emergencies more than ever, do not misuse 'off-the-record' openings. Make it quite clear to all who speak for the company in emergency situations that they should not make any statement that they are not prepared to see published. Before talking to journalists, try to list what you want to say, and also list items that, under the circumstances, you should avoid discussing.

Do not interfere with investigations to be made by the police, the fire service, your insurance company or government agencies. If in a tight corner, use expressions like 'it seems', 'it appears', 'as far as I can see', 'my impression at this time is'. In most emergency situations such 'personalized' wordings are by all accounts more justified than seemingly objective statements that can later prove to be wrong or at least ill-advised.

It is usually in the company's interest to make sure that every step taken to remedy the situation is conveyed to the public.

When an issue cannot be discussed appropriately, promise to get back to the reporter when the situation has cleared up – and do so!

Try to tape all interviews you give for the records, both for later checking and to draw experience for future cases. Be as positive as the situation permits.

Remember that the press are in an emergency situation just as much as the company is! Do your utmost to help them, despite your own difficulties. They have been assigned to make a story on the emergency. If they do not get enough material from you, they will pick up bits and pieces from less informed or directly hostile sources, just to get a story. Let them get as much as possible from you!

Temporary action groups

In most countries, business has had a long time to get used to working with the regular political parties and the various pressure groups. But it is a fairly recent trend in the business–community relations field to meet *ad hoc* groups, some formed around an issue that is fashionable for a certain period, some formed on the basis of a specific case, an 'unfair' appointment, an environmental disaster, an investment decision in an unpopular country, a product with alleged faults or similar incidents. The reaction may or may not be in reasonable proportion to the issue – company management will normally feel it is grossly exaggerated, if not completely misdirected.

Handling temporary action groups, from a communications point of view, is both easier and more difficult than handling emergencies. When an accident or other emergency happens, the company may well be blamed for negligence, lack of planning, etc. But basically, everybody knows that the company is a victim, is suffering, at least as much as it is responsible. There is a potential for sympathy with the company in most cases.

Action groups today have developed techniques for turning public opinion decidedly against a company or a group of companies. In presenting their case to the public, they choose the time, the phraseology, the examples and the media to support their views. Their action is deliberate – and the things they charge the company with are presented not as accidents but as deliberate wrongdoings from the company, part of an evil policy, of conscious negligence, of greed, excessive profit-seeking or lack of public spiritedness. Also, while a temporary action group is normally just that – temporary, the duration of its attack can be felt by the company as part of a long-time conspiracy against it and its basic principles, indeed, against business or the market economy as concepts.

Reaction – or pre-action?

There is another significant difference: while an accident normally strikes like a thunderbolt from a clear sky, the clouds have usually been gathering for some time in the case of temporary action groups, at least to the experienced and attentive listener to public opinions. Whereas the immediate reasons for an attack may be misconstrued, misinterpreted or totally wrong, the attack normally strikes a chord that has, at that specific time, a resonance among certain groups of people.

In principle, the situation of the communications manager is as follows. If an emergency hits the company, he should be prepared and capable of handling the communications side of it, but it is not his responsibility that the accident has happened. If the company is attacked by a group of citizens, customers or employees, he should at the very least have anticipated the attack, preferably even prevented it through appropriate action from the company.

The responsibilities of the communications manager include, perhaps even as the top item on the list, training, indoctrinating and assisting other managers in the company to be aware of opinions and attitudes as an ingredient in every decision they make. This does not mean that each decision should be made to satisfy all imaginable whims of public opinion. No company could work under those conditions. But it does mean that the opinion consequences of every decision should be anticipated and considered, they should be weighed and balanced among other pros and cons, before a position is chosen. The principle must be accepted by top management as part of management training programmes and in evaluating the achievements of individual managers. Once the principle has been integrated into the management philosophy of a company, there will be three specific advantages to the company:

1. In some cases, the company will be able to anticipate protests in time to modify decisions and procedures and thus avoid conflicts.
2. If this is not possible and unpopular decisions have to be made they can be presented on the company's terms. The timing, presentation, communicator (!) and media can, within reasonable limits, be chosen by the company.
3. If, despite this, protests flood in, the company has its line of defence in order – reasons for the decision or policy that is the immediate cause for protests sorted out and presentable with the poise and credibility that the matter deserves, and by the spokesman who is the right choice for the occasion.

Where more long-term interests are concerned, try to establish platforms for a true exchange of views – not only with the blind aim of defending the company's position at any price, but with an attitude of open-minded listening to the other side.

Not necessarily bad

Many companies have found, sometimes to their surprise, that environmentalists with a true concern for clean air, water and other aspects can contribute ideas and suggestions, which, when integrated into the company's planning system, not only add very little to the costs, but sometimes even reduce them, for example by extracting valuable heavy metals from the waste, or recycling hot water, saving fuel bills, or improving worker safety, thus cutting insurance costs – all this in addition to creating a better environment.

Similarly, racial groups, expressing their views on promotion policies, church groups with strong feelings about the company's presence in countries with poor records on human rights, consumer groups with definite ideas about product quality levels or design principles, youth groups concerned about employment opportunities and many others have often proved capable of contributing positive ideas, which, when tested with an open mind, provide additional input to the company's decision-making material.

It is here that the clue to the successful handling of temporary action groups lies, in the basic communications principle of listening twice as much as you talk. Even when the company cannot satisfy all demands, the attitude of positive listening is often rewarded by understanding, at least in part, the company's side, when it is explained in an understandable way, with the background and documentation necessary.

See it as a selling job

Again, not all conflicts can be eliminated – and it is perhaps not even desirable. It is, after all, one of the characteristics of a democracy that differences of opinion are allowed and respected. While most chief executives are prepared to accept this principle, in theory, it may take some strength and a great deal of inner balance to accept its consequences when important values – both moral and financial – are under fire from people 'who don't understand'.

Take it as a selling opportunity: listen to your 'customer's needs and interest', present your 'offer' as well and as convincingly as you can, try to get your 'customer' to accept your proposition; and do not be too disappointed if not all 'customers' buy your idea!

What methods are available?

In the different examples of communications tasks reflected in this section, the common denominator is the variety of contact areas concerned in each specific case.

The identity of the company influences – and is influenced by – all those who deal with the company, as clients, employees, owners, city authorities or others. Big business events affect all or most of the company's various contacts, as do special events, emergencies and temporary action groups. Similarly, these tasks often require full command of a wide range of tools from the kit of the communications engineer.

While the *press* is often a corner-stone – the general press as well as specialized media – *radio* and *television* have their roles to play and to take into account. But also *direct mail* – for example, to the shareholders immediately after an emergency; *exhibits* – for example, to explain to the local community the company's environmental aspirations, thus avoiding criticism based on lack of knowledge; *leaflets* – for example, giving students all the facts they need to understand the company's employment, training and promotion policies; *space advertising* – for example, to convey the company's views on an important issue, say taxation, co-determination or minority advancement programmes, your own *staff magazines* – on practically all issues; your *customer magazine* – for example, to discuss price–quality aspects, design resources, etc.; *audiovisual presentations* – for example, to show church groups what you are doing in developing countries (also perhaps in countries with other values and attitudes towards democracy and human rights than your own country); *conferences and speeches* – for example, in connection with new investments, closures or meeting political groups, and any other communications method that may be of use.

In these 'across-the-board' situations, no communications tool should be left without due attention: all of them may not be used on all occasions, but considering a wide array in a positive way opens up many more opportunities to do a good communications job than the traditional PR methods. It shows also why it creates such dangerous limitations to see 'PR' and 'advertising' in their traditional light, rather than seeing purposes, contact areas, communications objectives as the primary object, and the whole range of methods to be applied as called upon by opportunities and requirements.

How to budget

The variety of purposes, contact areas and communications methods under this heading is reflected in the budgeting methods to be applied. Obviously, planning and budgeting for an anniversary or an inauguration is entirely different from planning and budgeting for the launching of a new product. And how do you budget for the communications programme in connection with a merger, an environmental protest action or a fire in the factory?

Still, to make sure that communications, as well as other management functions, stay in line with normal planning methods in the company, don't give up on budgeting until you have presented to management something that can be believed in and that seems plausible to financial and general management. This usually means that the budget should be made:

- Primarily, in terms of communications objectives.
- Secondarily, by contact areas.
- Finally, by communications methods.

Identity programmes must be budgeted differently, depending on whether the programmes involve the creation of a new identity or a major change, on the one side, or the maintenance of a basically good identity. Not only are the amounts normally different, but they should also be considered in the company books as two different things.

While the first type of programme, the building of a new identity, should be considered as an investment, as much as building a new factory, acquiring a company or establishing a sales subsidiary in a new country, the other is more a continuous operation, an integrated part in every communications budget. In both cases, however, one of the important budget items is attitude measurements. Since the purpose of the identity work must always be to close the gap between opinions that key contact groups have about the company and opinions that the company itself experiences as its 'true' identity, continuous measurements of those opinions are the basic guideposts.

This is true about the regular identity maintenance work, but it is even more significant in the process of re-shaping a company's identity. Doing identity work without adequate opinion/attitude/awareness surveys would be equal to building a major factory or office without checking the geology of the site.

Depending on the results of the attitude surveys, one will find the categories where the need for action is the greatest, and that will give the background for budgeting by contact area according to needs and priorities.

The greatest needs, obviously, are in areas where the divergencies between the 'ideal' perception and the awareness/attitudes as measured are the widest. Those are areas where big changes have to be made and where, therefore, the major efforts should be made.

They may, however, not be the main priority areas and so one will have to balance the resources to make, perhaps, bigger efforts to create small improvements in key areas, at the expense of filling big awareness gaps among groups that are at present more dispensable.

Having analysed the survey results in these terms and evaluated the priority changes you want to create, and in which contact groups, the choice of methods to be applied will be a lot easier and safer. That is why the planning and budgeting by communications methods should be left to the later stages of the total process. Any media can be used: space advertising, manuals, leaflets, billboards, editorial work, direct mail, company publications, audiovisual programmes, conferences, training sessions or any combination of media, but the choice should not be made until the specific communications targets have been closely identified.

Budgeting for the communications parts of big business events or for special events should basically follow the same pattern:

1. Which are the key groups? The lower priority groups?
2. What are their present awareness levels/attitudes/opinions on the matters in question?
3. What is the change we want to achieve, what is our communications target?
4. Which are the appropriate media?
5. How do we check the degree of achievement of the targets?

Emergencies are by definition difficult to budget for. Depending on the situation one may find, however, that a general allocation may be in order. Include time and money for training and preparing management and others concerned how to handle various emergencies. Put some amounts towards 'fast action' – photo coverage – and plan and budget for 'follow-up' action, including surveys after the event.

Budgeting for handling temporary actions follows emergency budgeting but with some more room for pre-planning, including the monitoring of opinions and attitudes among potential action groups or on potentially sensitive subjects.

Budgeting for 'across-the-board' programmes will obviously have to be closely linked to the budgeting process for each contact area individually. In fact, some 'across-the-board' activities, such as good identity programmes, will be an indispensable basis for individual programmes geared to youngsters, local communities, employees or

166

various customer categories. Such individual programmes will also provide a 'safety net' from an opinion point of view, should you be exposed to broadside attacks or disasters.

It is always advisable for the professional communications manager to push his analysis, planning and budgeting a bit too far – and then allow for flexibility – even if some of the finer distinctions between budget items or areas may seem a waste of time. The alternative would be to leave it too indeterminate. With that, he would never have the opportunity to show to himself and to management that there is a clear connection between plans, targets, budgets, action and results in communications as in other management fields.

Part II

Communication channels and methods

Part II will help the reader choose the right tool or combination of tools for each communications task, to use the advantages of each kind of media or channel in each situation.

9

'Gutenberg – and then?':
The printed media

In this chapter the reader will find a review of the specific characteristics of communicating through printed matter of different kinds.

It will help the reader to plan concepts, design and production of printed matter and to budget, execute and evaluate brochures, leaflets and other forms of printed matter so that they become result-oriented components of a company's communications process.

Ever since Gutenberg, the printed word has been the main method to communicate thoughts and concepts publicly. Even today, with all the electronic and audiovisual media available, more information is probably transmitted through various printing methods than through any other channel.

The business communicator uses printed messages in leaflets, catalogues, brochures, booklets, manuals, books and other forms of literature, which he controls himself. He uses it in periodical publications originated in the company or he works with editors and journalists in different types of 'public' media. This chapter will discuss the advantages, difficulties and use of the first category of printed media, the literature produced by or for the company itself.

What is so special about printed matter?

Printed matter is a communication method used by practically all companies to communicate with practically all audiences or contact groups of interest. The employees get their personnel handbook on the first day they join the company, the shareholders get their annual report, one of the regular direct mail pieces of most publicly-owned companies, teachers and students may get technical literature for use in their classes, customers get the whole range, from simple leaflets to sophisticated technical documentation, instruction books and manuals, and printed corporate material is distributed across the board to a wide range of company contacts.

If the destinations of printed matter are widely varied, so are the products of the printing presses from other aspects. An industrial booklet can be as detailed as an encyclopaedia or it can be a two-page teaser. It can build its presentation on text only, on illustrations only – photographs, drawings, cartoons, sketches – or on any combination of text and illustrations, in any proportions. It can be black and white – for economy or for graphic purposes – or it can use all the colours on the traditional rainbow scale or from any daring creative trend – psychedelic, phosphorescent, metallic. It can use any base for the printed message, paper products, from newsprint to cardboard, rough or glossy, plastic, cloth or metal sheets. It can use any printing method, from traditional letterpress to photo typeset, electronically-controlled, high-speed offset, or desk-top with dot-matrix or laser.

All this goes to show that printed media can mean a lot more to the communications manager of a company than the traditional 16-

or 24-page sales booklet. Any printed product, from the business card to the instruction manual, has a role to play in the total communications process, a role it can play with varying degrees of success.

Just because it is so widely used, it may slip into a routine and lose much of its potential for doing a great job. The knowledgeable communications manager, making maximum use of artists, writers, graphic designers and printers, can find highly traditional or quite unconventional ways to put printing techniques to work for his communications objectives. The least he can do is to avoid some of the frequent mistakes, the traps that make big numbers of printed matter go to waste, or at least 'lose their name of action'.

Planning printed matter – working backwards

Planning a piece of printed matter is, if anything, something to do in reverse. The planning of any piece from letterhead or invoice forms to the company centenary history must begin with the recipient. Starting from there, the planning should work backwards through the distribution process, coordination with other media, choice of communicator, the printing process and end up with the creative aspects of the production process.

Here are some questions that may be used to start the thinking. Add to them, modify them or delete any of them to suit the situation and the project in mind. Above all, try to accept the discipline of not jumping to the production process too fast! It is sometimes difficult to keep calm when bosses and colleagues come to your desk and ask you to 'produce a leaflet'. Remember, the communication manager's task is to be the specialist in communications and that includes much more than producing leaflets. In other words, the first question may be:

Do we really want a leaflet?

(For simplicity, I use the word leaflet in this section. Of course, a piece of printed matter can take innumerable forms, all of them worth considering as the planning proceeds.)

What is the communications task to be performed? There might be other means of communication that would serve the purpose more effectively: advertising, a film, a press release, an article in the customer magazine, a conference or personal contacts. If the conclusion is that a piece of printed matter *is* the right method, or at least a good method of performing the communications objective, then proceed with more specific questions.

Who will read it – and why?

Who do you want to read the leaflet?
A student, a purchasing manager, a chief executive, an electronics engineer, an American, a Brazilian or a Japanese, a young woman, a senior citizen, a university professor, or what combination? Make an outline demographic description, or more sophisticated if the scope of the communications job warrants it, of the typical reader you are aiming at. If you are aiming at several different categories, write them down, set priorities on them and try to examine their common features and their differences in relation to your communications job.

Why would he or she want to read the leaflet?
Give much thought to this question – it may well be the key to the success or failure of your leaflet. When you have gathered the demographic facts, try to conjure up a live image of the potential reader and put yourself in his or her shoes. Why would she want to use valuable time reading your message? If it is the student market, would a student read it because he is interested in a job in your company, because he hopes to do better in his next examination, because he is politically interested in big business or because he is concerned about the environment? If it is a customer, would he read it to place an order, to find ideas for better productivity in his factory, to defend a purchasing decision he has already made, or to see what one of the potential suppliers might be up to? If it is an investor, would she read it to decide whether to keep her shares or buy more, to judge the likelihood for dividends in the future, or to estimate the capabilities and personalities of the top management team? Answers to this question, which should be specified as closely as possible, may directly influence the layout, cover, contents and form of the leaflet.

What does he/she know, feel, think or do now, in relation to the subject, before reading the leaflet?
In the process of change from A to B, it makes it easier to define B correctly and realistically if you know where A is. How much do the

target readers know now about the process you want to sell? How do they feel now about the role of multinational companies in developing countries? What do they think of the advantages of electronic versus hydraulic control systems? What is the prevailing attitude among the workers on the relations in size between profits, dividends and wages? The answers to questions of this type can be found through formal surveys, or they can be readily available for the asking among specialists or managers of the company. When established, the answers provide the starting point for the print production planning, as well as the basis against which to measure the success of your communications effort.

What do you want him/her to know, to think, to feel and to do after reading it?
Is your purpose basically to convey information, or to influence emotionally or to get the reader to act in a specific way? Linking the purpose to the reader's interest, what can you reasonably hope to achieve?

Be specific in defining your objectives, make them as personal as you can. In some respect, in some way, to some extent, you want your leaflet to change another person. The important thing is not what you want to tell about a process, a machine, a system, a company, a product, or a service. What is important is the awareness, knowledge, feeling or activity that should be generated in the reader.

The leaflet is not the end, it is the means to an end, a method to create change.

To make this part of the planning more concrete, try to define the specific reaction you want to achieve, the feedback. At the same time, consider how you will measure that reaction. Reply card, phone call, questionnaire, order, inquiry, survey?

How does it get there?

Working backwards from the receiving end, having identified the readers and their situation and, having established the communications objective as suitable for a leaflet, it is now time to look carefully at the question of how the readers will receive the leaflet. What distribution process is best for the purpose and how will it influence the design, creation and production of the leaflet?

The choice of distribution method is largely dependent on the number of people to reach, but also whether they are scattered over a wide area or concentrated, whether they belong to a specific group or category that can help define the distribution problem, on the time-frame you work in and on the impact you want to make.

Again, remember that your objective is not simply to 'produce a leaflet', not even to distribute a leaflet, nor physically to reach the target audience, in the sense of getting an envelope through their letter box, but to touch them fundamentally, to affect their mentality.

The distribution process has a lot to do with that objective; it is not just a mailing function.

The best way may be to deliver it personally – to your customers through the sales team, to students through their lecturers, to visitors through receptionists or the company hosts, to employees through their immediate supervisors, to local politicians through their party organization, to participants in meetings, conferences or courses through speakers or conference organizers. If controlled timing is not a primary target, and if immediate feedback is important, try to find methods for person-to-person delivery.

Person-to-person delivery has distinct advantages, but it is slow and expensive. The traditional way, therefore, is by mail.

If other mail, invoices, letters, tenders, etc., go to the same categories you want to reach, enclosing the leaflet with that mail may be a good way, not primarily to save postage, but to get some of the attention that the letter gets to 'spill over'. Of course, you take the risk of too much competition and thus end up in a less favourable situation in the struggle for attention. In the creative process, ways may be found to make the leaflet more competitive in such situations. Size, colour, printing techniques – you name it!

Alternatively, the leaflet may get more attention if it is sent with an accompanying letter, written and preferably signed personally. Indeed, it may even be advantageous to send just the letter, with a reply card to request the leaflet itself. Whole books and lots of articles in the specialized press have been written on the techniques of direct mail (also treated in Chapter 12), so there is no reason to duplicate them here.

Just one word of caution: mailing one leaflet alone is seldom going to change the world. Put yourself in the recipient's shoes and imagine what it would take to move you to the same reaction that you want to create. The conclusion is normally that more than the leaflet is needed: tie-ins with personal contacts, personal letters, serial mailings, advertising, editorial comments, special offers, play-back incentives, etc., are among the additional efforts that will be required to make the leaflet fully effective.

When the mailing method has been decided, make sure to have the postage regulations checked and fed back at an early stage into the creation and production process. A saving on the paper weight or the number of pages or the cover type may make a difference in total cost/value, either as reduced expenses or as an opportunity to add a personal letter, make a follow-up mailing or create a better reply offer within the same budget limits.

The distribution process is obviously also affected by such questions as frequency – is it a one-off shot or part of a regularly recurring programme? Timing – is the date all-important or is the leaflet in season for a long time, maybe years? Coordination – is the mailing a single action in itself or is it part of a campaign?

Who says?

This is a question that many companies give far too little attention to. It is perhaps seen as self-evident that the company as such must be the spokesman for itself.

The choice of communicator is often overlooked in other types of communication than printed matter, so any reflections you make here could be applied to other means of conveying messages.

Our perception of a message is not only a function of the value of the message itself, and perhaps even less of the form of the message. It is affected to a considerable degree by the status, relation, emotional involvement, respect or credibility that the sender has in our eyes.

To understand the importance of choosing the right sender, look back to the last two or three meetings you have had with different people. The way we give attention to a message, listen to it and act on it is very different, if it is our wife/husband, our boss or a colleague, whether it is somebody we like and respect or somebody we are indifferent or even hostile to.

In other forms of communications the choice of communicator may be freer than in printed matter. After all, it is clear in most cases that the company is the sponsor of a company leaflet. That makes it even more important to look for ways to find the right sender to improve the effectiveness of a leaflet.

One way is to 'personalize' the message. The staff manual may be more readily accepted if the employees themselves were represented in the creative group and if it is 'signed off' or at least endorsed by this group. The leaflet presenting a new product may be introduced by the team of development engineers who worked on the project or

177

by the customers who tested the first sample machines. Many companies personalize the annual and interim reports through a personal message from the chairman. The engineering handbook of a technical company may be personalized by featuring the VP Engineering (Technical Director). Leaflets with nationwide or international circulation could gain more credibility if they include personal references to local managers.

The graphic production process

Against the background of these considerations, the receiver and the impression you want to make on him (i.e., the reaction you want to create), the distribution and the discussion on sender–communicator, you have now worked your way backward to the production method.

Nobody expects the communications manager to be an expert in all the intricacies of modern printing technique. After remaining practically unchanged from the fifteenth century, printing methods have changed dramatically since the 1960s, and new technical development, such as the whole desk-top publishing concept, keeps coming upon us all the time.

While the printer or agency must naturally be trusted to supply the sophisticated skills, it is necessary for the communications manager to have enough knowledge especially of its main economic factors, to be a competent buyer of printing services.

- Learn about typesetting, printing methods, typefaces, graphic measurements, paper qualities, bookbinding, repro work, etc.
- Learn as much as possible about printers' requirements on manuscripts, photo originals, artwork, layouts, proof-reading and the approval process.
- Learn about calculation principles and the basic cost characteristics of stock qualities, letterpress and offset, of numbers, sizes, weights and colour, the cost effects of changes made at various stages of the production, and the result of such changes on delivery times.
- Learn to make a proper and complete request for price and delivery quotes, to check what is included in the quotes and what will come as extras.
- Learn about the rights and obligations of the printer/supplier and about the client's rights and obligations.

The best way to cover all of this is with an up-to-date reference book, which should be easy to find at the nearest public library or through the company's supplier of print work. Add one or two study visits to modern print shops and it will be easier to carry on a discussion, ask intelligent questions and help suppliers give a smoother print production job. And don't imagine that this short introduction has made you a full-fledged printing expert!

The main contribution to an efficient relationship with print suppliers will be clear, concise concepts of what to achieve through the planned print job. Put the objectives down in writing, in as specific terms as possible and with the stress on the process to be initiated in the reader's mind. This will give the agency or printer the opportunity to advise on printing methods, type of printed matter, binding, stock, general appearance, size, production time and other practical considerations that can substantially influence the costs and the impact of the final product.

And now for the creative work

At this stage, it is time to get started on the creative elements – copywriting, artwork/illustrations and layout. The printing job has a clear communications objective that has been defined and can be presented. Getting the suppliers to see that objective and to put their resources to work towards that goal and not in other directions, is the task in managing the creative aspects of printed projects. Graphic designers, artists and copywriters will make more appropriate contributions the better they are briefed on what to accomplish.

Encourage them to bring their ideas to your attention. Make it a point to relate all proposals, and the costs that will be involved, to the purpose of the project. If a new idea contributes to that purpose, fine! If not – leave it out! The task is not to create art for art's sake; it is to achieve a defined communications objective.

Some basic comments

Some of the comments below may seem obvious. The only excuse for including them is that too many of the brochures or leaflets produced neglect the simplest guidelines. Wasting good communications money through poor printed matter is bad in itself. Even worse is that it tends to make readers immune to printed matter as such, including some of the material they would benefit from.

Garbage, in terms of poor comunications material, is in nobody's interest. If these examples of basic graphic thinking can help eliminate some of it and make somebody's next brochure somewhat more cost-effective the more sophisticated reader may excuse some of the obvious.

Copy

The KISS principle – for 'Keep It Short, Stupid' – is not bad advice, in this case as in others. That does not mean that the copy has to be short in absolute terms. But it has to be concise, in the sense that only copy that contributes to the objectives is included.

Go back to the reader definition and keep a vivid picture of the target reader before the copywriter's mind! Make sure that the reader benefits are kept in focus all the time and not the company's interests. This is obviously true (although not always remembered) of a sales brochure, but also of an investor prospectus, a machine-operating instruction, an employee manual and – yes – a corporate brochure.

Make sure that the language is adapted to the educational background and the interests of the target reader. Watch out for superfluous adjectives, superlatives and clichés. A newspaper editor's instruction to his new – and old – journalists 'No sentences with more than five words – no words with more than three syllables!' may seem too restrictive, but contains a lot of common sense. Another famous journalist's guideline 'If in doubt, leave it out' may well apply to other copywriting as well. If a word, a sentence or a paragraph is not necessary for the purpose, cut it!

Reading and understanding becomes easier if long sentences and long paragraphs are broken down. Subheadings make it easier for the reader to get an overview and find the items he is most interested in.

Artwork/illustrations

Photo or artwork? It depends, of course.

A good artist can create additional reader interest, make important things stand out clearly, illustrate abstract items and issues, show things that cannot be accessed by the camera, emphasize and visualize for clarity and understanding. But nothing beats good photography for that feeling of authenticity, reality, credibility or impact.

Whatever suits your project best, make sure your pictures get full attention in the creative process. Keep photographs, drawings, charts, diagrams and other illustrations focused on the essentials. Crop photographs to make them tell the important story.

If pictures can be given a human touch without violating the purpose of the leaflet it usually adds to reader interest. If a machine or process involves people, let them be shown, in the right circumstances, doing the things they do in real life, and dressed appropriately.

Size is a necessary element in illustrations. Be generous on size and save, if necessary, on the number of illustrations.

Layout

Simplicity, again, makes for easier reading, easier understanding and a higher acceptance level.

Watch out for unnecessary graphic elements. They tend to clutter the pages and draw attention away from the message.

Reverse copy – white against a black or colour background – tends to be difficult to read. In multi-lingual print jobs it has cost disadvantages in addition to poor readability.

A good leaflet cover should do three things for the reader: present the subject, identify it with reader interest and arouse curiosity to open the leaflet. Titles that contain a surprising statement, a challenging question or the magic words 'How to . . .', 'Your guide to . . .', 'A new way to . . .', help create reader interest. Who can see the front page of the annual report stating: 'The first half of 1989 was lousy' without opening it to see what happened in the second half year?

Other creative aspects

As in other communications methods, an objective should be to upgrade one-way information to two-way communications. In printed matter this is often disregarded, partly because it is difficult at times, partly out of conventional neglect. Or what can you say about an attractive, four-colour brochure that does not feature the company's address in legible type?

Yet there are a few things that can easily be done to create response-orientation in business literature.

A clear readable address, with appropriate department identification, and with telephone, telex and fax numbers are minimum requirements. A coding of the address for proper identification within the company of the source of the answer helps to link answers to the brochure for result follow-up. By giving an address, the company also makes a commitment to handle the responses that come in.

A card with questions to be filled in by the respondent is a somewhat stronger indication that the company wants a dialogue. It should always be considered as a standard element in every leaflet.

A more detailed form of response challenge is a full-page questionnaire, raising specific matters relating to the subject of the leaflet. An annual report could challenge the reader to ask for additional details on the impact of currency changes, on dividend policies, on how inventory reduction is carried out or on open issues, to be asked by the shareholder. An environment leaflet could add a form letter, inviting questions on procedures and techniques the company uses to keep its effluents down. A recruitment brochure could enclose an application form to make it easy for readers to take direct action. A product leaflet, obviously, could include a request for a tender or an order form. A corporate brochure could invite the reader to ask further questions on items presented in the brochure, such as strategies and personnel policies, or it could invite the reader to ask for product brochures or sample copies of the company newsletter.

A reader competition, based on material in the leaflet, and with appropriate prizes, would be an additional underlining of the wish to create reader reaction. Whatever method is chosen, it shows that the company is interested in getting in touch with the audience that the leaflet addresses, that it does not only want to talk *to* this audience but to talk *with* the readers.

Multi-lingual printed matter

More and more companies recognize that their audiences are not restricted to their own language areas. Export opportunities call for customer-oriented literature, product descriptions and operation manuals in many languages.

A multi-lingual print job should be planned as such from the start. In addition to the practical printing aspects, multi-lingual printing projects need to be thoroughly planned for cultural acceptance of contents, approach, copy/language, layout, colour schemes, etc.

The contents and approach may have to differ from one language area to another, due to the different audiences: simple things such as Imperial or metric measurements, different product ranges or applications of similar products, photo material – faces, clothes, background or situations – or more complex aspects such as political or cultural taboos affecting some of the material. For some multi-lingual material, the audience analysis recommended above may even lead to decisions to produce separate pieces of printed matter.

The copy may need more than just a straightforward translation. Language adaptation should include a review of the whole presentation to suit the character and conditions of the language areas to be covered. Professional, multilingual management services should offer their clients more than just translations. They should also:

1. Understand the subject matter and the objective of the printing job to be made.
2. Understand the business situation of the company in the countries concerned.
3. Offer cultural adaptation and editing services.
4. Provide opportunities for copy checking in the countries concerned (although you may want to have the copy checked by your own contacts).
5. Offer print preparation and proof-reading services.

Layout and colour have cultural implications, but also require considerations of a very practical nature, such as the fact that copy in different languages, even as close as English, German, French or Spanish (not to mention Japanese, Arabic or Pharsi) have quite different space requirements.

From a purely printing point of view, three main possibilities are open to the company that needs to produce printed matter in many language versions:

1. Printing all versions with one printer, in one operation.
2. Producing blanks, for example, of the four-colour parts, and add black, usually the copy, in separate printing operations. The separate printings can be made on the blanks in the countries of the respective languages, or by the 'home' printer. One advantage of this procedure is that each new language version

can be finished when each separate copy version has gone through its review and adaptation process without waiting for all the others to be ready.

3. Sending colour-separated offset films to the respective countries for local printing, a practical way but not accepted in all countries for legal or job protection reasons.

Conditions in each case determine which is the best in terms of cost, speed, language checks, etc.

Back to the future – the objectives

If you find the printed matter procedure suggested in this chapter odd – well, it *is*, in a way. Most of the printed matter produced for communications purposes starts with a layout, or with some sketches, or with a manuscript, and then works its way forward step by step until it finally lands on the reader's desk – at best. The sender company seldom knows or follows up what happens to the leaflet, and even less what happens in the recipient's mind after that.

Considering the substantial amounts involved in producing and distributing, say, 20,000 copies of a 24-page, four-colour brochure, let alone one in three or four languages, the traditional procedure does not seem very professional. Few other investments of comparable size are made that way.

It does not necessarily mean that traditionally planned and produced brochures are flops (though in honesty, in most cases one does not know if they are successful either). Instinct can lead the producer to be successful without knowing why. The problem is, nobody knows.

What is wrong with the process? Much or all of the great literature in this world is created that way! That is exactly the reason why business literature, as a principle, should *not* be.

The big difference between literature as an art form and the type of commercial literature we are discussing is in its basic purpose. The main purpose of literature as an art form is to express the personality, philosophy, ambitions, ideals or experience of the writer. The main purpose of 'our' type of literature or printed matter is to create an impression in the reader.

Yes, that is a simplification – there are elements of both in either type. But with that reservation, the principle is there and it is a strong reason why all printed communications should start with the reader, with the planning process working from that point backwards through all the stages.

The process is not as linear as it may sound; there is room for a lot of back-couplings and regeneration of plans and ideas, but the main direction should be from the intended reader backward to the creative process.

How to budget printed matter for tangible results

Making the normal production budget for a piece of printed matter may have its problems, with its balancing acts between printing methods, size of the print order, colour/black and white, stock quality/price, choice between alternative suppliers and other considerations. Staying with the defined objectives and evaluating all options against the objectives usually helps overcome these problems.

A more sophisticated task is to make assumptions on, and subsequently budget for, the contributions that printed matter of different kinds can make to the wider communications objectives that are part of the total communications plan.

As we have already observed, printed matter, with its great flexibility, can be used for almost any number of communications tasks. As a guideline, therefore, it is advisable not to have an amalgamated 'printed matter budget' at all. The budget is better used as a control instrument if it is tied to the objectives, to the specific projects or to the contact areas, rather than to the methods, such as printed matter.

The respective budgets for staff communications, financial communications, local community relations and market communications would be linked to the overall objectives the company has for communicating with each contact area. Within each of these budgets, the various projects would be the next budgeting stage. Not until then, if indeed at all, would the communication methods, such as printed matter, be singled out and budgeted for.

In a company where the structure and the budgeting process has been by communications methods this may seem strange. It is, however, a natural consequence of the principle of 'communications by objectives'. It would also mean that the results are evaluated not by what people think of the look of the leaflet, not by the 'quality' of the paper or the print job, not even by the layout or copy. The results will be evaluated by the performance of the leaflet, in the context and against the objectives that have been assigned to it.

Some printed matter specialists may think that this approach downgrades the importance of printed matter. That is not the intention. On the contrary, printed matter is extremely important and the expert on printed matter should be given due reward.

That reward is not given, however, when the leaflet is delivered from the printers, not even when it reaches the desk or letterbox of its intended recipient, but when you get feedback confirming that it has done its communications job!

10

'Editor!':
Editorial work as a communications method

In this chapter the reader will find a presentation of the characteristics of editorial work in a company, focusing on three important aspects: getting input from the media, managing press contacts and editorial production inside the company (house magazines, etc.).

It will help the reader plan, budget, execute and evaluate editorial work as a result-oriented part of a company's total communications process.

A multifaceted method

The category 'editorial work' contains a wide range of communications methods. Many of those methods have traditionally been classified as 'PR' (as opposed to 'advertising') and have often in traditional PR literature been considered more as objectives of communications work than as methods. In result-oriented communications work, it is more appropriate to consider them as methods, to be used as an alternative or as a complement to other communications channels or techniques. In this context, editorial work is only rarely an objective in itself, it is a means to an end. Regarding editorial work this way puts it in an operational perspective and helps make it more manageable.

Also, conventional PR wisdom has often made editorial work a superior category as such, no matter for what purposes it has been used. To some extent this is understandable. The variety that editorial work offers makes it suitable, under certain conditions, for various communications tasks. Any contact area a company works with can be reached through editorial means, the staff, the shareholders, the local community, government, various sectors of the voting public, educational groups and all those decision influences that together form a company's opinion market.

Not only are editorial means useful for talking to the various contact groups, they are often also one of the best ways to listen. In most countries, the press and other public media provide a forum for opinions. Clearly expressed opinions on business and industry in general and on specific companies are not unusual. In fact, even in countries where critical views are not always available to the public, newspapers and magazines are given a certain leeway to air their thoughts on industrial companies and their performance, and in traditionally open countries every business manager knows that he can rarely open a magazine or other news media without reading more or less well-informed considerations on how business performs. Editorial work should therefore rightly be considered among the main opportunities for business to communicate in the true sense of both listening and talking.

Against this background, this chapter will review various forms of editorial work as it applies to business situations and offer suggestions on result-oriented applications of editorial work.

Three main forms

For the communications practitioner, it may be convenient to consider three main forms of editorial work to be familiar with and to apply in the daily programmes:

1. The input into his organization of material that public media produce which is of concern to his company.
2. Contacts with editors and journalists in media that are of interest to his company.
3. Editorial policy and direction for such periodical publications that are produced or controlled by his own company and production of editorial material for them.

All these three forms can be applied in communicating with the main priority contact groups that the company has and should be guided by the relative importance attached to the contact areas that the media represent to the company, rather than to the media as such. In other words, planning editorial work, just as all other types of communications planning, should start with a priority list of contact areas and go from there to a media preference list, not the other way round.

The natural next step is to make an analysis of the media consumption habits of the various key publics. Traditionally, this has been a working method used only by advertising experts, especially by the media planners. The reason why editorial workers used to give less attention to this phase of the planning process was that advertising involved more substantial tangible expenses. The need to be efficient in media selection thus appeared to be more important in advertising than in editorial work.

While it is true that the visible costs are higher in advertising, there are important cost factors involved in professional editorial work as well. The input of high-level management time is often considerable in editorial work of all kinds. If that is taken into account, it is worth the effort to plan editorial work by the same strict target audience standards as required by 'advertising' staff. Chapter 11 offers a discussion on media analysis which may also be applied to editorial work.

It is advisable to work out, for each important contact group, a 'media consumption profile', taking into account television, radio and newspaper habits of that particular group, as well as their

189

readership of more specialized media, technical press, business and trade magazines, etc. The readership potential of the media that the company publishes – or plans to publish – itself should be part of that analysis, namely, house magazines of various kinds for the staff, customers, shareholders or other groups.

The analysis should help define audience characteristics in such fields as:

- Subject-matter areas of interest.
- Language capacity (how 'technical' can a text be to be read by the target audience?).
- Reader preferences to illustrations (is a cartoon, a realistic photograph or a machine drawing most likely to make the target audience 'tick'?).
- Type of journalism (interviews, articles, feature stories, case descriptions?).
- Time available (nobody has time to spare for bad journalism, but most people take time for subjects of concern to them, if well presented).

An audience profile along these lines, which can gradually be refined, will be helpful in all three kinds of editorial work defined above, creating input, improving editorial contacts and editorial production.

Let us take a closer look at the three kinds of assignments.

Following public media for feedback into the organization

In most countries, the general and specialized public media present tremendous amounts of opinions and information that have a bearing on the life and decision-making process of any company. Although management in general are avid readers and give more than the average share of attention to media of value to them, they can only cover part of the total output, especially if foreign and international media have to be considered.

Today more than ever, management should always act in full awareness of opinions and attitudes among key contact areas and give them due consideration in the decision-making process. It is a natural part of the responsibilities of a communications function to support this by ensuring that the attention of top and middle management, and perhaps other categories, is drawn to relevant articles, statements and discussions in the public media.

This function can, to a greater or lesser degree, be covered by company staff or by outside service agencies. Plan to do those parts of it that require qualified judgement and specialized company know-how through company staff, library or communications, while those parts of it that aim at collecting 'raw material' from a wide range of sources may be suitable to assign to an outside press-cutting service. No matter what organizational solutions are practical in your company, the communications manager must ultimately be responsible for processing and feeding into the company relevant material that appears in the public media.

Several factors speak in favour of covering the media through company staff. It is difficult enough for insiders to follow the variety of interests that a company may have – for outside agencies it is next to impossible. Company staff, at least in theory, have more knowledge about people and roles in company management, about plans, trends, ambitions, competitors, customers and corporate conditions. That should make it easier for company staff to select the right type of material, to avoid piling too much on the desks of overloaded managers and to put clippings into a context, with or without commentaries. The work can be carried out by library personnel or by other types of communications staff.

There *are* good reasons for utilizing outside agencies, whether for routine press cuttings or for analysis and documentation of special subjects. The main advantage is that specialized press-cutting services cover a wider range of media than company staff can normally follow on a day-to-day basis. Thus, in those cases where articles or shorter stories of interest to the company appear in unexpected media, they stand a better chance of being observed if the assignment has been given to an outside press-cutting agency. Also, while these services are by no means cheap if one wants a quality job, they may be a better buy than hiring your own staff for some of the tasks.

One of the disadvantages is that, usually, the order will be limited to fairly mechanical clipping of articles with the indicated key-words. Only the key-words will be covered in the specified media categories. Related subjects may not be considered at all. In other cases one may get more than is wanted. Innumerable duplicates of rather unimportant mentions may pour in, as well as unwanted cuttings as a result of understandable misunderstandings. I recall a case when a colleague in a commercial bank ordered press cuttings on anything concerning banks and banking. One week he was truly inundated with stories on the results of that year's cod fishing on one of the banks in the North Atlantic!

To sum up: make sure that the organization receives systematic input of essential press material that originates from or reflects opinions among important contact areas. Give management the benefit of up-to-date press cuttings or press extracts, if possible with concentrated, balanced summaries and with conclusions or even recommendations for specific action by company managers. Editorial input is not the only way, but it is an important way to make managers conscious of what is expected of them today: managing their companies with clear awareness of what is going on within people that make up priority contact areas of the company.

Keeping in touch with editors and journalists of interest

One of the reasons why traditional PR officers often feel overworked is that they often are! Why? Is it a matter of inadequate resources put at their disposal? Yes, in many cases that is probably true. But in addition to inadequate resources, the reason may well be inadequate analysis of the specific jobs that have to be done. And the step may be short, indeed, between inadequate analysis and – paralysis! If the task of the press officer is defined in such general terms as 'to deal with the press' or 'to handle media relations' it is easy to feel frustrated. What an assignment to get to grips with!

Making press contacts manageable
The press, or even wider, the media may be conceived and felt as an amorphous body of good-will or ill-will. It includes journalists who wake you up in the middle of the night to inquire about your company's dealings with South Africa; the local radio station that wants comments on the effluents from your factory; the foreign journalist who wants an impromptu statement on alleged bribes to secure the company's recent contract for equipment in the Far East. It may also be the trade magazines that your boss sends you memoranda about – those who always seem to take your competition's stories, while they refuse all the fine press material you send them. Or the investigative journalists who report comprehensively on the trade union views of your plans for production cutbacks – before the decision has even been taken. If these and other difficult situations are allowed to create an unlimited volume of work for the press officer, no wonder if he or she ranks high on the future list of heart attack victims.

So, how to avoid it? The examples are realistic enough – anyone with a responsibility for press relations will confirm that, and come up with a dozen or so similar situations from their own experience.

There is certainly no way to avoid the situations as such. The task is to find a way to deal with them. Volumes of books, articles and courses are available on the subject of press relations. There is no reason to repeat their wisdom here, but it may be a good investment to get some new thinking started by taking a course, reading a few articles or a book on the subject. A library or the local chapter of the PR association can give good advice. A few suggestions are included in the Additional Reading at the end of this book, pp. 410–12.

Some of these sources may present an extremely broad picture of the task of press relations, thus adding to the problems rather than showing a practical way of handling them.

Try this definition for your own situation:

Press contacts are one of the methods to get our message across to such groups that are important to our company.

Every expansion to this definition is likely to add to the headaches and create more uncertainty as to the purpose and direction of the job to be done. If you feel you have the capacity for unspecified responsibilities, fine! If not, start from a tighter definition and then add gradually to the list!

Let us take a closer look at the practical implications of the definition:

1. Press contacts do not constitute the whole communications programme of any company. They are an important part of it, but only a part. They may be a channel to forward the company philosophy, but they are not the philosophy. They are a communications method among others, alongside printed matter, letters, advertising, exhibitions, etc.

2. While it may be in the company's interest to be of service to journalists in a very general way, the priority task is to help get the company's message across. There is nothing wrong in this. That means that sometimes it is legitimate to decline a request. While it may make you feel good always to be helpful to any journalist who calls, your role is primarily to further the aims of the company, both when you represent the media within the company and when you represent the company among media.

3. Setting clear priorities means that there are some journalists and

some media that are more important to you than others – not because the individual journalists or media are more important than others, but because their readers, listeners and viewers are among the key contact areas of your company. List those media, and individual journalists in them, preferably classified under your respective key contact areas, not as an unspecified group of media or 'journalists'. If the list tends to get too long for efficient handling, set priorities on the really important journalists under each contact area, giving each one of them a ***, a **, or a * mark, according to your evaluation. This will help you serve the key journalists well and in line with your own objectives, rather than being controlled by outside influences or pure chance, which may put you under stress and lead you away from 'communications-by-objectives'.

Media analysis by contact area

As a start, let us discuss briefly what kind of editorial contacts to consider under different contact areas.

Staff communications

In addition to the company's own staff publications, which will be discussed later, certain media may be part of the consumption patterns of wide groups of your staff. The local newspapers and radio stations in the communities where your company has many employees are one such media category. Trade union magazines, local or nation-wide, are other examples. Review if there are any other characteristics that are shared by groups of your staff and which may be reflected in their reading, listening or viewing habits. Make a list of the media you have come up with and specify individual journalists that are or should be on your 'short list' of editorial contacts.

Shareholder and financial groups

In addition to the company's own annual report and other material that is mailed directly, financial contacts are sure to have certain media consumption habits that could improve the links between them and the company. Do they read the financial columns in the big national dailies? The specific business magazines? Bankers and stock brokers have their own specialized publications. The bank that your company works with may have a staff magazine. Do your shareholders have any common features that could guide you to creative media thinking, geographic, age-wise or other? List the media – and the journalists – and you have an excellent starting point for long-range as well as emergency action.

The local communities
The local daily newspapers and radio stations are obvious contact points. In addition, local service clubs and local civic organizations may have regular publications for their members. The local council may have a staff magazine for the employees of local government.

Government
The big national media, newspapers, news magazines, television and radio networks, etc. are, of course, already on your list. Have you also listed individual editors, with their special interests and preferences? Some branches of government may be closer to the company's interest than others, such as consumer protection agencies, occupational safety and health authorities, engineering standardization and business regulation agencies, national or regional business 'advisory' boards, etc. These boards, agencies and offices often run their own periodical publications for their staff or for outside circulation. Which are they, who are the readers, who are the editors and what types of material might they be interested in?

The educational world
Teachers' unions often have their own local or national magazines. They may be general, with a bearing on the elementary and secondary general school system, or reflect more specialized aspects of the educational system, such as technical schools, business schools, etc. Other magazines deal with various types of education, with educational aids and methods and with principles and philosophies of the educational world. Reviewing these publications may create ideas for editorial contacts with schools, school authorities and teachers.

The market
The technical and trade press serving important customer categories are high up on the priority list already. How specific is the list and does it exist, physically? How much data are included about reader categories, readership analysis, types of material covered, etc.? How much information does it include about individual editors, staff and freelance, working for those magazines, their interests, personalities, background, experience, etc.? A worksheet for each one of the media, with facts and figures about the magazine on one side and your contacts with it on the other side may be helpful. List material you send, acceptance/rejection notes, personal meetings with journalists, inquiry statistics, etc. (Such a worksheet is useful not only for the market-oriented media but others too.)

While the technical and trade press are important as editorial channels to your market, these media are not the only ones to consider. Technical and business pages of the major dailies, specialized editors of the radio and television networks, magazines published by the business associations in your customer fields, all should be listed and evaluated. The trade union press of customer industries should be listed among market influences.

Material and methods
This analysis and evaluation of potential editorial contact opportunities will generate ideas on material that is available or can be developed, material that will fit into the editorial programmes of the media concerned at the same time as they fit company plans and ambitions. It will also create ideas on methods for establishing or improving contacts with the priority publications, and for keeping these contacts alive and active. Informal personal contacts, planned meetings with company management or specialists, demonstrations and news presentations on company premises, press visits to interesting worksites or customer plants, financial or technical press releases, appointments and other staff news, changes in organization and management, case stories, specially written articles, photograph and caption releases, comments by top management or company specialists on business trends or events, and so on. Your own creative thinking is the only limit.

The mechanics of handling press relations, editing press releases, staging press conferences and dealing with journalists have been well covered in many books, and there is no need to duplicate here what will be easy to find elsewhere. However, a few aspects on training management in press and other media relations might be worthwhile.

Training management in media relations
The need for business managers to get appropriate training in press relations is growing. This need is being recognized by increasing numbers of managers as well as journalists. Reasons behind it include the growing public interest in business (consumerism, regulatory trends, the role of business in developing countries, employee participation, etc.), freer access to data about business, partly forced upon, partly voluntarily offered by the business community, and a less respectful, or openly aggressive, attitude towards business from editors and journalists.

For the company it is vital to have an adequate number of executives with authority and the ability to present the company's position on important issues. A secretary or press officer who has to say 'No, I am sorry, but only the Chief Executive Officer and the Chief Operating Officer are authorized to make statements on that issue, and none of them is available today' is not in an enviable position, and the company misses an opportunity to get its views across. Each one of the media discussed above, not only the more spectacular media like television, radio or the major dailies, offers opportunities to make the company and its position accepted or at least understood by an audience that may influence the future of the company.

The communications manager should not be the only company representative. It is his or her responsibility to see to it that the company is represented by the best spokesman in each case. That calls for an acceptable number of executives and specialists who can handle an interview and come out of it unscathed. Even otherwise well-endowed executives need training to feel at ease in interviews. They must feel that they are able to explain the company's views in terms that a layman/voter/reader/viewer can understand and, hopefully, agree with.

Many industrial associations provide training for managers from their member companies in dealing with the media. The advantage of such courses is that they offer an opportunity for exchange and learning across the company lines. On the other hand, in-company courses offer the great advantage of choosing examples, cases and situations directly taken from the company's situation and which, for that reason, are perceived as realistic by all participants. It also gives the communications manager a better chance to evaluate how well each individual manager can handle relations to journalists. Knowing this gives the communications manager invaluable insight in guiding who should be 'on the air'.

Whether such courses or training sessions are set up 'in-house' or for managers from a group of companies, certain items should be on the agenda:

1. Briefings to help participants understand the role and work situation of the journalists, the job they have to do, how they experience working with businessmen, priorities, difficulties and limitations in their work, principles for news evaluation, problems in meeting tight deadlines, etc.
2. Simple guidelines on what to consider before, during and after an interview, preferably developed during the training session by the participants.

3. Concrete examples, taken from real television programmes, radio broadcasts, daily newspapers and trade press, in form of videotapes, audiotapes and real cuttings, to discuss and analyse.
4. Practical training in news evaluation.
5. Realistic interview situations, in front of video cameras, on subjects of direct relevance to the participants. They should have a chance to experience situations as close to their own reality as possible, including difficult cases, perhaps even 'leaks' and 'disasters' – as long as they are realistic – but also 'positive' cases.
6. A discussion on how the company could prepare itself for better relations with the media. That discussion should lead to full familiarity on principles and guidelines for the company's editorial relations, including who has the right and obligation to speak for the company on what subjects, etc.

Some additional suggestions: allow at least one full day for the course. Engage one or more qualified journalists in the preparation work and to conduct live interviews during the course. Limit the number of participants each time to ten to twelve. Use video and audiotape to give participants an immediate learning experience from their own performance in interview situations.

One of the 'fringe benefits' in running training programmes of this kind is that the communications manager gets a clear understanding of who in a management group is best suited for various types of interview assignments, who he can 'send in' when the press calls.

Editorial work under your immediate control – the house magazines

Advantages and pitfalls

Many big companies – and a growing number of smaller companies – are publishers of periodical publications in their own right, using consultants, freelancers or company staff to do the editorial work. Staff publications, customer magazines, shareholder newsletters or other editorial products, bearing the company hallmark, are ingredients in the communications mix of thousands of companies. They represent big investments in money and manpower, aiming at improved communications.

What are the advantages of periodical publications in the total corporate communications work? For what reasons and under what circumstances are they chosen instead of or as a complement to other communications methods?

If sound journalistic methods are used, so that the publication does not appear too 'slick', in paper, printing, use of colour or in the editorial treatment of the material, a company periodical can have certain distinct advantages. However, these 'ifs' are important. Far too often a house magazine editor or publisher, especially if his or her background is in conventional advertising, hides a lack of substance behind a nice four-colour, heavy stock appearance. This only fools the reader for a short while.

That leads us to one of the strong advantages of the periodical publication: that it is periodical. The fact that the publication reaches the recipient at regular intervals is a key factor towards reaching the goals that should have been set up for it. Few other corporate communication channels can match the publication, newspaper style, magazine style or newsletter style, in such qualities as consistency, long-range awareness-building and a capacity to build human interest around the company and its life.

Editorial policy

Before starting or redesigning a house magazine or other editorial product, be sure to put some time into considering its editorial policy. The policy outline should be discussed, modified if necessary, and then approved by as many as possible of those who will have a hand in the final outcome, from the chief executive to the printers. Lots of problems can be avoided and lots of good thinking and practical advice can be generated in that process. Here are a few points to be thrown in – with more or less validity in each specific case:

1. *What is the audience?*
If it is an employee publication, the question may seem easy. After all, the personnel department has all the statistical data in their files. Still, for the editorial policy, take time to analyse the statistics, reflect on them and draw conclusions from them. Draw up an 'age pyramid' – what is the predominant age group? Keep the key age groups in mind in the editorial work. What are the male/female proportions? Are the majority of your employees blue-collar or white-collar? Does that have any implications on editorial policy? Are all your employees located in one spot or do they work in far-flung locations, nationwide or worldwide?

Follow the same procedure for a customer magazine. What is the geographical spread? What branches of industry do they represent? What levels in the customer companies is the publication aimed for?

A shareholder publication requires the same kind of initial analysis of the composition of the audience. What is the shareholder profile, in terms of age, sex and geographically? Are the shareholders a group of big owners, small investors or a mixture of both? Are most of them investors in many other companies as well, or does their interest in your company play a dominant role? Do many of them have an interest in the real business of the company or do they look upon their holdings only as an investment? Is the publication to be distributed strictly to the shareholders or do you plan to include other financial interests as well?

Answers to these questions could strongly influence decisions on the kind of material, layout, frequency and editorial style of a company magazine.

2.   What is the specific purpose of the publication?
In general terms, the purpose is probably to create good-will and understanding for the company among the audience selected. But such a wide definition is not enough to help establish guidelines for the editor's work. Try to reach more in-depth criteria for why the company considers the expense and effort of establishing the publication. Go back to the chapters in Part I and review the overall ambitions and goals that your company has set for the contact area in question, and from that base, work out the specific role that the periodical publication can be expected to play, in cooperation with and as reinforcement of other channels, both personal and non-personal.

3.   Who is responsible for what?
Discuss how the material should be generated, who is responsible for the day-to-day editorial work and who has the last word in approving material for publication and include the conclusions in the editorial policy document. Leaving considerable freedom to the editor, within the framework of company policy, is much more likely to produce a publication with journalistic integrity than a tightly controlled, CEO-approved magazine. An editorial council, with representatives of readers and other interested parties, meeting a few times a year is usually an asset in keeping a company magazine active and responsive to various legitimate interests.

The editorial process

What subject matter should be aimed for?
A company-sponsored magazine is normally sent out free to its
target audience. Some industrial editors, or their superiors, often
believe that this means they do not have to consider reader interest
at all and that the subject matter can be selected with the sponsoring
company interest as the only guiding factor. The fact that this guides
so many sponsored publications directly to the wastepaper basket
should be a warning.

An employee publication can and should deal with much more
than the latest office party, new employees and the wisdom of the
managing director. A customer magazine is not a leaflet presenting
the newest products in glowing four-colour pictures. A shareholder
newsletter containing only the profit development of the last six
months and other strictly financial information is an insult to the
shareholder.

The following types of material should be actively considered for
company-sponsored publications. The list applies as a 'think-list' for
various types of company publication, although the material could
be treated differently for a staff magazine, a customer magazine or a
shareholder magazine. Sometimes, however, the same item may
serve several audiences, with only light adaptations: headlines,
illustrations, lead-ins or captions.

1. Topical, up-to-date reports on company progress and achieve-
    ments and on set-backs and problems. The sun does not always
    shine on your company. The best way to learn about that for
    people interested in the company is from the company itself!

2. Feature stories on departments, plants and special functions in
    the company, their characteristics, their development and
    particular roles in the overall organization.

3. Case stories about products at work, preferably written by or in
    cooperation with customers. What happens to the products,
    which customers use them, what requirements do customers
    have, what problems can our products solve among our
    customers, why does a customer choose our products rather
    than competing brands?

4. Presentations of key people in the organization – not only senior
    managament or 'shop-window' staff, but also the important
    back-up people that no company can do without.

5. Reports on the industry in general, its ups and downs, trends,

perhaps written by a guest writer representing the manufacturers' organization, an independent magazine or an educational institution.

6. Reader feedback – important to all editors. A simple way is to establish and encourage a 'Letter to the Editor' section. Alternatively – or as a complement – create an advisory board with representatives of the employees, of the customers or of the other categories that your house magazine is supposed to serve. Other feedback methods include various types of readership measurements.

7. Frequency. Should you aim for a frequent, 'newsy' publication or for a low-frequency, heavier type of magazine character? There are good reasons for both, although it seems as if frequency is gaining ground. Whatever you decide, make sure that the agreed timetable is carefully observed.

What is the graphic quality level you want to keep?
In too many cases, the simple answer to that question is: 'We certainly want nothing but the best.' A $10,000 answer.

Go through this question carefully, for it *is* a question of editorial policy as well as one of cost. Take time to discuss it with several printers but not only in terms of printing techniques. The stock and the print method have a direct bearing on such things as the use of colour, the layout principles, the general looks and character of the publication. And 'nothing but the best' may have unwanted side-effects. Discuss it your with readers. Their reactions may be totally different from what is intended.

A graphic level to match the purpose of the publication, well in line with corporate graphic guidelines, but preferably on the 'low-key' side should be your ambition. A check-point on paper stock may be what similar commercial publications use – don't go much higher! And if that is a choice, put money and efforts into the contents (and frequency) of the publication rather than into heavier stock and an expensive printing process. Bad journalism will never be accepted, least of all if it appears on glossy, high-quality paper, while interesting reading, arriving on the reader's desk in time, will be received with sympathy even if the stock is bad.

Evaluating editorial work

What we shall discuss here is not the literary or journalistic quality of editorial work, but purely its value in the corporate environment, to promote the interests of the company. Not that journalistic quality is unimportant, nor for that matter literary qualities, but in business communications they have a distinct value only in as much as they contribute to corporate success, to communicate the cause of the company. In this respect they are similar to political, ideological or educational writing, as opposed to literature as a 'pure' art.

Evaluating 'input'

Of the three main types of editorial work we have treated, it is paradoxically most difficult to measure the results of the type we control most, the feedback into the company of attitudes, opinions and awareness of what is going on around the company. Naturally, one can measure the physical input into the organization of press cuttings, extracts, etc., and the distribution of the material among the managers who should be exposed to it.

But the important part of this process, the changes in awareness and attitudes it creates, and the influence it has on the long-range and the day-to-day, is a lot more difficult to evaluate, even more the contributions that this process makes to company success. This is especially true since the main contribution it *can* make is to help management avoid making serious mistakes – and who can measure the value of the disastrous, detrimental or just plain bad decisions that were never made? The plant closure that was not brought about in one month but over a six-month period giving everybody a chance to adjust – or perhaps not even made, because management included social consequences in the planning process. The dangerous product that was not launched because management was made aware of its environmental consequences. The questionable payments that were stopped, the shoddy deals that were not made.

Adequate input of ideas from the outside world may not be the only factor to help influence decision-making and bring it closer to valid social trends, but it should certainly contribute to more responsive policies.

Evaluating editorial contact work

Evaluating good editorial contacts with public media is slightly easier. The quantity of it can be adequately measured through press cuttings and similar registration methods for radio and television. The 'quality' from the company viewpoint can also be assessed and preferably in more qualified terms than 'positive' or 'negative' publicity. But what is the relative impact of what is written or said?

One way to measure it is to compare the editorial coverage of one company with that of similar companies in the same or similar media. In the local community one can make a direct, physical comparison of what is published about three or four local companies of similar size and importance. In national media, one can do the same thing with a selection of comparable companies. In the trade press, take the closest competitors as a yardstick, collect and evaluate material about them against the company's record. Measuring the quantity and quality as such is not enough. Try to go beyond that, asking the more important 'how' and 'why' questions. One thing this will give is a 'bench-mark' from which to set new targets. The analysis will reveal areas where the company's performance is not up to par, which will indicate potential improvement areas. And the next time, maybe after a year, progress can be measured and discussed with management in terms that they will understand.

Evaluating company publications

The editorial products that a company produces or sponsors are perhaps the easiest category to evaluate. That does not mean that it is done without effort, neither does it mean that all companies really make such evaluations, despite the time and effort invested in house magazines. A few per cent of the total investment in a staff magazine or a customer journal goes a long way towards estimating the return on the investment, especially if the effort is made at periodical intervals, so that changes and possibly trends can be traced.

A regular commercial publication gets automatic feedback through the fact that somebody has to pay for it. A newspaper or a magazine can follow the development of news-stand sales issue by issue and subscription renewals monthly, quarterly or at least annually. A house magazine, distributed free of charge, does not get this kind of direct feedback.

One easy way to measure reader response is to request, as most 'controlled circulation' magazines do, that a reader must express his interest in the publication at periodic intervals to remain on the circulation list. For customer and shareholder magazines this method has been tried successfully by many companies. A simple return card is mailed to all recipients, with one or two follow-up cards if necessary. The degree of interest expressed provides valuable feedback. It creates the possibility of weeding out those who do not want the magazine and replacing them with readers who may be more responsive to your message. The non-return rate will of course be subject to careful analysis to help find out how the publication can be adjusted and improved to make it better suited for the purpose you have set up.

This method is normally not applicable to staff magazines nor to publications for other groups of readers, where the company definitely wishes that the target audience should be exposed to its message in this form. In such cases feedback can be generated through an editorial council with reader representation. A reader panel, which may not meet as often, but can include a bigger number than a council, is another way. More accurate evaluation of reader interest and appreciation can be received through a readership survey. Get a professional adviser or consultant to help in order to avoid some of the traps. One trap may be, as is so often the case, overambition. In most cases a questionnaire of ten to twelve simple questions (such as Figure 10.1), mailed to every fifth or tenth reader, will provide very valuable clues for the future, especially if the same procedure is repeated once a year or every other year. (For further details on survey techniques, see Part III, Chapter 17.)

Reader response, in various forms, represents one side of the evaluation work. The other equally important side is represented by the degree to which the publication fulfils the ambitions and objectives outlined by the publisher, that is, the management of the company. After analysing the results of a reader survey, call a meeting with those concerned in corporate management, recall the written objectives of the publication and encourage enlightened comments based on the objectives and on the registered reader reactions. Should the objectives be modified, should the editorial product be changed to match better the objectives and generate more reader interest, could management contribute more actively, should budget allocations be adjusted to better match the ambitions?

The road to professional editorial work

Editorial work is an important part of every communications function in the three main forms discussed in this chapter. It is certainly important enough to deserve frequent evaluations of performance versus objectives. Such periodical evaluations help keep the communications department professional and create a

WE WANT YOUR OPINION!

Please help us make *Transamerica Magazine* more interesting and useful to you by answering these 20 questions. Except where indicated, select the *one* answer that most closely reflects your feelings. And please add your comments in the spaces provided.

We'll summarize your opinions in the next issue of *Transamerica Magazine*.

1. **How thoroughly do you read most issues of *Transamerica Magazine?***

☐ Read most stories   ☐ Read some stories
☐ Skim stories   ☐ Do not read
☐ I've never received an issue before

2. **Overall, do you find the articles in *Transamerica Magazine*:**

	Strongly Agree	Agree	No Opinion	Disagree	Strongly Disagree
Interesting	☐	☐	☐	☐	☐
Relevant to your work at Transamerica	☐	☐	☐	☐	☐
Believable	☐	☐	☐	☐	☐
Timely	☐	☐	☐	☐	☐
Informative	☐	☐	☐	☐	☐
Lively and readable	☐	☐	☐	☐	☐

3. **Do you find most articles in *Transamerica Magazine*:**

A. ☐ Too long   ☐ About right   ☐ Too short

B. ☐ Too formal   ☐ About right   ☐ Too informal

4. **Overall, do you find the appearance of *Transamerica Magazine*:**

☐ Well-designed and modern
☐ Average and ordinary
☐ Outdated and uninviting

If you checked "average and ordinary" or "outdated and uninviting," please give us suggestions for improving our design (check all that apply):

☐ Use more photos and illustrations
☐ Use fewer photos and illustrations
☐ Use more color
☐ Use less color
☐ Change format to newspaper

☐ Other: (please specify) _____

5. **How well do you feel *Transamerica Magazine* performs in each of the following categories?**

	Excellent	Good	Fair	Poor
Helps you understand Transamerica's goals and plans for the future	☐	☐	☐	☐
Motivates you to be more productive	☐	☐	☐	☐
Makes you appreciate being a part of the Transamerica "family"	☐	☐	☐	☐
Suggests solutions to help you solve work-related problems	☐	☐	☐	☐
Encourages you to help Transamerica reach its goals	☐	☐	☐	☐
Helps you understand how your job fits into Transamerica	☐	☐	☐	☐
Offers information that you don't get from other sources	☐	☐	☐	☐
Helps you understand how Transamerica Corporation adds value to your company	☐	☐	☐	☐
Overall, an interesting and useful publication	☐	☐	☐	☐

6. ***Transamerica Magazine* features stories on a variety of topics that affect all Transamerica companies and employees.**

Would you like to see more (or less) information on the following topics?

	More	Okay As Is	Less
Effect on Transamerica of external economic and legislative events	☐	☐	☐
Our performance vs. the competition	☐	☐	☐
Our community involvement	☐	☐	☐
Insurance and financial services industry updates	☐	☐	☐
Our products and services	☐	☐	☐
Our benefits plans and policies	☐	☐	☐
Customer service	☐	☐	☐
Our financial results and how we use our profits	☐	☐	☐
Our stand on current legislative issues	☐	☐	☐
Our goals and plans for the future	☐	☐	☐
Our advertising and promotional plans	☐	☐	☐

7. **What kinds of articles would you like to see more (or less) of?**

	More	Okay As Is	Less
In-depth interviews (Q&A format)	☐	☐	☐
In-depth feature articles	☐	☐	☐
Profiles of employees on the job	☐	☐	☐
Messages to employees from chairman Jim Harvey	☐	☐	☐
"Question Man" column (pose one question to several employees)	☐	☐	☐
Contests and puzzles (with questions related to articles in *Transamerica Magazine*)	☐	☐	☐
"Hard news" stories about events at Transamerica companies	☐	☐	☐

8. **What other topics would you like to see covered in future issues of *Transamerica Magazine*?**

_____
_____

9. **How often would you prefer to receive *Transamerica Magazine*?**

☐ Three times a year   ☐ Quarterly   ☐ Every other month

☐ Other (please specify): _____

10. **How would you rate the distribution system for *Transamerica Magazine*?**

☐ Excellent, I always receive a copy
☐ Good, but sometimes I have trouble getting a copy
☐ Poor, I rarely receive a copy

11. **How do you receive *Transamerica Magazine*?**

☐ Copy delivered directly to me by U.S. mail or inter-office mail
☐ My supervisor gives me a copy
☐ I take a copy from a general supply located in a central area

☐ Other (please specify): _____

On about what date did you receive the latest copy? _____

Figure 10.1 *Questionnaire for a house magazine readership survey Transamerica Inc., reprinted with permission.*

platform for increased understanding of the role and value of professional communications work. The initiative for such evaluations should therefore be taken by the communications manager. They should be one way for the communications manager constantly to improve his efficiency and performance.

Budgeting editorial work

The editorial parts of a company's communications programme are more personnel-intensive than most other elements. The budgeting process, therefore, is very much one of allocating staff resources. In most companies, this budgeting process is less developed than the budgeting of immediate monetary outlays. Advertising agencies and other consultants usually have better methods for keeping tabs on time consumption for various types of work, including editorial work. Ask for their help in reaching reasonable budget figures for the types and amounts of editorial work the company is planning, both 'input', media relations and editorial production.

The material and services purchased from outside sources are easier to calculate. That includes press-cutting and press-extract services needed for the input parts, as well as consultancy, press release services, press conference assistance, photography work and other external services for editorial contact work.

For the company's editorial production, especially the customer magazine, you may have to make interesting choices between various ways to use a set budget or modifying a budget in different directions. You may get into a situation of choosing between higher or lower frequency, increased or reduced circulation, using more or less editorial time, staff, consultants, free-lancers, artists, photographers, etc., improving or reducing the quality of the stock, the printing process, colour printing, mailing procedures, etc.

Balancing these demands is not easy, but reliable reader reactions matched with the priorities and objectives of the publication provide valuable input.

Comparing alternatives, it is obviously necessary to know what makes up the basic creative costs, the paper and printing costs and the distribution costs of each issue. Try the following model and fill in your own figures:

Fixed Costs
    Per issue

Editorial costs (including staff time)
Photos, artwork, layout, etc.
'Fixed' mailing list costs
'Fixed' printing costs
    (typesetting, engravings, plates, etc.)

    Total fixed costs per issue   ———————

Flexible costs
    Per 1,000 copies

Paper costs
Printing costs
Mailing and distribution costs
Postage

    Total flexible costs per 1,000 copies   ———————

When you have made this breakdown, you will be in a better position to take appropriate action. Based on relations between fixed costs and flexible costs you may find that an increase in circulation of your customer magazine adds substantially to its reach without adding a lot to the total investment. You may also find that the total cost of photography, artwork, etc., is rather limited. In such cases, increased use of professional illustration work may add considerably to readership, reader understanding and reader response. The cost breakdown may point to a need for lower costs/new methods for typesetting, printing method, maybe desk-top or mailing list handling. You may find methods to save on paper and printing and apply those savings towards higher frequency, if one of your prime aims is improved contacts with your audience.

Finally, in the budgeting process you will of course compare communications costs not only within the channel of editorial work, but also between the various channels that are or could be used for communications with each contact area.

What are the costs of the staff magazine, compared to meetings, committees and other staff communications methods? What are the staff communications costs as a percentage of total salary and wage costs? And compared with the benefits of good staff relations?

What are the total costs of the customer magazine in relation to sales literature, customer-oriented direct mail, market-oriented space advertising, participation in trade shows and in relation to salesmen's costs?

In many companies, a cost-benefit analysis of this kind will indicate that, even including staff time, editorial work is one of the most indispensable communications methods – and one of the best, on the basis of value for money or return on investment.

11

'Let's put an ad in!':
Media advertising

In this chapter the reader will find a presentation of the characteristics of media advertising as a communications tool, not only in the traditional marketing context, with a clear focus on response-orientation.

It will help the reader plan, budget, execute and evaluate advertising projects as result-oriented parts of a company's total communications process.

Media advertising – a communications tool

Media advertising, defined as the use of other (mostly commercial) communications vehicles, in which you place your own message, usually differentiated from the 'editorial' contents, is probably the most used – and mis-used – of all the tools in the communications manager's tool-box. It is less dominating in business-to-business than in consumer-oriented communications. Yet, it often takes half the budget, in competition with direct mail, literature, audiovisual media, exhibitions and other contact forms which, together, take the other half.

In fact, it is so dominating that the word advertising is often used as a synonym of communications. Such confusion should be avoided in the interest of intellectual clarity as well as practical use. Advertising is not the same as communications. It is, at best, one of the tools of the communications trade, one of the techniques or methods that can be used to reach communications goals, to establish or improve relations between people. If media advertising is regarded this way, as one of the tools in the tool-box, it is easier to recognize its advantages and shortcomings and create a basis for more intelligent, more cost-efficient choices in building the total communications network for a company.

Serving many contact areas

Media advertising is not a marketing tool, it is a communications tool that can be used for market communications, as well as for other contact areas. It has advantages that make it easy to understand its strong position compared to other communications methods.

This chapter will discuss media advertising as a communications tool serving many contact areas to be used for a wider variety of purposes than just selling a product:

- To convey a message to local or national political influences.
- To make the general public aware of a problem or a solution.
- To present a company to potential employees.
- To make wide or specialized audiences understand the importance of research, technology, productivity, profits, international trade or other concepts that may be significant to your company.

- To make the financial position of your company known and appreciated by shareholders, brokers, banks and others in the financial community.

Media advertising is such a powerful communications method that it should enter into practically any discussion aiming at solving a communications problem or improving a communications situation. It would limit the communicator's imagination if media advertising were to be seen exclusively in its marketing applications.

Considering advertising in these terms would defuse the political discussion in many countries on the role and dangers of advertising. The method, as all human implements, can be used more or less intelligently or responsibly. In itself it is neither good or bad, 'but thinking makes it so'.

Characteristics of media advertising in business communications

Some of the main characteristics of media advertising in business communications are listed below. To keep the presentation within reasonable limits it is by necessity fairly general. It must, therefore, be applied judicially and adapted to specific situations.

Different audiences

Media advertising, as has already been mentioned, can be used quite successfully to communicate with very different audiences or contact areas. In many countries it is possible to find media that, with reasonable accuracy, reach quite specialized audiences within a company's sphere of interest.

This flexibility in reach is, indeed, one of the main general characteristics of media advertising, and the main reason for considering media advertising for many other communications purposes than marketing. The financial community have their reading or listening habits that a company can link their message to. The residents of a small community in which you intend to set up a new plant – or close down an existing business – may have their local media in which you can explain your reasons, your intentions and your procedures. Lawyers read certain magazines in which your advertisement for a new corporate solicitor has a good chance of reaching the right individuals. Government employees of certain levels, or with certain specialities, may habitually read certain sections of newspapers or certain magazines, so your message has a fair chance to reach them there.

Probing the unknown

You can 'send your beam in the general direction' of your target audience, but you can rarely reach any target audience through media advertising without a certain percentage of waste. This is in the definition of media advertising: 'using other communications vehicles, in which you place your own message'. Only in exceptional cases, indeed, is every reader of a newspaper or magazine, or every listener to a radio or television channel, of specific interest to you.

This may seem to be a weakness in media advertising, since all waste tends to reduce the cost-efficiency of your communications work, but it is also one of the positive factors of media advertising, comparing it with other methods. The positive side of the 'waste' is that it offers you one of the unique opportunities to reach people who may be interested in your message, without being known to you. This quality of probing the unknown, of exploring an undefined interest potential, makes media advertising a preferred choice in many situations. The first stages of a screening process, aiming at selecting categories or individuals who fill the double criterion of being interested in your message, and being of interest to you, can be implemented through media advertising. This is often made in practice, but mainly in the conventional contexts of market-oriented advertising. If it were applied more consciously, many companies could improve their total communications process.

'One-way' or 'two-way'?

The word communications is used in this book to emphasize the two-way character of a contact process. Media advertising, by nature, is in itself a one-way process. 'You send a beam in the general direction . . .'

It is said in gastronomic contexts that some kinds of food are not necessarily excellent by themselves, but you can 'force them to be good', if you apply enough creative thinking, skill and the right spices. By the same token, media advertising can be 'forced' to play a two-way communications role, if you apply enough of creativity, skill . . . and the right kinds of spices. How to do that is part of the art director's secret, but it is the communications manager's responsibility to insist that it is being done: to make sure that no effort is spared to 'create a reflection', not only 'send the beam'; to force media advertising to take the step up to communications.

Full control

Full control can be achieved in most cases. The reason why is the fourth characteristic of media advertising: the sender has full control over the message, both its contents and the form in which it is presented.

In editorial work, even when working with the same media as those used for advertising, the contents and the presentation of your message is entirely in the hands of the editorial staff. You can 'help' in various ways to get the editors to see things your way, but if they have any guts – in other words, if the media are independent and qualified enough – they will make a personal and professional evaluation of your press release or any other contact form you use. The final form of your material when it reaches the reader or listener may be far from what you imagined. Also direct mail, audiovisuals and exhibitions have their limitations, both in form and presentation. Media advertising gives you more control than most other methods over your message, all the way, until it reaches the individual for whom it was designed.

The Wheel of Fortune – a continuous planning cycle

The advertiser, however, has no guarantee whatsoever that his message is penetrating and creating the effects he is after. Much advertising is still misdirected and inefficient. The planning process can be improved and the waste factor reduced if a few clearly discernible elements are given more attention.

Choose your starting number!

These elements do not necessarily function as steps where you start

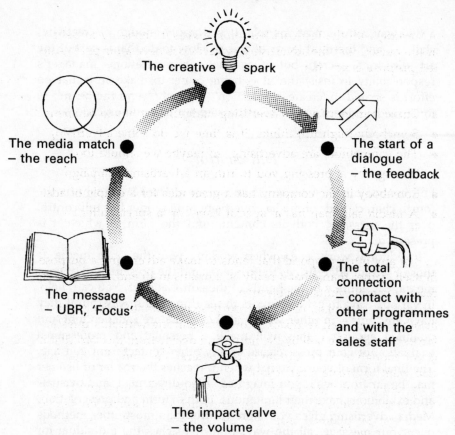

Figure 11.1 *'The Wheel of Fortune' – six key factors to observe in designing a communications programme*

at the bottom and climb your way upwards. They are rather like a wheel or a merry-go-round. One can start anywhere on the wheel, as long as all elements are covered in the total planning/feedback process. In other words, the order in which I am presenting the elements is not the only line to follow. If any other order seems more natural, try it that way. I believe, though, that all the numbers of the wheel should be examined well before the button is pressed for any media advertising project.

If the order does not count, why not be a little 'Alice in Wonderland'-ish and start at the end?

What feedback do you want?

As often with Alice in Wonderland, what seems very odd may, in the end, turn out to be surprisingly logical.

216

Starting with the feedback question makes it necessary to define, at the outset, that the advertising project does have a purpose. And the purpose is *not* that:

- There is money in the advertising budget, so it has to be spent.
- Somebody (high up) thinks 'it is time we do some advertising'.
- The competitors are advertising, so maybe we should too.
- The agency is pressing you to run an advertising campaign.
- Somebody in the company has a great idea for a couple of ads.
- A media salesman has a 'special issue' or 'a special offer'.

. . . or any other proposal that tends to make advertising a purpose in itself, rather than what it really is, a means to an end, a method to reach a communications objective.

One can, of course, define the purpose of your advertisng project in other terms than feedback. However, starting with that question forces you take the bull by the horns and decide from the start that it is not enough 'to send a beam in the general direction', but that you also want to 'create a reflection'.

By defining at the start the desired results, the foundation is laid for the subsequent evaluation. Any research or measurements to be made can be planned from the beginning – including the initial benchmark measurements.

Clearly-defined feedback requirements influence all other numbers on the media advertising 'Wheel of Fortune': media selection, the message, the creative process, the impact selector, the budgeting and cost/value analysis, and the interface with other communications efforts.

So how can we define the purpose?

More often than not, the purpose of business communications is change. It can sometimes be 'non-change', the maintenance of certain patterns of thinking, feeling and doing, but even then, the communications efforts are made to deflect a development, such as attrition, which would have taken place if the contact areas had been left to competitor influence or non-influence. Basically, it can be assumed that any media advertising project has a purpose that can be defined as change, from the present situation or from an anticipated trend.

The feedback wanted, then, is an assurance that the objective has been reached, that the media advertising project has created change.

Try the following table to see if it helps define your objectives, and then define how to measure the results, the feedback.

Objective/purpose	Feedback/measurement

A change in awareness
  of your company
  of certain characteristics
    of your company
  of products/product range benefits
  of important issues
  of positions your company takes
	'What do they know about this?'
	  (before/after)
	Ad measurements 'Seen',
	  'Read most or all'
	
	Ad recall

A change in attitudes
  to the company
  to certain characteristics
    of your company
  to qualities/benefits
    of your products
  to company positions/actions
	'What do they feel or think
	  about this?'
	  (before/after)
	Preference surveys
	Ranking questions

A change in behaviour
  new patterns of action
	Coupon or 'bingo cards'
	Phone calls, letters
	Requests for literature, studies
	  assistance, sales calls
	Visits
	Sales

When you have gone through the list and decided on general objectives/purposes and on the measurement methods that correspond best to these objectives it is time to quantify your objectives, to transform them into measurable goals.

It will probably be useful to make a benchmark study to know where to start from, unless other recent data can be used with confidence as a starting point. Normally, a specific benchmark study is advisable. If made properly, it can conveniently be repeated after the project has been carried through. In most cases this is the simplest and most reliable way to measure the result of the project.

Yes, it does add to the cost: usually, however, not as much as one thinks. And both in the short and the long run, it is better to take that money out of the total campaign budget and make appropriate measurements. Using 5 or even 10 per cent of the budget to ascertain the results achieved with the other 90–95 per cent certainly makes the job a great deal more professional and creates the only basis for 'value for money' discussions.

The Big Match: 'target audience' versus 'media reach'

The key questions in the media choice cannot be answered by the media experts. The questions can only be answered within the four walls of the advertising company.

Who do we want to talk with? What are the features of the people we are interested in and who may be interested in our message?

Any effort to 'get under the skin' of the target audience will pay off in the planning process. That means going beyond statistical data. Meet people from the target audience in person, talk with them, get to know them, try to learn how they think, feel, act and react.

The general parameters that consumer companies work with, such as age, sex and income levels, are not always the main parameters that business-to-business companies are interested in. They may be important, however, for certain communications projects, those of a more general, political or educational nature, so they also belong on the business communicator's checklist.

The three most significant dimensions in defining the 'who' of business-to-business communications projects in general are:

1.   Industrial classification.
2.   Job function.
3.   Geographic location.

These are also the dimensions on which most business and trade publications break down their readership – or should do. In many countries, even some of the industrially advanced countries, it is difficult to obtain certified readership data with this kind of three-dimensional classification.

International and national industrial advertisers would do well in setting up their own internal registers to define their audiences by those classifications and then put strong demands, alone or through their advertiser associations, on industrial media to give full information along the same lines – to make it possible to get 'the Big Match' to work.

It is rare, indeed, to find a situation in which the defined target audience completely matches the media reach. In most cases there is only a partial overlap between what you wish and what media offer. Finding out how big that overlap is and estimating the cost per person or per 1,000 of those that you are interested in, rather than

219

the full circulation, is the basic step in the quantitative parts of the 'Big Match'.

A suggested sequence in the quantitative part of matching target audience with media reach would be as follows.

Review of the audited statement

Every respectable magazine, newspaper or other publication, as well as other media, should have an audited circulation statement, certified by a reliable, independent organization. This seems obvious to some advertisers. It is, regrettably, not quite so obvious in all countries. The audited statement shows the net number of copies that are subscribed, mailed or sold, issue by issue, not the number of copies printed.

Statement of real readers per copy

Many publishers claim that each copy of their publication is passed along to other readers than the original buyer or receiver. If the publisher can prove this, allow him the benefit of an addition to the circulation statement. By the same token, everybody knows that every issue of a publication is not read cover to cover by every potential reader. Check with the media representative what (documented) figures he can give on real readership and adjust the cost calculations accordingly.

Circulation breakdown

This is the time to get a certified breakdown of the total circulation by branch of industry, job function and geographical area, and any other breakdown that is necessary or helpful in order to get the media data to match with your definitions of the target audience.

Circulation of primary interest

With your definitions of target audience and the circulation data of the media under consideration you can now get to a percentage figure showing how big a share of the total readership that is of primary interest.

Theoretical contact cost

With this background you can calculate the theoretical cost to expose your message to your target audience: the theoretical cost only – whether you can expose it in practice to this audience depends on other factors as well, including the quality of the media and the impact of your ad; to expose only – for the cost of establishing a contact with your audience depends on additional factors, such as the capacity of your advertisement to evoke a reaction.

The quantitative factors in the 'Big Match' are, after all, relatively easy to assess. It is when one gets to the qualitative aspects of the process that things get really interesting.

Starting with assumptions about the interests of the defined target audience, try to estimate the qualitative aspects of the media under consideration. Look at the following factors.

Editorial direction

Are the editors working in a general direction that makes your message fit? Most readers choose, by instinct or by a conscious process, those publications that are in line with their own thoughts and beliefs. This selection process is obvious in their professional reading, chosen to help them in their professional endeavours. Does the editorial direction of the media you are considering reasonably coincide with the ideas and basic beliefs of the target audience you want to reach? Or is it a contrast that you want, so that your message really stands out? The ambition may be to convert the readers to an entirely different way of thinking, as if the advantages of a technological society are advertised in a publication that generally caters for the 'green wave' people, or when the advantages of steam turbines for ship propulsion are advertised in *The Motor Ship* (as I did once). Whatever the choice, it must be made in full awareness of the editorial direction of the media, so that the creative team gets the necessary guidance.

Editorial quality

Independent of the direction, is the editorial quality of the media considered suitable to create a good environment for the message? Editorial independence, adequate professionalism in the editorial work, the right technical level, appropriate 'depth' in articles and news stories are factors that contribute to reader appreciation and acceptance also of advertiser messages. They put similar requirements on the quality and contents of the advertisements.

Ratio of editorial to advertising

The editorial contents are normally what readers profess to be interested in, even if, in reality, the advertisements may take as much reader time as the editorial material. Thus, it is advisable to evaluate the ratio of advertising to editorial content as one of the quality factors. With too big a share of advertising, say more than 50 per cent, advertisement messages may be in for sharp competition.

Preference studies

The best judges of the quality of 'your' media are members of your target audience. Multi-media studies of reader preferences, or comparability studies sponsored by independent organizations, may provide a background for evaluations based on your groups of interest. As a regular advertiser or before a big campaign, you may find it worthwhile to sponsor a study of your own.

Paid versus free circulation

This used to be considered as an important factor in assessing the quality of magazine readership – and still is by some. The assumption is that people put more value on a publication for which they pay than for one that comes free. In reality, most business publications are free to their readers, subscriptions being paid for by their companies. It may still be a factor to consider, although in general there is little reason to attach a great deal of weight to it. Editorial independence and quality can come in 'free' as well as in 'paid' publications and are more significant in the total evaluation. Also, as a natural consequence of the circulation method, 'free' magazines can usually provide higher-quality readership data.

And so the 'Big Match' goes on, defining target audiences, assessing media from quantitative and qualitative aspects, arriving at acceptable contact costs to reach an attractive audience in a good editorial environment that creates an appropriate 'backdrop' for your message.

Intelligent media analysis is certainly an aspect of business communications work that can improve the cost-effectiveness more than most other aspects. A challenge, indeed!

'You are telling me?' – making a reader-oriented proposition

The message you want to get across is as good a starting point in the planning process as any other. What do you actually say or plan to say?

You expect to get X,000 individual persons to spend time, maybe many minutes, looking at the ad and reading it. More than that, you expect them to relate the ad to their own situation, to accept what you say and to change their thinking, feelings and behaviour as a result of the ad. It is a heavy responsibility to place on the advertising message. The odds of success do not seem very impressive. How would you rate the odds? Would you be prepared to stake your own money against them?

Why make things more difficult than they have to be?

There is no guaranteed key to success in defining your message, but there is a safe way to make things more difficult. Surprisingly, many industrial advertisers take that road because they are interested in their own subject – themselves, their company, their own products, the fascinating new technical features that clever technicians in their R & D departments have designed. But the ads were meant to be interesting to the readers, weren't they?

The simple, and yet so often neglected, way to give the message a better chance to get across is obviously to talk in terms of the other person's interest. When you defined the target audience, a group of people came alive before your eyes. You could visualize their profile based on their industrial affiliation, job function and geographic location, perhaps also on their age, sex, income, educational background and other characteristics. So what is their interest in the matter you want to claim their time for?

In every message there must be a reader benefit. The reader must feel, after reading the advertisement, that it gave him something he could use, something pleasant or interesting, something that increased his knowledge, that will be valuable to him, or that he can apply. This guideline can be applied to all kinds of advertising, pure customer-oriented advertising as well as personnel advertising, financial advertising, issue advertising, 'constituency' advertising and any other type.

An industrial production tools company adopted as its policy that all product presentations should be customer benefit-oriented. It was found that all their products were of benefit to their customers in one, two, three or all four of the following parameters:

1. They improved the customer's production economy.
2. They improved the customer's delivery capacity.
3. They improved the customer's products, making them more competitive in the customer's market-place.
4. They improved the working conditions in the customer's workshop.

All advertisements for all the company's products could be related to one or more of these factors. Can you imagine a production manager who is not interested in improving one or more of them?

For each product category it was clearly defined on which of the factors to base the advertisements, which customer benefits that were the key message and how a clear, specific proposition could be made from those customer benefits. The definitions were given to the creative staff as their working material for ads, but they were also used in sales literature and for the salesmen's presentations. Product qualities or product features were used only to prove the customer benefits.

Some years ago the USP concept – Unique Selling Proposition – was launched. It has been widely applied and has probably been useful in many respects. Still, I feel the time has now come to replace it, with a more customer benefit-related concept. I would suggest the UBR – the Unique Buying Reason – as a replacement. Working to find the UBR is bound to lead to a customer-oriented or reader-oriented way of defining a message and to transform the message into a proposition. Take a few financial ads as an exercise and try to make them reader interest-oriented, to rework their message into a reader-centred proposition.

One group of advertisements that tends to neglect the reader orientation more than others are the so-called 'institutional' ads. To some extent, this can probably be blamed on the label as such, which, by the way, does not improve very much if it is changed to 'corporate'. Both labels are ego-centred rather than reader-centred.

Much poor advertising would be eliminated, and great amounts of misspent advertising money would be saved, if institutional or corporate advertising were reconsidered completely. Focusing on the feedback wanted, on the people to establish contacts with and on reader-oriented messages, would help improve a lot of loosely defined advertising to the benefit of all parties concerned, except possibly certain general, top-level or executive magazines that thrive on 'prestige' advertising.

I am *not* against presenting a company, its qualities or characteristics, its people, research resources, technical proficiency, financial success or any other features that may be worthwhile to enhance. But the analysis of objectives, reader categories and messages – from a reader-oriented viewpoint – should be just as close as any so-called 'product ad' analysis. If anything, the scrutiny should be tougher, since the money involved is often much bigger.

In concluding these brief remarks about defining the message, the proposition, one topic that has a magic attraction to most readers, in addition to benefits of direct importance to them, is people. If the message can be made reader-related and human, then you have taken two big steps towards acceptance. Most people like to read about people. And in addition to the immediate benefits this is likely to give your own advertising programmes, it also serves an essential long-range purpose, that of making business and industry in general more people-centred.

Getting the message across – the creative spark

What makes some advertisements go unnoticed while others are remembered longer than any Ebbinghaus memory curve would ever warrant? What makes readers spend their valuable time at the office or at home reading some ads while grimacing at others or not even noticing them? What makes well-paid executives fill in coupons in response to some ads, while others might possibly get students to write in for a leaflet?

General Electric is one of the major companies that not only asked these questions – as many other big companies have – but that put some of their best brains and talents to find answers to them. They spent several man-years studying high-scoring and low-scoring ads, trying to find what were the common features of high-scoring ads, ads that really conveyed the message they were intended to convey, to the people the ads were aimed at, and what the differences were between these ads and the low-scoring ones.

Was it the use of colour, the size or the frequency? Yes, such items did certainly make a difference. But the main difference, and the one that gave the name to the GE programme, was that the effective ads were 'in focus'. The high-scoring advertisements aimed at clearly-defined readers – they had the audience in 'focus'. They also had a clear message, a proposition that was 'in focus'.

Thus the creative process does not start when the legendary bearded man at the agency sits down at his drawing board. It does not even start, when he is thoroughly briefed on the target audience, the feedback wanted, the media to be used and the message or proposition to be conveyed. It starts when you are working actively to get all this information together.

But, if that homework has not been done and if it has not been properly conveyed to the creative staff, then the chances are slim of creating an ad or an advertising campaign that is really creative, in the sense that it generates the desired results.

Some people feel that giving the creative staff all this information limits the creativity. If creativity were synonymous with the free use of form, colour and words without relation to a purpose, there might be some sense in this view. However, industrial (or

225

consumer) advertising is not an art in itself. It has a purpose. Creativity in advertising, therefore, is useful only when it helps towards that purpose. If it does not, it is a nuisance – to the advertiser, to the agency and to the 'creator'.

Few things are more frustrating for an advertising artist, photographer, writer or layout artist than having to go back to the drawingboard or word processor and start from scratch, just because the task had not been clearly defined to him in the first place. And the other alternative, that the ad passes the screening and goes through the whole process of production, ordering and insertion – and then fails to do its job of communicating the right message is hardly less satisfying. No 'creative award' in the world can do much to alleviate the pain of knowing that so much human effort and money was spent in vain.

The illustration of an advertisement is not good just because it is different – only if that helps attract the right readers and gives them a good start towards acceptance of the message. The headline meets the same purpose – attracting the right readers and promising them a benefit if they read the copy. The copy should fulfil that promise, offer a real benefit to the right reader, or at least make it credible that the promise will be substantiated if the reader takes appropriate action. The more specific the copy is, the higher the probability that the reader will accept its proposition – and be happy for making this move.

As the General Electric team found when they worked on the FOCUS concept, the element that really made the difference, the really creative element, is the dramatization of the message, the proposition. Not getting away from the message, not 'adding decorative elements', be it models, original typefaces, unusual layouts, extra big or extra small headlines, no irrelevant puns or jokes, but real dramatization of the message. And while the dramatization requires really creative people, whose value can hardly be overestimated, it has to be based on the analytical process of defining the reader, the receiver, the target audience, and on the strategic process of hammering out the message, the proposition.

What, then, about artwork versus photography, about colour versus black and white, about fancy typefaces, cunning headlines, long or short copy, sophisticated layouts and other traditional issues of advertising creativity?

All these and many other aspects of creativity may be good and useful to consider, but should only be applied to the extent that they help to strenghten the purpose of the ad. Headlines and typography should make reading easier, not more difficult. Illustrations should lead and explain, not confuse. Copy may well be long if it gives the reader valuable information. But if you can give the reader enough valuable information in less space, so much the better – for you and for the reader. If you have no valuable information to give, it does not help if your copy is short, has subheadings or is set in a fancy typeface. The only thing that helps is to reconsider your message entirely. Colour should attract and illuminate, not distract. Logotype and address should make it easy to take action. Don't expect the reader to look for a magnifying glass to read your address.

Advertising is a functional artform. The creative staff has a goal to work towards. Provided that the creative team gets the right briefing, they will have ample opportunities to use their talents towards this goal. They will get the satisfaction of seeing their capacity used, not misused, their efforts contributing to a team result, their work accepted, because it works as it should. I have seldom heard creative people complain about getting the right guidance – so why not give it to them and let them use their creative talent to dramatize, activate the message in reader-benefit terms?

The impact valve

The other factors we have discussed, the feedback, the audience–media match, the message definition and the creative process, contain several important elements of judgement, evaluation, strategy – almost philosophy. The impact valve is easier to handle. It is basically a matter of money.

The impact valve controls the factors that are almost entirely dependent on how much money you are prepared to spend, or 'invest'. The impact valve is the instrument to use in deciding the number of insertions, the frequency, the size of the ads, the duration of the campaign and the length of your media list.

The impact valve factors are, in a way, the category of advertising decisions that are more closely related to regular return-on-investment thinking than others. They are also fairly different in business-to-business advertising compared to consumer advertising. The preparatory costs, that is, all the costs involved in the planning, preparation, creation and production of an advertising campaign, are high, both in business and in consumer advertising. But, as a general rule, the business advertiser works with a much smaller media schedule. As a share of the total programme, therefore, the pre-insertion costs are much more significant to the business/professional advertiser. The cost-conscious industrial advertiser may benefit from Figure 11.2, which shows that he has to dig deeply into his pocket before he has any return at all on his money.

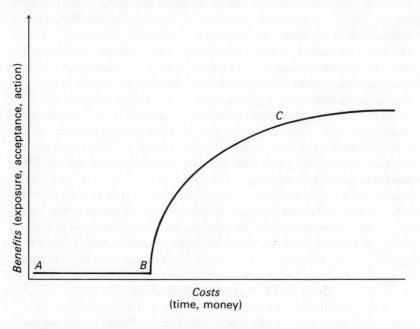

Figure 11.2 *Cost/benefits of many communications projects, related to the time factor*

The insertions he makes in the primary media should give the best return. His main question is to decide when he reaches point C, the point where any additional space buy will only give him marginal return, in terms of the benefits he has set up for the campaign.

A – project starts
B – insertions start
C – 'saturation point'

Benefits
(exposure, acceptance, changes, reactions)

A   B

Costs
(Time, money)
A–B preparation costs
B–C space costs.

Given the advertisement material, he can increase the number of insertions through higher frequency and/or longer time for the campaign in the primary media. This should give better penetration, up to an optimal point, among his primary audience.

He can, as an alternative, include secondary media in his list, the media that came close to primary selection in the first round. This way he widens the circle and gives himself the opportunity, at a cost, of getting positive reactions from less expected interest areas. He uses the advertisements for the screening process discussed earlier.

Some of the major industrial publishers have plenty of material available to illustrate and document the values of additional use of existing advertisements. In very general terms, I believe it is fair to say that most industrial advertisers would find it advantageous to put more effort (or money) into the production of good advertising material – and then use it more. Good ads stand a lot of use and it takes a lot longer for the target audience to get tired of the ads than for the corporate staff, for the communications manager – or for the advertising agency.

If you have a built-in feedback system, for example coupons, it is easy to count, ad by ad, the return you get on each insertion. You can physically count when the curve starts to flatten out or turn downward. If your ad or advertising campaign does not include coupons, you will have to test the feedback through other procedures. Simple, small-sample telephone interviews may be the easiest way to check recall, awareness or acceptance.

The message of this discussion about the impact valve factors is really that, in many cases, one should *not* decide in detail, in advance, the duration or volume of an advertising programme. The targets should be defined in such terms as awareness or acceptance of the main ideas of the advertising campaign by a sufficient percentage of your target audience – or, even better, by action in terms of response, coupons, letters, telephone calls – or specific steps towards 'purchasing'. (The word purchasing is not necessarily used here in the direct, commercial sense!)

Certain amounts of the money needed to operate the impact valve are kept in reserve. If additional insertions are needed to reach your target – make them! If not, so much better! The objective of your media advertising work is not to spend money, it is not even to put in advertisements, nor 'to make good advertisements'. The objective is to make a certain impact, to change awareness, attitudes and behaviour. The less resources you need to deploy in order to reach those objectives, the better is your professionalism!

Interface with other communications efforts

Although media advertising is highly flexible and also, when applied intelligently, a very cost-efficient communications method, it does not stand alone. In fact, its efficiency is often increased substantially when it is linked with other methods to form an integrated communications programme. (Principles and practice for such coordination are discussed in more detail in Chapter 15.)

Just because media advertising is so flexible, it is also eminently suitable for coordination with other communications methods.

- Combine media advertising with your exhibition activities, to reinforce your exhibition messages, to get more visitors to your show, to follow up on your exhibition programmes.
- Use media advertising to get your printed matter into the right hands.
- Media advertising can tell potential audiences about the great films you have available.

The way in which the special qualities of media advertising comes out best is perhaps using it for screening purposes. In industrial marketing and other functions where media advertising is used, it is only very seldom that you can achieve the complete change you want through media advertising alone. But you can, quite often, scan the horizon with media advertising and distinguish or call up the points of interest that warrant the deployment of more expensive contact forms. For an excellent summary of factors that make effective advertising see Figure 11.3.

Send in the coupon!

Above all, use media advertising to find those who state an interest in the same subject. 'Send in the coupon and we will mail our new leaflet!'

Since this is such a routine measure, many industrial advertisers let it slip into just that – routine. And yet, it should not be. For in that interface between media advertising and literature lies one of the most powerful keys to obtain – and prove! – the profits of industrial media advertising. Use it, put your creative talents to that interface, work with it, experiment with it and follow up on it!

Make that coupon the gateway to your company, to its staff, its expertise and to all the benefits your company can offer. Make it the sign of acceptance of your ad message, or at least proof of positive curiosity! Get the respondent to feel that you are interested in his situation, that you want to get the opportunity to help him.

The examples below give just a few possibilities to stretch your

I. THE SUCCESSFUL AD HAS A HIGH DEGREE OF VISUAL MAGNETISM

On average, only a small number of ads in an issue of a magazine will capture the attention of any one reader. Some ads will be passed by because the subject matter is of no concern. But others, even though they may have something to offer, fail the very first test of stopping the reader in his scanning of the pages.

Ads perish right at the start because, at one extreme, they just lie there on the page, flat and gray, and at the other extreme, they are cluttered and noisy and hard to read.

An ad should be constructed so that a single component dominates the area—a picture, the headline or the text—but not the company name or the logo.

Obviously, the more pertinent the picture, the more arresting the headline, the more informative the copy appears to be, the better.

II. THE SUCCESSFUL AD SELECTS THE RIGHT AUDIENCE

Often, an ad is the first meeting-place of two parties looking for each other.

So there should be something in the ad that at the reader's first glance will identify it as a source of information relating to *his* job interest—a problem he has or an opportunity he will welcome.

This is done by means either of a picture or a headline—preferably both—the ad should say to him, right away, "Hey, this is for you."

III. THE SUCCESSFUL AD INVITES THE READER INTO THE SCENE

Within the framework of the layout, the art director's job is to visualize, illuminate and dramatize the selling proposition.

And he must take into consideration the fact that the type of job a reader has dictates the selection of the illustrative material. Design engineers work with drawings. Construction engineers like to see products at work. Chemical engineers are comfortable with flow charts. And so on.

IV. THE SUCCESSFUL AD PROMISES A REWARD

An ad will survive the qualifying round only if the reader is given reason to expect that if he continues on, he will learn something of value. A brag-and-boast headline, a generalization, an advertising platitude will turn him off before he gets into the message.

The reward that the ad offers can be explicit or implicit, and can even be stated negatively, in the form of a warning of a possible loss.

The promise should be specific. The headline "Less maintenance cost" is not as effective as "You can cut maintenance costs 25%."

V. THE SUCCESSFUL AD BACKS UP THE PROMISE

To make the promise believable, the ad must provide hard evidence that the claim is valid.

Sometimes, a description of the product's design or operating characteristics will be enough to support the claim.

Comparisons with competition can be convincing. Case histories make the reward appear attainable. Best of all are testimonials; "They say" advertising carries more weight than "We say" advertising.

VI. THE SUCCESSFUL AD PRESENTS THE SELLING PROPOSITION IN LOGICAL SEQUENCE

The job of the art director is to organize the parts of an ad so that there is an unmistakable entry point (the single dominant component referred to earlier) and the reader is guided through the material in a sequence consistent with the logical development of the selling proposition.

A layout should be only a frame within which the various components are arranged.

VII. THE SUCCESSFUL AD TALKS "PERSON-TO-PERSON"

Much industrial advertising, unlike the advertising of consumer goods, is one company talking to another company—or even to an entire industry.

But copy is more persuasive when it speaks to the reader as an individual—as if it were one friend telling another friend about a good thing.

First, of course, the terms should be the terms of the reader's business, not the advertiser's business. But more than that, the writing style should be simple: short words, short sentences, short paragraphs, active rather than passive voice, no advertising cliches. Frequent use of the personal pronoun *you.*

VIII. SUCCESSFUL ADVERTISING IS EASY TO READ

This is a principle that shouldn't need to be stated, but the fact is that typography is the least understood part of our business.

The business press is loaded with ads in which the most essential part of the advertiser's message—the copy—appears in type too small for easy reading or is squeezed into a corner or is printed over part of the illustration.

Text type should be no smaller than 9-point. It should appear black on white. It should stand clear of interference from any other part of the ad. Column width should not be more than half the width of the ad.

IX. SUCCESSFUL ADVERTISING EMPHASIZES THE SERVICE, NOT THE SOURCE

Many industrial advertisers insist that the company name or logo be the biggest thing in the ad, that the company name appear in the headline, that it be set in boldface wherever it appears in the copy.

Too much.

An ad should make the reader want to buy—or at least consider buying—before telling him *where* to buy it.

X. SUCCESSFUL ADVERTISING REFLECTS THE COMPANY'S CHARACTER

A company's advertising represents the best opportunity it has—better than the sales force—to portray the company's personality—the things that will make the company liked, respected, admired.

A messy ad tends to indicate a messy company. A brag-and-boast ad suggests the company is *maker*-oriented, not *user*-oriented. A dull-looking ad raises the possibility that the company has nothing to get excited about, is behind the times, is slowing down.

What we are talking about is a matter of subtleties, but the fact remains: like sex appeal (which is not easy to define), some companies have it, some don't. And whatever it is, it should be consistent over time and across the spectrum of corporate structure and product lines.

Figure 11.3 *The Copy Chaser principles of* Business Marketing *magazine* © *Crain Communications Inc., reprinted with permission.*

231

imagination, but I am convinced that you can do much better yourself, when you link creative coupon design with your own specific purposes.

Make the coupon big enough – the coupon does not intrude on the ad, it is one of the main elements of the advertisement! Give the respondent enough space for his name, company name and address; a chance to say something about himself, his company, his job, his problem. It shows your interest in him and helps you to be more specific in your reply – an essential element in the screening process! Here are the examples:

YES,

I am interested in saving fuel. Show me how I can do it!
My job function is: ....
Our factory works with: ....
We now use gas/oil/ ....**/mainly for:** ....

....

☐ **I would prefer to talk with one of your specialists.**
☐ **Have him call!**
☐ **Right now, I only want documentation.**

My name: ....
Company: ....
Department: ....
Address: ....
Telephone: ....

YES,

We use cutting tools **in our business for:** ....
....

Our main problem with cutting tools is: ....
....
....

Can you do something about that?

My name: ....
Job function: ....
Company: ....
Department: ....
Address: ....

YES,

I have read your ad about your company's environmental work. It sounds good, but can your really prove what you say?

My special interest in environmental protection is: ....

....

....

Let me know what you do in this field, if anything!

I am interested in it as a
☐ professional ....
☐ student of ....
☐ concerned citizen

My name: ....
Title: ....
Address: ....

YES,

I have read your president's statement on your company's results for 1990. Please let me see if the complete annual report gives more facts.

I am interested in your company mainly as a
☐ shareholder
☐ potential investor
☐ customer
☐ supplier
☐ citizen
☐ student of ....
☐ ....

My name: ....
Title: ....
Address: ....

With coupons like these – or the better ones you design – your screening process is working. You are likely to get a satisfactory return in quantity *and* quality. You will have a chance to mail your literature to people who can benefit from it, and you will get a foot in the door for additional contact steps. You have a chance to build a mailing list and to classify it for progressive mailings, without the junk-mail label being attached to them, since you know at least some of the parameters. The interface between media advertising and literature is working.

Other contact forms where media advertising can act as a creative screening tool are exhibitions, shows, trade fairs and demonstrations. As discussed in more detail in Chapter 14, you have a big element of fixed costs in exhibitions, etc. Your great chance to improve the cost-efficiency of such events is to increase the attendance of qualified visitors. Active pre-show advertising is a proven tool to obtain just that. Give enough information in the ads about what you intend to show, and why it would be worthwhile to visit the exhibit, without giving all the details in the ad. Your purpose is to attract the right visitors. To do that, make specific offers in the ad:

1. Most importantly, give clear indications why a visit to your show will be beneficial: a new method to drill holes in hard metal will be demonstrated. Your factory expansion plans will be shown and the environmental measures will be explained. Experts will be available for consultation on surface coating problems. A film on training and job opportunities for college students will be shown – and you can register your interest at the show.

2. Offer special advantages to those who pre-register in response to the advertisement.
    (a) A new manual on material handling, a personal demonstration of high-temperature shock treatment, an accuracy test of the measuring equipment he currently uses.
    (b) As a last resource – offer special price cuts, 'introduction prices', 'free test use', etc., for those who register in advance.

As with exhibitions, pre-event advertising can increase the qualified attendance, and thus bring down per capita costs, of other communications events, film shows, audiovisual programmes, conferences and so forth. The interface between media advertising and other communications methods is there for you to use actively and creatively.

The story of Bill and Bob

The successful story about Bill's way through the efficiency score card of media advertising, and the not so successful way that his colleague and competitor Bob took, and the difference it made in the end.

Once upon a time there were two competing companies that were both starting their planning for a small advertising campaign. The names of the communications managers of the two companies were Bill and Bob. Both of them did their homework in defining their target audience and, independently of each other, came to the same definitions as to industry classification, job functions and geographical location. They both found two magazines, let us call them *Industrial Systems* (*IS*) and *Industrial Technique* (*IT*), that seemed to be on the right lines. Both magazines had an audited circulation of 10,000 copies per issue, and one black and white page cost $1,000 in both of them. But *Industrial Technique* had a pass-along readership (proven) 1.8/copy, while *Industrial Systems* had only 1.4/copy. So the total readership figures were:

	IT	IS
Circulation	10,000	10,000
Pass-along	18,000	14,000
Total	28,000	24,000

Industrial Technique seemed a better buy, with, as the space salesman put it, 'a contact cost of only $0.04 per reader'. Bob decided to choose *IT* without checking the figures of how *IT*'s and *IS*'s reader profiles in detail matched his own reader profile.

Bill did check, and he found that only 15 per cent of *IT*'s readers were in his target audience while 25 per cent of the other magazine were right on his target, so he chose *IS*. Thus, for the same $1,000, his theoretical reach was 25 per cent of 24,000 or 6,000, while Bob's was 15 per cent of 28,000 or 4,200. Bob found later in his evaluation that he consequently paid $0.24 per theoretical contact, while Bill got away with $0.17.

But those amounts, of course, were only theoretical. No matter how good an advertisement is, it is hard to get everybody in the target audience to see it, even less to read it and respond to it.

Bill's staff and agency worked hard and came up with a super ad. Preparation and production costs were $10,000. Since they planned to use it for at least ten insertions, the advertisement production cost was $1,000 per insertion.

They could have got away with lower production costs, but then they would perhaps not have used it so many times, so the difference in production cost per insertion might not have been all that significant.

Maybe that was how Bob figured it, for when the two advertisements appeared, they had both cost $1,000 (space) + $1,000 (production), adding up to a total of $2,000.

Bill's advertisement had a tremendous appeal. In fact, it was the best advertisement in the whole book, as far as the 'seen' figure went. Eighty per cent of the audience registered having seen his advertisement. His exposure cost (cost/'seen') came to just over 40 cents.

Bob's advertisement was not bad. It reached a fairly average figure of 30 per cent 'seen'. Combined with his less successful media choice, that gave him an exposure cost figure of about $1.60, four times as high as Bill's.

Now, of course it was great that people *saw* their advertisements. But did they *read* them, too?

Well, Bill's copywriter seemed to have done a great job: 60 per cent reported to have 'read most or all', a top-notch performance. With 80 per cent 'seen' and 60 per cent 'read most or all', the cost per reader of his advertisement came to around 70 cents. 'Hmmm, costs are creeping up', said the old accountant to Bill.

His competitor was even worse off though. With 30 per cent having 'read most or all' of his advertisement, his cost per reader stands at a huge $5. At this stage, he found that less than one out of ten of his theoretical contact audience had read his advertisement.

Bill felt that, after all, maybe it was not such a bad investment that he had taken so much time in defining his message, that he had gone to a good but expensive agency and briefed the creative staff so thoroughly.

How about the final part of the advertisement's performance record, reader reactions?

As with other parts of the advertisement, Bill's creative staff had put a lot of thought into designing an attractive coupon with a good offer, and as a result Bill got 500 good quality coupons from his advertisement. That was one out of six readers of the advertisement.

Bill's competitor got one coupon response for every eight

readers. It was really more than could be expected with that lousy 'Send me your leaflet' coupon of his, but anyway . . . . His cost per coupon response was $42, while Bill's was $4.

With such an investment behind each coupon received, one would certainly hope that Bob's company takes really good care of each coupon, that they answer promptly with the right type of information, that they follow up with good quality sales calls and that they file the addresses properly for future contacts.

For that is what Bill's company does even if they only paid $4 per coupon.

After all, that is how he got the company's money back, with that nice profit margin that keeps the whole game going, and that proves that Bill and his function are valuable parts of the company's business.

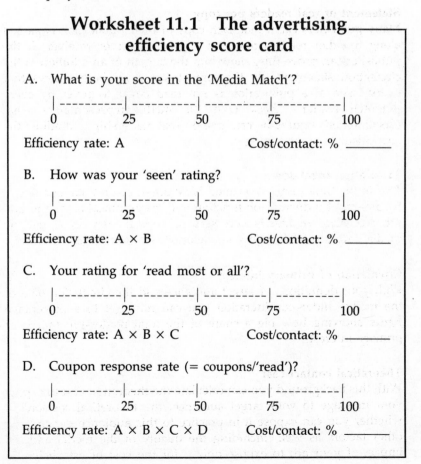

Worksheet 11.1   The advertising efficiency score card

A.   What is your score in the 'Media Match'?

```
| ---------- | ---------- | ---------- | ---------- |
0          25          50          75          100
```

Efficiency rate: A   Cost/contact: % _____

B.   How was your 'seen' rating?

```
| ---------- | ---------- | ---------- | ---------- |
0          25          50          75          100
```

Efficiency rate: A × B   Cost/contact: % _____

C.   Your rating for 'read most or all'?

```
| ---------- | ---------- | ---------- | ---------- |
0          25          50          75          100
```

Efficiency rate: A × B × C   Cost/contact: % _____

D.   Coupon response rate (= coupons/'read')?

```
| ---------- | ---------- | ---------- | ---------- |
0          25          50          75          100
```

Efficiency rate: A × B × C × D   Cost/contact: % _____

12

'The direct approach':
Direct mail and similar methods

In this chapter the reader will find a presentation of the characteristics of 'direct mail' and similar methods as communications tools, not only in the traditional marketing context but also in staff relations, financial communications and for other purposes.

It will help the reader plan, budget, execute and evaluate direct mail projects as result-oriented parts of a company's total communications process.

Is 'direct mail' a good term?

'Direct Mail' is the accepted term for a whole family of communications methods with a wide variety of applications and with great potential. Since it has been used very much for marketing purposes, the concept, just like 'advertising', has sometimes been thought of as a marketing method rather than as a communications method. Let us start by examining the following definition. Direct mail is:

- A systematic effort
- to establish or improve direct relations
- with individuals in selected contact areas
- for a specific purpose
- through the use of mail, telephone, telex or similar methods.

'A systematic effort . . .'

Sending a letter is not direct mail (DM). The mailing has to be put into a system. It does not, however, have to be a mass mailing. Especially in business-to-business communications, DM can often be used for small-scale activities, where the direct shot is more productive than a broadside.

'. . . to establish or improve direct relations'

The effort is always made in order to bring the relationship between the two parties, the sender and the recipient, to a higher level of awareness, attitudes or action. It can be made to create relations, where they have been non-existent, or to improve them, maybe even from an already high level, such as between the company and a special group of employees.

'. . . with individuals in selected contact areas'

Even if, in some cases, one has to accept collective addressees of one kind or another, such as 'The Purchasing Director', 'Dear Investor', 'To all new employees', the objective is always to build a relationship with an individual, to 'personalize' in the best sense of that word. Modern administrative techniques, guided by a

240

communications manager's ambition to make business human, can go a long way towards this objective. As we shall discuss later, this also takes DM a long way from the 'junk mail' label that is so often attached to it.

'. . . for a specific purpose'

All business communications are made for a purpose and various DM methods can be successfully applied to very specific purposes. Again, those purposes can very well be marketing-related – but they don't have to be! The purpose can quite well be to make shareholders willing to participate in a new shares issue, to explain to local neighbours the reason for that unusual smell from the factory or to give older employees the full story of the new retirement programme.

'. . . through the use of mail, telephone, telex, telefax or other similar methods'

This, of course, is what really differentiates the whole category of DM methods from other communications methods. It is also in this field that new, sophisticated technologies are coming in wholesale. That does not mean that the old duplicated letter is redundant. It only means that it has been joined by a whole range of new techniques for producing letters, new mailing systems – for letters and any other items you want to mail and new electronic ways to get your message across, all giving new openings for creativity in communications.

So, after this short resumé, is direct mail a good term for this family of communications methods, with wide and increasing opportunities for creative applications? Considering all the electronics involved, one might want another term, 'direct response' perhaps or 'direct approach'. Due to its long traditions, however, the term DM may have to be accepted for practical use. It is important to note, then, that DM is a group of communications methods, not limited to market communications, and that it can use a wide range of techniques, not only traditional mail.

This chapter will provide the reader with thoughts and ideas on how these versatile methods can be used successfully and with result-orientation to improve an organization's communications with its important contact areas.

What's so special about direct mail?

Like all other communications methods, DM has its special characteristics that make it a good choice for certain communications tasks, alone or in combination with other methods. Here are some characteristic features that may be useful to consider:

Selectivity

Whereas media advertising 'sends a beam in the general direction' of the target audience, DM can come closer to the target. DM has a potential to be more selective and thus reduce the waste. This potential should always be used, not only for the savings it brings the sender. Every mailing that goes to a company or person with little or no interest in the message also discredits the method as such. The mass of information that hits almost everybody in the industrialized world is not only wasteful, it also tends to build a general resistance, which is able to hamper seriously the ability to read, listen and learn. No function of society has greater responsibility to stop this situation from getting worse than the communications experts. Information that is inappropriate for those who get it is as bad as other forms of pollution and as damaging to people's well-being. Fortunately, modern technology can do a lot to help reduce this form of pollution as much or more than other forms, if only we decide to take advantage of it. In practice this means that every mailing list, whether generated inside the company or acquired from external sources, should be carefully screened against the purpose of each specific mailing. Intelligent use of computer technology is a great help, but the computer does not eliminate the responsibility or the need for good judgement of the communications manager, who defines the purpose and the scope of a mailing. Incidentally, I have yet to see a mailing that is not considerably improved by personal screening of every outgoing envelope, if the mailing is not too big, or of an adequate sample, if the mailing operation is too big to be 100 per cent screened.

Flexibility

In addition to various marketing applications, there is hardly any contact area in a company's range of interest where DM, in one form or another, cannot be considered and applied. Specific ideas and suggestions will be presented later in this chapter.

All the five senses

The standard content of a DM piece is printed information in one form or the other. Even within this framework, DM offers great freedom of opportunity for creative thinking and production. But the DM technique is not limited to printed matter. Records or taped messages give a chance to engage *hearing*, an authentic spoken message from the chairman, the results of noise abatement efforts on new products, the noise of happy vacationers at the company's new holiday camp, testimonials from real customers. Videodiscs or video-cassettes give the same possibilities to engage the *vision* of the recipients. So do pictures, slides, scale models and, at times, a sample of the 'real thing'. *Smells*, pleasant or unpleasant, can underline a product message or a community relations message. A 3-D item, a sample with rough or smooth surfaces, a soft or hard item, or an unusual shape, can put the receiver's sense of *feeling* to work for your communications purpose. *Taste*, as well, can be a remarkable resource for creative direct mailers.

Direct mail is the only communications channel, in addition to the personal representative of your company, that can activate all the senses in a communications process.

A solo game

If you manage to reach the right person, and *if* you manage to catch his attention enough for him to take a first look (or feel, or smell) then the direct mail piece plays it solo for a while, undisturbed by other advertisers or editorial reading material, by exhibitors in the next booth or by any other messages. If a DM piece can overcome the threshold problems, then it has almost the same attention chances as a good company representative sitting in the same office.

Easy to time

It is a general complaint in most countries that the postal systems leave a lot to be desired. Even so, it is fairly easy to calculate a DM operation and to time it so that it matches other elements in a total communications programme, advertising, personal presentations, exhibitions, openings, annual shareholder' meetings, inaugurations or other events. This makes DM a natural partner in wider communications efforts, as well a good method for follow-up action, for example, of media advertising. A special form, very useful in business-to-business communications, is to use media advertising, preferably with attractive coupons, as the first sweep and then link DM action to the coupon responses.

Easy to measure

Most DM methods lend themselves excellently to direct measurement of reactions or other communications results. In fact, creating an immediate result is such a natural element of DM that it is almost part of the definition. Make it a rule, when considering DM, always to try to define the purpose in terms of measurable reactions. Make reasonable assumptions and set targets in such terms as X per cent reply cards, requests, phone calls, yes votes, orders, contributions or other forms of return contacts. Such return targets help make DM a form of two-way communication. They also make it possible to calculate the cost of a programme on the basis of response rates rather than on the number of mailings.

Before a substantial mailing, it may be worthwhile to consider test mailings to check whether the response assumptions are realistic. Such test mailings can be extended to examine different types of creative approach, different 'offers' or virtually any element of the mailing programme that is important enough to be tested.

There are other facets of DM that may, in specific applications, be equally important as those suggested above. Also, some of the six factors listed are not always applicable. Even so, they give an indication that DM has certain specific features that make it worth looking into in many communications situations, as a single communications method or in combination with others. Creative thinking, coupled to good judgement, will help create tangible results.

A communications method for many purposes

Since DM can be used for so many different purposes it may be useful to look at some ideas and examples of DM applied to other contact areas than the market and then to add some market-oriented applications from the business-to-business field.

In staff relations

Personal contacts may seem to be the only natural choice in developing and improving the staff relations in a company. And certainly, common sense as well as formal research prove that information directly from the immediate boss has great credibility and is the method most often preferred by the staff.

But there are occasions when the normal person-to-person contacts are not enough. In those cases various forms of DM can come to use. In fact, the staff magazine or paper is a regular DM programme, and so is an internal staff memorandum. Just imagine the improvements in readership and reader acceptance that might result if the communications manager were to put some DM experience into the layout and copy of internal staff memoranda!

Other cases where an intelligent DM approach could help get an internal message across are:

1. The annual Christmas and New Year greeting from your chairman and/or chief executive could be read and accepted almost to the degree that your CEO currently believes it is! Incidentally, have you ever dared to make a survey on how that message is actually read? Take it through the basics of the DM planning process:

    (a) Analyse the recipients and their interests (should you adapt the message for blue-collar/white-collar, young/old employees, home office/overseas, men/women, other categories?).

    (b) Analyse the purpose and define a specific objective (build pride, awareness of difficulties ahead, prepare for changes, tell success story, bring out specific contributions, new business ventures).

    (c) Analyse the optimum distribution method (deliver on site, hand through foreman, include in staff magazine, send by personalized mail to home, pick up at factory exit).

    (d) Encourage reactions (make it easy to answer, invite comments, ask follow-up questions, even question the message).

    (e) Evaluate the results (did the main points get across, how many reacted and in what way, who were those who reacted?).

2. The annual reports of many companies are difficult to understand, even for investors. Why not apply a true communications-oriented DM approach to make sure that the employees get a good idea of how the company developed last year? Make it easily accessible, distribute it the right way, invite reactions – and measure results!

3. New product launch. There are top managers in big companies who complain that their employees do not take an active interest in the real business of the company. Use new product launches to build better understanding – and take a look at DM methods to bring such messages across:

    (a) Analyse who has been directly involved in getting the new product on line, research staff, purchasing staff, workers, engineers, salesmen and take a look at those who have only been indirectly involved. Maybe two different messages are needed?

    (b) Put some DM creativity to work: show the new product in real applications, enclose authentic customer statements, tell the staff about some of the snags in the development process and how (by whom?) they were overcome, tell them the benefits financially and in employment terms if the expectations materialize, enclose a sample (if possible) or a promotion gift related to the new product, etc.

    (c) Encourage questions about the new product or about the launching process.

    (d) Check the reactions – to what extent did the employees read and appreciate this information?

In shareholder and financial relations

Very often, the only contact a shareholder has with the company in which he has put his confidence and savings is the annual report. (Some progressive companies send out half-yearly or even quarterly reports.)

If companies in general regarded these mailings as DM and applied some of the accepted DM practices, they would be generously rewarded by increased investor loyalty and appreciation. Just imagine what a product sample, or a card to order one, could do to add life to an annual report mailing, or, say, a regionalized cover letter, emphasizing what the company does in that area. Companies that take these and other opportunities to build and maintain good relations with their owners and with others in the financial community will find that they help enhance their standing in investor and money markets, sometimes equally important as the customers.

Most companies have one asset in this field – they have an up-to-date shareholder register, an ideal mailing list, which can be mouth-watering to any DM fan. Furthermore, this list is often set up so that it offers break-down possibilities, geographically, by shareholding size or by other criteria, which can add to the adaptability of a good DM programme.

In addition to the regular reports – which in many cases could do with a face-lift from an experienced DM consultant – what are the occasions that could initiate a good mailing to the financial contacts? There are many. Here are a few examples:

1. Important events in a company's life, such as big or unusual orders, new factories or administrative centres, high-level staff appointments, new business ventures – at home or abroad – or new product introductions are examples of news that share-holders are or could be interested in. If presented with a touch of DM creativity, there is little doubt that many shareholders would appreciate such information.

2. Financial news about the company, not only 'hot stuff' but also information of a 'backgrounder' character, is worthwhile for investors in increasing their understanding of the company and its situation. Information about the general business situation in the industries that the company serves, trends to be observed, personal statements, comments and reflections by high-level corporate officers can contribute to make the investors familiar with the company, build confidence and loyalty. Even 'bad news', when presented intelligently, can help stabilize the company's financial relations and thus avoid panic sell-outs.

3. Takeover bids, real or anticipated, are the kind of event that have made even old-fashioned companies find the DM road to their shareholders. Some of them wish they had tried it before – and perhaps with a higher level of communications thinking.

4. Speeches made by high corporate officers to branch associations, government authorities, community groups, staff meetings and on other occasions create excellent material for a shareholder

mailing. Just remember that even a good speech with valuable information, when presented live, can be very boring if poorly mimeographed on standard office letterhead. Try to find, through good DM thinking, ways to substitute in the mailing some of the life and action that were put across by the speaker when the presentation was made in person.

There is no doubt that you can find other opportunities, as good as these or better, in your own situation. Allow yourself some time for creative thinking – why not with your advertising agency, your DM consultant or your financial director, or all of them together?

By the way, do you send your staff magazine to interested shareholders? Or do you offer them the opportunity to get your customer magazine? Or, even better, have you considered creating a shareholder newsletter or a regular shareholder magazine, to appear four to six times a year? All these are, of course, excellent ideas and they fall within the DM category, as well as within the category of editorial work.

Your mailing list to shareholders and other financial contacts is a great asset in building good financial relations. Looking at that list with DM eyes can transform that asset from dormant to active, something that should appeal especially to the financial officers of your company! Why not give it a try?

In community relations

Contacts with the local community can be made at many levels. One may want to keep in regular touch with the town or city council or similar bodies, with administrators in the city hall, with the immediate neighbours of the factory or with specific interest groups such as service clubs, youth organizations, 'green' groups and other local groups.

Local newspapers are an obvious way to keep in touch; so are speeches, plant tours, etc. But in many cases, these methods can be systematically complemented with DM programmes. Mailing lists of city or town officials are usually public, lists of board members or even complete membership lists of clubs and organizations are often easy to obtain or build up. Such lists can be the framework to which can gradually be added opinion-builders that would benefit from closer, more direct information from the company. To make this communications method two-way, use these lists to invite comments and questions, or as invitation lists for special meetings with local management. Obviously, such contacts, once they have been established, can go a long way to build local pride and attachment to a company, understanding of its difficulties, if and when they come, and an atmosphere of confidence in situations of potential conflicts or grievances.

Here are some specific examples that may help start a planning process:

1. News events in the company often have a value outside the factory gates. Take such opportunities as plant extensions, appointment of local managers, changes in product range, significant orders, etc., to send a mailing to the community list or parts of it. Make it personal, creative, interesting. And make sure 'the local touch' is there!

2. Give background material on a regular or occasional basis. Why not a resumé of the history of the specific plant, the reasons why it was located in that community, how it has grown, etc.? Include information on employment, tax contributions, but don't push too hard. Also, explain how the local plan links in with other units, domestic or abroad, how it forms part of a bigger system. On another occasion, give information about the product lines, its development trends, customers, exports, etc. Tell them about the company training and staff development systems, how they relate to the local school system and about the skills and know-how that are represented among company staff. Present individuals and/or teams of employees who have made special contributions or are noteworthy in some other way, maybe for the active part they play in community affairs. Using DM methods for such presentations makes it easier to give each presentation the appropriate bulk, timing, direction, form for each group of recipients, and to encourage reactions and comments.

3. Send copies of local or national speeches made by corporate or local plant officers to a suitable selection from your community list. 'Personalize' and 'localize' them through cover letters, special underlinings and colour markings. Add photos from the occasion and other illustrations. Invite comments, perhaps on a reply coupon.

In government relations

Various government bodies have one thing in common: their names and addresses are usually accurately listed. Also individual names of decision influences are publicly known and can thus be integrated into a DM system, to be taken out collectively or by specific parameters for mailing purposes. In many countries, outside mailing houses can help build up such systems or have them ready for use on a time-to-time basis.

Structural changes in the business situation in general are normally passed on to the right government agencies through the industry association concerned, but if this is not done, or if they affect a specific company more than others, there is no reason why the company should not inform the government agencies concerned themselves. Even companies that run efficient government relations programmes often fail to take the numbers into account. Government bureaucracies throughout the world have grown tremendously in numbers. This means that internal communications within the governmental system do not always function as one would hope. Consequently, to be sure that a message comes across to all those who may have an influence on the subject, it is not enough to send one official letter to one agency. Analyse, as for other DM operations, who in terms of agencies, departments or, preferably, individual staff members is involved. (You will often be surprised at the length of the lists you arrive at!)

When businessmen complain, as they sometimes do, of mistakes made by government bodies, they do not often turn that criticism to themselves: why didn't they share their views effectively while there was time? The slow speed of the governmental process, which is sometimes a nuisance, is also a help. It is normally fairly easy if you keep your ear to the ground to hear the noise of upcoming government action, long before it is irrevocable.

Why not, then, make DM methods part of your government relations programme? Examples are easy to find and it will be just as easy to develop appropriate ideas to suit your company. Occasions can be found or generated in your own organization, at home or abroad.

1. When products or services have a relation to such government concerns as health, education, employment, exports, environment, worker safety, use DM methods to keep government staff and politicians informed.

2. Major investment programmes may affect several government agencies, from different viewpoints. Make a presentation, with appropriate facts, but also with illustrations and well-documented reasons, and send it on your government mailing list, possibly with variations in the cover letter. Present new export programmes in a similar way.

3. Also, much that happens in government, at broad preparatory levels as well as at top decision levels, has a bearing on your company and its business. If it does, your company probably has expertise and viewpoints that could contribute to the legal or administrative process, before it has gone too far to be influenced. If you have built a system of government mailing lists, using up-to-date DM techniques, it will be easy to make your views known to many of those who will deal with the issue, offer expertise, invite government officials and politicians to round-table discussions, provide facts and documentation and explain why you want to contribute to a good solution. More often than not, when government decisions are seen as negative to business, the reason is lack of knowledge rather than ill-will. Why not use DM methods to help?

4. Much information material produced for other purposes may double up to inform government staff or politicians as 'backgrounders' on a specific subject or to provide general understanding of your business. With a proper mailing system, such additional use of staff magazines, customer magazines, general news releases, copies of speeches, leaflets, photographs, etc., can be highly effective, producing important results at low cost. As always with DM techniques, do your utmost to personalize mailings, encourage receivers to react and measure the results!

In relations with the educational world

Schools, universities and other educational institutions have the same advantage from a DM point of view as politicians and government institutions. It is relatively easy to build relevant mailing lists. Direct mail, along with other communications methods, should therefore be considered in communications programmes for the educational world. Also, compared with some other audiences, teachers still tend to receive relatively small amounts of mail that may be of direct help to them in their jobs. Good mailings stand a decent chance of being read and used! This is especially true if modern DM technology plus human consideration is used to create mailings that are really helpful.

Teachers in engineering, business and social sciences are among those to be considered in such mailing categories. Other criteria, such as level, geographic locations and previous contacts with the company, may also be important. Categorizing along such lines, and then personalizing as much as possible, creates great opportunities to build fruitful two-way communications with the educational world with the help of DM methods.

Here are some examples:

1. Send your engineering handbooks, product presentations, method and application manuals, case stories, copies of customer feedback, technical newsletters and non-classified research reports to engineering teachers.

2. Let those teachers concerned know about new slide presentations in their field, films and other audiovisual material that your company can provide them with, either free or at nominal charges.

3. Staff- or customer-oriented training material can often be used, with or without adaptations, in other educational situations, at schools or universities. Let teachers know about it through DM.

4. Business teachers may benefit from the company's annual report, with or without side-material, such as slides, overheads, 'short versions', staff reviews of it, etc. Other corporate material may also be useful, such as corporate leaflets, speeches, export progress stories, investment project reports (at home or abroad), corporate films, slide presentations, and so on.

5. Employment trends and consequences may be of interest to business teachers, but also to teachers of social sciences, who may include it in their programmes to explain how companies interrelate with other aspects of society. Any material provided to document this may therefore be of interest. Documentation of a 'social audit' nature, showing the company's influence on society through employment, taxes and rates, environment, training and education, preferably presented in an intelligent, educationally acceptable way, may be of help.

6. This applies also to documentation on the function of the company's products and services, in housing projects, road-building, well drilling, agriculture, administration, electrification,

production processes or any type of activity where products from the company are engaged. If a company is working in developing countries, material from projects there might be of great interest in social sciences.

7. Obviously, the company may produce and distribute material specifically produced for the educational system. However, with a good DM system it is easy to complement such material with creative distribution of existing material, originally made for other purposes. With light adaptations, or 'as is', it may come to new life and help give teachers and students a broader understanding of the wide world of business and industry. Who would deny that this could be extremely valuable, both short- and long-range?

In market communications

With the increasing costs of salesman time, there is little doubt that most companies in business and industry can improve their marketing profitability through DM, the medium that is second only to the salesman himself in personal approach, flexibility and measurability.

Practically all that has been written on DM has treated it exclusively or mainly as a market communications tool, mostly in consumer marketing. As shown above, it is my conviction that it has many other applications as well. A few conclusions can be drawn from this:

1. It would not be easy to find new angles to add to the subject of DM in market communications. The reader would probably be better off looking to other sources for information on DM in marketing.

2. Some of the general literature on DM, although consumer-oriented, offers suggestions, checklists and advice, and is also useful for business-to-business marketing applications. It includes case stories, some of which may certainly generate ideas suitable for the company, products and business situation that you are in.

3. Much of that literature, while dealing with DM in marketing, can offer the open-minded reader lots of ideas, which can also be applied to other communications tasks.

Consequently, I shall be very brief on DM in market communications and, in line with the general purpose of this book, touch mainly on its role in business-to-business market communications.

Some of the roles that DM techniques can play in business and industrial market communications are:

- Creating inquiries and sales leads.
- Building recognition of the company and its product range.
- Introducing a new product or service.
- Generating direct sales.
- Introducing and supporting the salesmen/distributors.
- Breathing new life into weak sales areas.
- Developing areas and customer categories not adequately covered by salesmen.
- Keeping contacts with customers between sales calls.
- Winning back inactive customers.
- Bringing buyers into your premises/to your outlets.
- Educating and motivating your sales staff.

For any of these tasks, DM will be one alternative to be assessed against other communications methods, or to be used in combination with other communications forms.

As an aid in that process, the following points may be worth considering. Each one of them can be crucial for the success of a DM project:

1. Can I turn my general objective into a specific, quantifiable target?
2. Do I have or can I obtain a good list, preferably with individual names and business functions?
3. Can I formulate my message into one, two or three short points suitable for DM?
4. Can my message be personalized and dramatized to get adequate attention?
5. Are the external conditions (season, business-cycle, competitive situation, other marketing activities, technological trends) acceptable?
6. What can I offer the receiver to induce him to answer?
7. What cost ranges would be reasonable to reach the targets?

8. How will I evaluate, after the project is over, if it has been a success, if it was acceptable or if it was a flop?

With these points as a basis for discussion with the marketing staff and with your advertising agency or DM consultants, you can make a pre-evaluation, thereby substantially increasing your chances of success.

The backbone of the direct mail system – the mailing lists

The success of a DM programme is entirely dependent on the quality of the mailing lists. All the creativity in the world does not help, if the mailings do not reach the target audiences.

Building high-quality mailing lists – and maintaining them – is a chore where dogged patience plays the main role. It is time-consuming, tedious at times, expensive, but also highly rewarding if the lists are used with reasonable regularity.

Bearing in mind the reduced prices of computer equipment and computer time and the steep costs of manual work, only computer-ized systems should be considered, at least if you go beyond the mailing needs of, e.g., the local stamp collectors' club. Computers, however, do not take away the necessity of full personal respon-sibility for continuous list management.

External services can do part of the list work. Many mailing houses offer complete maintenance and operation packages. The need for somebody within the user company to be responsible is still there. A company can also choose to set up an internal system and operate it completely in-house. In most cases, combinations of internal and external services work out very well.

Quite a number of potential contacts are already listed, one way or another, within the company. The personnel department or various line functions have the whole staff listed and probably have some logical breakdown system. The financial or legal department has the shareholders listed, and may also have banks, financial analysts and other contacts. The purchasing department and/or certain line functions have the important suppliers on file. The marketing and sales organization has distributors, other outlets and certain (or all) of its customers listed. Other functions may contribute additional material for an overall mailing system.

In a big company it may not be necessary to coordinate physically all mailing lists into one huge operation. It will probably be indispensable, though, to agree on certain criteria to be applied to all mailing lists that will be used. If these criteria also facilitate coordination with potential or existing external suppliers of address material, operations will gain in efficiency.

Before deciding on how to set up or improve mailing systems, make an analysis of anticipated needs, so that the system is built on the right level of sophistication. Each additional classification category adds to the complexity and hence costs of the system. On the other hand, it may also significantly improve the selectivity of the system, the ability to have messages geared directly to those who are likely to benefit from them and will thus reduce the waste factor. And, although even a computerized system is more expensive the higher the degree of sophistication, it is still marginal to add such factors that will help in the selection process.

Once your company has come to appreciate the possibilities of DM, they will want to use it more and more; selectivity is one of the important advantages of the DM method.

These are the selector codes that you will certainly require for each entry, with possibilities for cross-reference with other classifications:

- Industrial code, SIC or similar in other countries.
- Geographic code, in the form of ZIP code (US) or Postcode (UK), also for addresses abroad.
- Job classification on all individual names.
- Broad contact area classification (e.g., staff, shareholder, teacher, supplier, distributor, etc.).

For each contact area, you may want the following additional classifications:

- Staff
    Age/birth date
    Employment date
    Educational background, in broad categories
    Plant location
    Home address

    (Note: the above are examples of classifications you may want for mailing purposes; obviously the Personnel Department has additional material on file.)

256

- Shareholder/financial
  Shareholders, individual
  Shareholders, institutional
  Size of shareholding
  Banks
  Brokers
  Financial analysts
  Financial editors
- Local community (for each location)
  Town council
  Important boards and committees
  Key administrative staff
  Immediate plant neighbours
  Other important companies, with individual names of CEOs,
    etc.
  Clubs and organizations
  Editorial staff of local news media
- Government
  Agencies, boards, committees, etc., by field of interest/
    responsibility (with individual names)
  Politicians, by geographic interest
  Politicians, by subject-matter interest
  Government staff members of special interest
  Your national branch organization, if it has 'lobby' functions
  Other government contacts
  National 'pressure groups', environmental, health and safety,
    trade unions, export/import, industrial relations, etc.
  Political editors
- Education
  Teachers, by level and subject area (engineering/technology,
    business/economy, social sciences, others)
  University institutions
  Libraries
  Educational writers and publishers
- Market
  Customers: by product interest
            by size
            by purchasing frequency
  Distributors and other outlets
  Sales managers, salesmen
  Suppliers
  Competitors
  Editors of technical publications related to your markets

Keeping lists up-to-date is one of the main problems of DM operations. It is also an absolute requirement that lists should be fully up-to-date when used. A well-conceived, personally addressed letter with the correct touch of warmth and individual interest is not only wasted, it creates a very bad impression if sent to somebody who left the company, or died, six months ago.

There are two things that may be more important than others in keeping your listings in shape. One is the support from various corners of your own organization, from personnel department clerks to financial directors and field salesmen, in reporting immediately all changes they hear about. The other is frequent use of the lists, with strong feedback and follow-up.

How does one measure if a mailing list is acceptably updated? Ask mailing house contacts for advice and make test mailings or checks on an nth basis. If in a mailing one gets a 5 per cent return of wrongly addressed mail, then the list is certainly substandard. If the return figure is 1 per cent or less, then the staff can feel reasonably satisfied, at least if the registered mistakes are not directly offensive.

The creative touch – the life and breath of your direct mail programme

The creative process

A response rate of 3 per cent is what many companies consider standard in their DM programmes. What about a response rate of 68 per cent? That is what one company achieved in a mailing to a group of construction engineers, a rather sophisticated target group for DM. How did they do it? By applying their thinking to what 'the other guy' thinks and wants, and, with that as a base, replacing one of the mailings in a package with a phone call.

Their example shows that creative thinking is not a question of 'gimmicks'. The creative process starts at the receiving end of a mailing. It also shows that the M in DM should not be taken too literally. The direct approach can be made not only with mail but with other media – telex, telephone, 'mailgrams', telefax or others: the choice of channels can also be part of the creative process.

Advertising agencies – with or without special DM experts – and DM houses are the outside experts who can help assure the right creative touch in your mailing programme. Their help, incidentally, is not necessarily limited to market-oriented DM programmes, but can often be successfully applied to DM programmes geared to other contact areas as well.

Whether you use external or in-house creative staff, make sure that full information about 'the receiving end' is part of the briefing. Hand them a copy of the mailing list, or an extract of it, so that they can see the names, titles, types of companies and addresses that their creation will reach. Fill in with background about their relations with the company, earlier contacts, earlier experiences. What documentation do you have on their awareness, attitudes and feelings toward the company?

Then, give full briefings on the objective of the specific mailing package to be made. How would you define 'success' with this mailing operation? Why not state clearly: 'I would consider this mailing very successful if . . .' or 'I would consider it acceptable if . . .'.

What is the basic message or theme? You may or may not want to give the creative staff some latitude in phrasing this. Indicate that at the briefing session!

Are any enclosures already specified to be part of this mailing action? If so, show them and explain them and their role.

Do you have one specific offer in mind? Are you prepared to accept creative alternatives to that offer?

Fill in as much as possible about other activities or conditions that could influence the success, format and timing of the mailing. Is the mailing tied in with any special events, with other programmes or with external conditions of some kind?

What are the budget considerations or limits that you are working against? Is the budget linked with the degree of response or other success measurement?

With this kind of briefing, your chances of getting a creative solution increase considerably. And in DM, there are hardly any limits to creativity in the medium as such. Also, DM applied in business and industrial communications offers great opportunities for creative solutions.

The four elements of creative direct mail

The four elements that lend themselves to creative ideas more than any others are the cover letter(s), the enclosures, the offer and the reply. Allow the creative staff to play around with these elements, and DM can be an extremely rewarding occupation.

1. The letter(s)

Start with the envelope or the packaging. Its function is to help get your letter before the eyes of the recipient, over the barriers that are built by secretaries, mail room clerks and assistants. Neat personal addressing is essential.

That's the end of rules. Sometimes the envelope can be as discreet and high-brow as a City banker, sometimes it can be as colourful as a circus programme. You can state the offer, or hint at it, right there on the envelope. You can use illustrations, graphics, unusual shapes, anything you like. Some phrases are useful to print on the envelope: 'Here is news about your . . .'/investment/teaching job/neighbour/promotion opportunities/ 'A better way to . . .' /evaluate your shareholding/teach chemistry/keep our river clean/get on-the-job training/make perfect screw joints/increase exports.

When writing the letter, don't get stuck on business jargon. Start the letter with a direct, clear appeal to the reader's interest that links immediately with the objective of the whole mailing. Compare the two examples below, to a shareholder, offering free subscriptions to a new, shareholder-oriented house magazine:

Dear Sir/Madam,
It is a great pleasure for us to announce the launching of a new periodical magazine, *Company News and Views*. The magazine will cover important events in XYZ company, and discuss market, staff, business and financial trends from the company's viewpoint. Since you are a shareholder in our company, we thought it would be of interest for you to follow these trends. We are therefore pleased to offer you a free one-year subscription to this magazine. The enclosed reply card can be used to express your interest in the new magazine – please return it to us immediately! Sincerely,

S. Jones
Chairman

Dear Mr Peterson,
You have invested some of your savings in the XYZ company. To make it easier for you to follow how *your* company develops, here is the first copy of a new magazine *Company News and Views*. Please take a look at it and send us your comments on the enclosed reply card. I appreciate your interest in XYZ. The new magazine may help us keep in touch.
Sincerely,

S. Jones
Chairman

I am sure the reader can improve on both these letters. Why not take a couple of minutes and write your own version? Then make up your own file of good and bad examples by collecting all DM letters that come your way during the next two to three weeks, review them, rewrite them or mark the passages that appeal very much to you – as well as those that put you off. In a short time you will get a set of examples that you can use the next time you are faced with the task of initiating a DM cover letter!

2. The enclosure(s)

First, does there have to be one? Maybe the letter can be so clear and persuasive, and the offer so attractive, that the reader can go straight to the reply device? Then again, the 'enclosure' may be the important thing and the letter (if there is one) only an introduction. An ad reprint, a leaflet, a catalogue, a manual, a fact-sheet, the copy of a speech, the annual report or some other printed matter is the 'standard' enclosure. And, by all means, there is nothing wrong with that. The printed word and picture are still very useful communicators.

But the printed matter should not be the limit of your imagination! Devote a touch of creative thinking to the enclosure and any number of alternatives will come to mind. To get you started:

- Send a part of your full offer: a grinding disc if you are offering a grinder; one overhead picture if you are offering a series; one slide if you are offering a show. This principle can, of course, also be adapted to printed matter. Send the index, or a few pages if you are offering a manual; the introductory text if you offer your staff a training course.

- Send something that gives a natural association to your subject or offer: a drinking glass or a fishing hook, if you inform about your efforts to clean the river; a golf ball, if your subject is staff professionalism; a binder, if you offer a magazine; a small coin to the financial analysts and editors to dramatize the message of your increased dividends; a record or tape that illustrates the new noise abatement programme.

- Send something that contrasts with your subject or offer: a piece of dirty cloth if you offer a new cleaning agent; a full attendance card if you talk about absenteeism; a photo of a yawning student if you offer an interesting educational aid model.

- If that is the best you can come up with, send something that may not be directly related to your subject, but can create interest

261

and trigger a response: a small gift, as a token of thanks for the time given to your letter/proposal; part of a gift, of which the other part comes after you have got the reply; a sample of your company's products, or a gift that reminds them.

The difference between a thoughtful, albeit small, gift and a 'gimmick' that may be uninteresting or even offensive, is in the consideration of receiver interest. If you are in the slightest doubt, test your idea on a selection from the same mailing list that you are going to use.

3. The offer
Basic rule: make sure that the offer is really helpful to the recipient, then express that in terms of his interest.

Any offer that follows this simple guideline meets with response, any offer that fails to follow it gets a cold reception – and deserves it.

When we analyse what the recipient wants, we sometimes run the risk of getting trapped in clichés.

Your staff, of course, want higher wages/salaries, shorter working hours and longer vacations, but they also want assured employment, good working conditions, good relations with their colleagues and bosses, pride and satisfaction in their jobs.

The shareholders obviously want a good return on their investment, security and growth, but they also want to know their company better, feel convinced that it is doing a good job, that its products are useful and that it acts responsibly at home and abroad.

Suppliers obviously want to sell and they want to get paid on time, but they also want to be assured of lasting relations, reliable and positive contacts and understanding when/if something goes wrong.

The local town council is certainly happy to get the rates and taxes your company generates, but they also want assurance that the company treats workers fairly, that the production process is safe and healthy, that the products have a reputation that enhances the community name.

The list could be made much longer, and it could be applied to any of the contact areas that you may want to reach by DM. What is essential is that, in analysing receiver interests, to make your offer attractive, by all means use the first degree, immediate interests, if they can be linked to your offer. But every recipient is more than his role according to the mailing list classification, he is also a human being, with interests, ambitions and desires in that capacity. Don't hesitate to go beyond the professional role and make your offer human – as you will recall from the introductory chapter, all business relations are human relations. Or, as Dale Carnegie expressed it long ago, 'Appeal to the nobler motives'.

4. The reply device

Even if an immediate reply is not always the primary objective in DM programmes, for example, in those aimed at building corporate reputation, it would be good if every DM programme were planned as if an immediate reply was the goal. In 95 per cent of all cases it is.

As you want to be personal in your approach, give the recipient the opportunity to be personal in his answer. Do not simply ask him to tick a box and return a card. Give him the opportunity to fill in more about himself and his requirements. Offer alternative boxes to tick, ask him to specify his situation in relation to your offer, let him indicate quantities, give him free space for additional comments.

Imagine that you have devised an educational package for social science teachers about your company's international operations. The coupon could look like this:

☐ **YES, relations between business and society is part of what I teach, so I would be interested in your new educational package.**

I teach at these levels: ....
....

In all, about .... **students would be involved.**

☐ **I would be interested in the whole package, as you describe it.**

☐ **I would only be interested in** ☐ **the basic text material**
                                      ☐ **the overheads**
                                      ☐ **the slides**
                                      ☐ **the statistics and charts**

☐ **NO, your offer is not applicable to my teaching right now.**

This is what would be useful to me: ....
....
....

My name and address ☐ **is correct as shown**
                              ☐ **should be corrected as**
                              I have indicated
The colleagues I have listed overleaf might also be interested in your material.

Although the reply card, simple or folded, is the most commonly used response form, there are alternatives. For extensive answers, that is, questionnaires, the prepaid envelope is the obvious choice and is also useful to encourage frank, personal or even controversial answers. Answers by telephone can be encouraged, with or without the use of collect calls. Another form of 'response' is that you as a sender follow up by calling, indicated already in the first mailing by a phrase such as: 'May we call you next week to hear about your interest in this package?'

How many responses can you expect? Several studies seem to indicate that the low quartile of response percentages for industrial/business DM is somewhere around 3–5 per cent, and the high quartile is 15–20 per cent, with an average around 10 per cent. However, the spread ranges between 0 and (close to) 100 per cent. There is no single, easy way to a high response. All elements contribute: the quality of the mailing list, the type of addresses, the value and creativity of the message, the letter, the enclosure, the offer and the response device. This in turn means that there are tremendous opportunities for every industrial company to make DM a valuable method in the total communications system. The return is in your own hands!

Direct mail – the communications method with built-in research

Evaluating the effectiveness of industrial communications work is as important as continuous evaluation of all other business activities. In this respect, DM offers interesting opportunities.

Two different reasons for systematic evaluation of DM programmes, as of other forms of communications work, may guide your research activities, indicate what to do, how to do it and how much resources to put into the research mix.

The first reason is to show what value you got for the money invested in the DM project, how well you reached the pre-specified objectives in relation to the budget.

The other reason is your ambition to improve the future performance of your DM work.

If the objective of a DM programme is to change awareness and attitudes, the fulfilment of your objectives has to be measured by the same research methods as applied to other communications programmes: personal interviews, telephone surveys, DM question-naires(!) and so forth.

But if, as is usually the case, the objective is to trigger a direct response, to get the receiver to take specific action, then obviously the actual response reaction, evaluated by quantity and quality factors, planned and designed from the beginning as part of the total project, *is* the research one wants. Is there any need for additional, systematic evaluation?

As we have said earlier, variations in response percentages in industrial DM projects are very big, from a few per cent to more than 50 per cent. If one could find a simple formula to success in industrial DM, a fortune would be in the finder's hands. Until that simple formula comes forward, there is no other way to improve-ments than continuous evaluations, made in such a way as to create useful input into the next DM project. Consequently, measuring has to be integrated with the planning process.

If, as has been suggested in this chapter, the planning considers the following steps:

- Objective (in qualitative/quantitative terms)
- Mailing list
- The creative process
  Letter(s)
  Enclosure(s)
  Offer
  Reply device
- Result

then it is natural to make the steps leading from objectives to results the objects of the evaluation efforts.

Pre-testing, split-run, 'bird-banding' and response analysis are four research methods to look into and try.

Pre-testing

Careful pre-testing of the mailing list against your objectives is probably the area where your research money produces the most tangible results. If you make a small mailing, especially on a list that you have not used recently, screen every address. Ask somebody who knows the category to run through the list manually and cross out or put question marks on all doubtful names, then get those names verified. For big mailings, proceed in the same way, but on an every nth name basis. Evaluate the whole list on that screening, making further verifications as necessary. This may seem a very expensive procedure – and it is. But remember also that every irrelevant name, or incorrect name, is a cost burden and may create serious bad-will, in addition to reducing the response rates and putting the professionalism of DM work in jeopardy. The whole idea of the D in DM is that your message goes directly to the person one really wants to reach, not to irrelevant or even non-existent persons. Consumer DM can sometimes afford a more cavalier attitude to list qualities – in business-to-business communications it should not be tolerated.

If the creative process brings up, on either one of the four main elements, two or more alternative proposals that have merits in your judgement, then it may be worthwhile pre-testing the creative alternatives. Pre-testing does not have to be a big thing. The scope of it is obviously related to the dimensions of the full mailing project, but two things must be observed for a pre-test to have any value whatsoever. Those who comment on the alternatives must be representative of the target category and you should not test more than one element at a time. Make mock-ups of the two alternatives and submit them to a selection from the list you are planning to use. Submit them at personal interviews or by mail and use the comments as additional input to your own judgement.

Split-run

Split-run is easy to set up in DM projects, in fact so easy that the technique should be used far more often than it is. There is hardly any better way to get substantial DM experience quickly than by using split-run. Again, test only one variable at a time, making sure that all other factors are identical. If you want to test two mailing list approaches, say one list with personal names and one with job functions only, make sure that geographic spread and the mailing package are identical. If you want to test two different letters in a shareholder or staff mailing, ensure complete identity on all other scores. Just mark the reply devices discreetly, in a way that cannot in itself produce any difference in acceptance. I would go so far as to say that, if you have not used DM to any great extent before, put in split-run to test the main elements, one at a time, into every mailing project for the first three to six months. You will gain invaluable experience, and the money and effort you spend will give you significant returns for years of successful DM!

'Bird-banding'

'Bird-banding' is a technique developed some years ago by the Marketing Communications Research Center in Princeton. Basically, the technique means that you enclose a separate questionnaire with every nth mailing. This questionnaire, in the form of a self-mailer, pre-paid, addressed to a separate entity, is used for awareness, attitude or preference questions related to the main mailing.

Response analysis

But then, the main research work in DM projects should be related to careful analysis of the responses as such. This analysis, which comes in addition to the processing of requests, orders, comments, etc., that the mailing was intended to generate, has qualitative aspects as well as just counting the numbers.

Some of the questions to be answered in that process include:

1. Was the total number of reactions in line with your objectives? If not, was the difference significant? Conclusions to be drawn?

2. Was the average quality of the respondents in line with your objectives? Differences? Conclusions?

3. Was the total cost per qualified respondent in line with your budget? Was it reasonable in comparison with what you could have achieved through other methods?

4. Were there any significant trends in the responses, any comments that came back often, any suggestions to be observed?

5. Were there any differences in response rates/qualities based on geographic location, job function, branch or industry, age, sex or other factor that can be specified? Conclusions?

6. Can you make a 'cluster analysis' of the typical pattern of the respondent versus the pattern of the non-respondent? Would it be worthwhile to make an analysis, by personal interviews, telephone or a separate questionnaire to a sample of the non-respondents?

Through a combination of pre-testing, split-run, 'bird-banding' and analysis of the reactions received, your DM work could gradually reach a degree of precisions and predictability which is hard to get with any other communications method. This will, in all likelihood, mean that DM will get a fair share of your total communications budget, with 'satisfaction guaranteed', to borrow a classic phrase from consumer DM.

New technologies in direct mail

In addition to the new computer technologies, with great opportunities for combining local, decentralized PCs with mini-computers and main computer files for refined selection of addresses, there are other aspects of communications technology that will give variety and flexibility to the creative business communicator.

A 'direct mail' campaign by telex, which I was the target of many years ago, led me into an advertising agency relationship that has lasted ever since. Indeed, telex offers excellent possibilities for 'direct mail' campaigns and information programmes, where the character of immediacy can make the receiver react more directly than with any other media. Technically, it is fairly easy to make targeted distribution of identical or varied messages to a number of receivers by using computerized base tapes at the sending end.

Cables and *telegrams*, although almost surpassed by telex in many countries, can still be used for fast reactions and attention value, not least in multinational 'direct mail' campaigns.

Personal computers and *micro-computers*, tied with such delivery systems as Western Union's Mailgram, or which link computer to computer, have the potential of delivering messages with higher speed and reliability than today's mail systems seem to offer. Systems of this kind, with a combination of the speed of electronics and desk delivery on paper, are being offered by the tele and mail systems in many countries.

Telefax or *telecopiers* are another method used for DM purposes – although with great caution.

The *word processor* technique, combined with desktop publishing resources, is getting more and more useful for DM applications as modems and new software packages develop.

Video-discs and *video-tapes* give 'show and tell' opportunities to the DM user who wants to improve internal communications worldwide, financial communications, educational contacts or various aspects of market communications.

The list of opportunities, existing or in the development stage, is endless. They raise doubts, as was suggested at the beginning of this chapter, of the appropriateness of the term 'direct mail' for this family of communications methods. There are no doubts whatsoever about the future growth potential of direct approach work as a powerful ingredient in any business communications manager's mix of tools for his trade.

13

'Is one picture worth a thousand words?':

Visual and audiovisual communications methods

In this chapter the reader will find a presentation of the specific roles of pictures and audiovisual media as communications tools.

It will help the reader plan, budget, execute and evaluate communications projects where pictures are an essential part, such as film and video projects, slide presentations and art and photographic work for other purposes, and make them result-oriented parts of a company's total communications process.

'In the beginning was the picture'

Planned human communications, in prehistoric times, started with the picture. Palaeolithic cave paintings, Asian and Pacific area picture-writing, the 'annual reports' of the Dakota Indians, the first alphabets of the Mediterranean and Near East peoples, the rock carvings of Stone Age Scandinavians, all originated in people's efforts to use pictures, naturalistic or more formalized, to convey a message.

Alphabets started as picture-writing. Later, they developed so that letters and words became more and more distinguished from pictures. The relative communications value of pictures and words came to be compared and confronted with each other, as in the standard quote about one picture and a thousand words that I have transformed to a question in the chapter title above.

Why the question mark?

With today's technology and communications thinking, we may again be able to unite the two elements of communications, words and pictures, more closely and more effectively than they have been since the early days of human thought. Desk terminals can help us dig into bottomless mines of stored information, words and figures, and turn them directly into all kinds of shapes and forms of presentation, for our own use or for communication with others. Similarly, pictures can be dissolved into signals, sent across the world and reappear somewhere else almost instantaneously. Pictures alone or combinations of pictures and words are captured, stored, retrieved, relayed and received with magnetic, electronic and photographic methods.

The business communicator today is being offered the age-old advantages of the picture, with the speed and accuracy of modern technology as an additional bonus.

Pictures with a purpose

The value of pictures in planned communications work is as strong as it has ever been. If anything, it is reinforced by today's picture-oriented media consumption habits. It has also been made easier and more effective through modern photography, illustrations and artwork technology.

In business communications, pictures, including graphs and charts, are an essential ingredient in establishing or improving contacts with all the business and non-business contact areas that a company is interested in. The skilful communications manager uses pictures in communicating with the staff, with the shareholders, with the local community and with other groups, obviously including customers and other market influences.

Pictures, in the form of photographs, artwork and computer graphics, are also a part of practically all communications methods, media advertising, direct mail, printed matter, exhibitions, editorial work, conferences and meetings, and so on. In other cases pictures, still or motion, are the backbone of presentation forms, for example, in slide shows, photo exhibitions, films and videos. Pictures, and presentations based on pictures, are a significant part of the budgets of most communications departments.

Whole books have been written about the creative aspects of pictures, company films, etc. This chapter will not try to add to that. It will instead focus on some management aspects of (audio-)visual communications material – how to plan and get maximum value out of the investment in picture and illustration material. Commissioning and guiding photo and film production work are important parts of that, including copyright aspects.

Later sections will discuss those specific media categories, where pictures play the dominating role, visual and audiovisual media.

A well-managed photograph file is a condition for cost-effective use of pictures in a company. One section of this chapter will discuss that aspect, starting with very basic details.

When the picture is part of the show

Pictures as communications support

Photographs and artwork provide essential raw material for practically all communications purposes and methods. Some methods are, however, more dependent on pictures than others. It is hard to draw a strict line: 'printed matter' includes text-loaded technical descriptions, where the illustrations play a minor role, but also sales leaflets with full-colour pictures and posters which are only a picture and a caption. Media advertising may use pictures as a minor or a major element. So do other communication forms.

In all those cases, pictures serve to strengthen, dramatize, 'emotionalize' or sometimes 'intellectualize' a message, to make it more easily accessible, comprehensible or acceptable. It is a more or less significant 'part of the show'.

When the picture *is* the show

Visual and audiovisual media

What is traditionally called (audio)visual media are those that rely entirely on pictures, with or without copy or sound.

Slide series or filmstrips with prepared copy for live presentations, slides or filmstrips with recorded sound, motion pictures, video-cassettes, video-discs and television are normally included. Whether television-type computer terminals should be included is still an open question.

The art of commissioning artwork

Your company may have excellent art and photo services in-house. If so, you are to be congratulated. Having such services in-house make them quicker and easier to use, although not necessarily cheaper. Less need for lengthy instructions and an easier access and permission process often follow the in-house creative picture resource.

If you do not have your own staff photographer, you will need to commission outside help on a regular basis. And even if one has in-house resources available, there may be times when external service is called in. You may need specialized photographic or art services that your own staff can not adequately cover. You may need work done in other parts of the world, where it is more rational to use local talent than sending your own staff. You may have capacity to produce stills but not film work. The freelance photographer may be able to command more respect and may be allowed more creative freedom than 'good old Joe'.

From a management point of view, commissioning film and

photographic work offers a lot of challenges and problems. Film, video and major photographic projects tend to involve substantial budget amounts, which puts a heavy responsibility on the manager who orders them. Time is often a considerable factor. Sending a film producer or photographer to a site, perhaps far away, means that logistics must work, permissions be obtained, time and cost limits be met. Copyright aspects may come in. And in the end, when the project is ready for presentation, everybody has an opinion on the result.

Given the efforts involved, commissioning photo and audiovisual work is a task that requires some consideration and a great deal of preparation. The following suggestions may be helpful.

Choosing a good photographer/artist

First, check your photo files for existing photos. Good photo files may save you the time, effort and expense of ordering a new job at all.

If you need to hire a photographer, nothing beats the confidence based on experience, preferably your own, but if your experience is limited, check with colleagues or friends, with the advertising agency or PR agency.

Define for yourself and together with the user of the pictures, as closely as possible, what kind of pictures you want to get done, and for what purposes: people, machinery, outdoor, indoor, details, large views. If people, is it 'real' people or will models be needed?

Use of the photos: for slide presentations, printed matter (what are the printing specifications?), exhibitions, other. Usually, but not always, you will want both colour and black and white, print and transparency.

Before you commission

- Check that the object is available and that you can get the permissions required.

- Get a cost estimate, and a contract (standard contracts available?), covering prices for copies, retouching, etc. Check such items as *per diem* allowances, travelling costs, transportation of equipment, lighting requirements, copyright rules, responsibility (deadlines, etc.), liability/insurance (for people and equipment), model fees, etc.

275

- Compare the costs with your budget. Also, check if others in the company have similar needs and are interested in 'sharing' the photographer for better economy.

After commissioning

- File contracts, etc. Make sure that all verbal agreements are properly confirmed in writing.
- Well before the photography session: recheck and confirm dates, times, places, availability of power (enough for studio lights?), equipment and people, permissions, back-up service (transportation, ladders, platforms), props, etc.
- Inform everyone involved, from managers in the area concerned to doormen and service staff.

The photography session

- Contact everybody involved and give them background briefing.
- Check object and area carefully (power outlet, fuses, safety and security regulations and material).
- Give instructions to people involved. Make-up, dress, etc.
- Check the object and the background (clean object and floor, correct signs, nothing irrelevant in the picture)?
- Check product safety/liability regulations (hard hats, safety shoes, hearing protection, etc.). If a machine operator is involved, check natural work position.
- Check that all useful shots (angles, black and white, colour, prints, transparencies, close-ups) have been taken before session is over.
- Get (or reconfirm) delivery commitment from photographer.
- Restore area, notify and thank those involved.

After the session

- Check quality and creative work. Check usefulness for purpose.
- Check bills against contract.
- Make notes of experiences for your own future use.
- Evaluate photographer for future reference.

Commissioning and managing film and video projects

A film or video project can well come close to $1,000,000 and few projects will be below $100,000. It may take anywhere from three months to a year of 'normal' production time. This alone indicates that commissioning a film project is a major responsibility, almost equal to commissioning the building of a small factory, or at least a substantial machinery investment. Consequently, it should deserve a planning process of the same scale, in terms of definition of purpose, calculation of return-on-investment, PERT diagrams and other sophisticated forms of support to be really manageable. Only seldom does a film project get this kind of professional handling from the buyer's side. Why?

Without going too deeply into the planning process, it should be useful to consider some of the steps on the road from the first idea to the presentation of the new masterpiece.

Why a film?

Is the idea to produce a film based on a real communications problem or is it based on somebody's desire 'to have a film'?

There are several essential communications tasks that can be met excellently with a film. Processes that are hard to show in other forms can be understandable on film. You can show remote installations and live action on film. Films can demonstrate abstract thoughts and make them acceptable. Films can probably help present the human aspects of a company better than any other media.

There may be many other good reasons why a film is being considered. Be sure to put down these reasons in writing before the project proceeds any further. Evaluate carefully if the reasons are strong enough to warrant the investment or if the same communications task can be met with other, less expensive media.

In this process, also consider what kind of complementary material that will be needed – brochures, leaflets, worksheets or other support material.

Who is the target audience?

Establish one primary target audience, and add, if applicable, secondary and other audiences. In planning the film, focus on the primary audience to ensure that you get a film that does its main job and avoid looking too much on the other categories.

Ask the usual questions about the typical target audience, such as age, sex, nationality (languages?), educational background, professional characteristics, industry affiliation, etc.

What is the typical situation?

Under what conditions will the film normally be shown? With or without company representatives present? At serious conferences and meetings, at exhibitions and shows or as entertainment? On your own premises, at the viewers' location, in other places? For large audiences or small? Film or video, or both?

What do you want to create with the film?

A change in awareness, attitudes or knowledge? Direct action? Of what kind? How do you plan to measure the results?

Take time for this discussion. At the end of it, you should be able to complete the sentence: 'This film project will be considered successful, if . . .', in specific terms.

What would a reasonable budget be?

To create these results in these audiences, what would be a reasonable investment?

And *now* – time to talk with producers!

When you have come up with well-defined – although tentative – answers to these questions within the company, it might be time to discuss the project with one or more potential producers or with a specialized consultant.

Be prepared to pay for producer time spent on these discussions, especially for those producers who do not get the job. Also, be careful about ideas generated in this process – the producer may well feel that he has a copyright to such ideas, and he may not take it lightly if the ideas are included in a film produced by a competitor.

Go through your items with the producer(s) and listen very carefully to the comments and advice you get. New questions are likely to come up in this process. Involve representatives of company management and company staff in the discussions.

Test ideas and listen to suggestions both from insiders, such as those who will be directly involved in using the film, when produced, and from professional outsiders. See examples of films produced for similar purposes by other companies. Check company experiences of earlier film productions. Ask questions! Allow enough time for this process – it will pay off later!

It is time to home in on a new line of specifics, such as:

A manuscript or synopsis

Ask for a separate price for manuscript or synopsis and possibly get one from more than one potential producer. See above on copyright!

Ask for a price for the rest of the production project.

Select your producer

Previous experience of working with one or more of the potential producers is, of course, helpful in the selection. Otherwise, do not hesitate to ask the producers for relevant references – and check them!

Look for resources, creative talent, financial stability, experience relevant to your project and people you will be able to work with.

Long life is a good quality for a company, but companies go up and down, so be sure to get references from recent projects, preferably from a colleague you know.

At the end of this phase, you will have come to a decision on which producer you will select.

Make a written contract

Before you sign, discuss (and be sure to get the answers into the contract):

1. What is included, and what is not, in the quoted price: external actors, travel and expenses, external services, music, artwork, copy, translation/language versions, etc.
2. Copyright: what rights are transferred to you and what rights remain with the producer?
3. Production plan, with a specific delivery time (list foreseeable problems that may affect the delivery time).

279

4. Authority: who is entitled to take decisions on behalf of the client and on behalf of the producer during the production process?

5. Payment rates.

6. Approval process.

7. Number of copies included, and price for additional copies.

8. Insurance: the producer should have adequate insurance for all material during the production time and for his personnel involved in the production.

9. Responsibility: the producer should take full responsibility for complying with all legal, trade union and copyright regulations that apply to the production.

10. Cancellation: if, for any reason, the project is not completed, what are the cancellation procedures and what damages will apply?

The production process

Make sure that the producer gets full support from your department and from all other company functions involved. Telling people in advance that the project is on its way, and what the purpose of the film is, usually helps get support from the company functions that may get called upon to assist during the production process.

See to it that the production of collateral material is coordinated along the same timetable, so that the whole project is ready at the same time.

Final cutting and editing of the film may be a phase where the producer will want your presence and assistance. If so, be sure to take the opportunity – being involved in the finishing touches usually means a lot.

Approval

When a work copy is ready, it is time for formal approval of the production. Any alterations at this stage, not directly due to mistakes by the producer, are normally at the client's expense.

The launch

Going back to the earlier comparison with the factory, a project of this magnitude deserves to be launched professionally. Make some noise about it, invite top management, the production crew and those in the company who were involved at different stages to the first showing.

Launch it through the whole organization so that the film is used for its purposes without delay.

Follow-up

Be sure to get feedback from all presentations, preferably with numbers of viewers, categories, description of situation, and reactions to the film and to the collateral material.

Report on the utilization of the film to management and guide and control the continued use of it so that the objectives that were set up at the time of the decision are met.

The photo/artwork file - garbage dump or treasure chest?

Think of all the times you have said: 'If only I could find the picture we took last year – I [or my boss] need[s] it now!' You know it's there – but where?

Then imagine the cost and trouble it takes to get good photographs and artwork produced. The average photograph or illustration may well cost as much to acquire as the average book in the library (often many times more) and yet even companies with well-equipped and well-staffed technical and business libraries often put much less resources into the maintencance and handling of their 'illustration libraries', their photo and artwork files.

Why is that so?

Perhaps the reason is that top management takes more pride in the laboratory and research departments, and sees the library very much as a service function to those departments, whereas the photography file is for 'the advertising guys'. Or maybe communications managers have often concentrated their interest more on the creative side than on planning and managing. It is great to have good pictures taken or good artwork made, but then, after it has been used the first time, one tends to lose interest in the potentially long future life of that creation.

Whatever the reason, companies who have changed this situation and got their photography and art files in order have found that it does pay off in savings and good use of investments made, and that it provides smooth and efficient service for several departments and functions, not least for top management.

Do not build a filing system . . .

There is one thing that librarians know, as well as warehousing experts, storage hands, stevedores, housewives, secretaries and squirrels: the problem of storing or filing is never at the storing end – it is always when you try to retrieve what you have stored.

Anyone can make the most sophisticated filing system for photographs, with or without the help of computers, and it can be as efficient in accommodating your pictures and absorbing them forever, as the famous 'black holes' of the universe. The KISS principle (Keep It Simple, Sweetheart) is seldom more appropriate than in building your picture collection, your treasure chest.

. . . build a retrieval system

The good secretary, the good librarian, the good squirrel or the good stevedore supervisor thinks of the retrieval when he stores his stuff away. In other words, he tries to make finding almost as easy as hiding.

- Who are the users of photographs in your company? The communications staff are likely to be major users. In addition, what about the sales and marketing staff, maybe the research staff and probably top management?
- What do they need them for – for printing purposes, for advertising, for meetings and presentations, for trade shows, for manuals, press releases, reports or other purposes?
- What types of question do they ask when they want to find those hidden treasures?

- How quickly do they need the pictures? Put yourself in the user's shoes in such matters as how long the user can accept to wait for his picture, depending on the situation.

If the normal user is one of your communications staff who deals with the daily press, then he may need the picture he is looking for in a matter of minutes. If not, the opportunity may be gone forever. If the typical user needs a certain picture for a corporate presentation leaflet, then he may have more time. Your president, who is working on his Chamber of Commerce speech, may have plenty of time in preparing his slides, until he decides to make some last-minute changes.

Working from that end may make it possible to build up a photography file that really works, whether it contains a few hundred pictures or hundreds of thousands. In designing or reshaping your photography filing system, put yourself at the retrieval end, time and again. Ask the questions that potential users would ask.

Working from the user's viewpoint does not mean that you have to accommodate all kinds of user whims. It only means that, in building up the system, in applying the system and, actually, in every single filing situation you think in user terms. Rather than a filing system, you build a retrieval system.

Looking for a picture in a photography file often makes you think of the proverbial needle in the haystack. Obviously, the bigger the haystack, the more difficult it is to find the needle.

If you build a retrieval system rather than a filing system, you may want to consider whether one big file is the best solution, or whether it is easier for the user to find what he is looking for if the system is built on small separate files, based on (user-oriented) logical or organizational splits.

'It may be useful one day'

A safe way to destroy any storage system and make it difficult to retrieve anything from it is to store things that 'may be useful some day'. Your own garage or attic may be proof if you need it. Admittedly, it is difficult to select one or two pictures from a sequence of twelve and throw away the rest. I also admit that it does happen more than once that one says afterwards: 'Why on earth did I throw away that picture?' Still, in building a functioning photograph retrieval system, every decision to include a photograph in it must be based on the high probability that *someone* will want to retrieve that picture again.

Whoever makes the decisions to scrap eight out of ten photographs that have cost the company lots of money (yes, scrap them, not put them aside!) has to have good judgement, plenty of experience and, above all, courage galore! For he will be criticized by others and he will regret his own decisions more than once. And yet, there is no way to build a working photograph retrieval system without careful screening of what goes into it. And if you check your own experience, you know that even in a system where rigorous screening is applied, less than 10 per cent of all the pictures are used more than 50 per cent of the time. Right?

Is there an ideal system?

How should the ideal system for easy retrieval of photographs and other illustrations be designed?

Since each system has to be user-oriented, and the users are different from company to company, the question is impossible to answer. What follows should thus not be considered as the once-and-for-all recipe for a successful photograph retrieval system for your company or any other company. Look at it rather as an example, which you can compare with your own existing system, or the system you have in mind to introduce. You may end up finding that your existing system is, indeed, quite good. Alternatively, you may take one or two ideas from the presentation and use them to improve your own thoughts.

An example of a photo filing/retrieval system

Manual or computerized?

The system outlined here can be applied, depending on your own needs and resources, as a manual card file or it can be computerized. Cost trends seem to favour computerization, so if you plan a new system now, make sure it can be transformed for computerization in the future without a total overhaul, even if you make it manual now.

Five main categories

Do you recognize some of the following questions:

- 'Do we have a good photograph of Peter Henderson in the sales department?'
- 'I would like to put in a slide of our service shop in Brazil in a presentation tomorrow. Can you help me?'
- 'What pictures do we have of the machines we delivered to the Philippines last year?'
- 'That exhibition in Hanover. Do we have any photographs yet?'
- 'I think I remember seeing an overhead of our sales development in Turkey. Could you find it for me?'

Retrieval questions like these point to a need for *five* (or possibly more) *main categories* or classifications:

01	Persons
02	Facilities
03	Products
04	Events
05	Diagrams, drawings, maps, etc.

Subdivisions
For each one of these main categories, there is obviously a need for *subdivisions*, such as those discussed below:

01 Persons
    (a) Individuals, perhaps in alphabetical order, by family name.
    (b) Groups, by the occasion of their meeting: 'Visit by the Dusseldorf Chamber of Commerce'; 'Sales conference at HQ'; 'International seminar on communications'.

02 Facilities
    By geographic areas or by function (factories, shops, offices, retail outlets, service places, or similar).

03 Products
    Subdivided by your own company's product codes or other system.

04 Events
    Subdivided by category, such as exhibitions, inaugurations, conferences, disasters, etc.

05 Diagrams, drawings, maps, etc.
Subdivided by category of contents, such as financial, market, technical, product applications, etc.

With these five main categories, and suitable subdivisions, carried through in your system, your 'Immediate Retrieval Quotient' (IRQ) probably gets somewhere around 90 per cent already.

If you want to reach higher than that, add another two categories or classification factors: *place* and *time*. For *place*, a country code may be enough. If it is not, add the first two or, if really necessary, all digits from the Post or Zip code. For *time*, add year (and month): 82 (03) for (March) 1982. The exact date is seldom necessary.

With these factors added, your IRQ might climb from the 90 per cent level to the 96–8 per cent level. So, the questions you were asked above may end up in retrieval of some photographs or artwork under the following classifications:

01	1	01	82 03
(Persons)	(Individuals)	(USA)	(photo taken March 1982)
02	5	55	79 11
(Facilities)	(Service facility)	(Brazil)	(photo taken November 1979)
03	39	99	81 12
(Products)	(Paper machine)	(Other countries)	(photo taken December 1981)
04	1	49	82 04
(Events)	(Exhibitions)	(Germany)	(photo taken April 1982)
05	2	90	80 02
(Diagrams, etc.)	(Marketing)	(Turkey)	(diagram made February 1980)

The register cards you find in the manual file or that flash up on your desk terminal screen may look like this example:

XYZ Company	02	5	55	79	11
B/w copy	Main Subdivision Classification		Geography	Year	Month
	Special remarks Sandoz Mesa Producer (photographer/artist/agency)				
	3285 Product no.	13527 Our no.	Copyright our prod.		
	Negative original	B/w Colour	Size: 24 × 30 Mtrl: Pos.		

cont

286

cont

Caption	Approved	Photo dep.	Service dep.
XYZ has service facilities in most countries. This one, in Brazil, was built in 1979.	for publication		

What you really do with a system like this, of course, is to split up the huge haystack into many smaller ones, first the five big ones, then each one of these in smaller heaps, then again by place/country and time. If this is in line with user interests, it should make it much easier to relocate what he is looking for.

In a big company, it may still not be enough. A product division may want an even finer division of their products and the competitor products they meet, or by parts or components or by special applications. Or a local factory will have photographs of their own installation going to much more detail than the photography department at head office is interested in. There may still be satisfactory coordination within a group, as long as the broad classification system is the same, with reasonable liberty for departments, divisions or local plants or companies to refine their own specific categories to greater depth.

A further division that this system allows you is to 'start afresh' each January. Since it is often the new photographs that have the highest user frequency, you gain substantial improvements in IRQ by not having to go through, manually or even electronically, all the old material every time you are looking for a certain photograph. You would still, of course, have the photographs of previous years accessible, although perhaps with gradually less demands on 'prime space', as they get older.

Budgeting visual communications

In the cases where photographs and artwork come as part of a project, such as a brochure, an advertising programme or an exhibition, the photography budget is obviously part of the total project. In these cases, the willingness to allocate enough resources to the illustration parts depends on the overall communications objectives. More often than not, however, such projects would gain from more attention to illustrations. A good job on illustrations can, in most cases, add substantially to the communicative value of any kind of communications project for any communications purpose.

In most companies, special visual production projects go through a high level of budget scrutiny. If, as happens in some companies, budgeting is allowed to become a pure cost exercise, rather than a professional cost-benefit analysis process, then the whole thing is rather useless. The important thing to remember in the budgeting phase is that a definition of clear-cut objectives is, and should be, an integral part of the budgeting, just as it is an integral part of most other major investment plans in a company.

Evaluating the results of visual communications

As always, evaluation of the results starts when you decide on the objectives of your project.

In space advertising, the values for 'seen' or 'noted' of an advertisement are often a good measurement of the visual impact, and the illustration normally contributes a great deal to the visual impact. You cannot, however, fully equate a high (or a low) value on the 'seen/noted' factors to the illustration. Such factors as the headline, colour/no colour, size and, not least, the relevance of the message have great influence on those factors as well.

In sales literature, annual reports and other forms of printed matter it is obvious that quality artwork and photographs play an important role for reader interest, understanding and acceptance. Formal qualitative research can show how big a role, but one can come a long way with small sample reader panels.

In editorial productions, such as employee and customer magazines, as well as in relations with outside print media editors, readership evaluations can give important clues to how much the illustration material contributes to the total communications result.

The impact of exhibition photo and artwork can be studied through simple observation of visitor behaviour.

Major visual productions, such as films, videos, major slide presentations, etc., should be studied and evaluated more formally, and a percentage of the production cost, say 3–5 per cent, should be allocated for an impact study, with the defined objective of the project as the starting point.

14

'Show and tell!':
Exhibitions, fairs and shows

In this chapter the reader will find a presentation of the characteristics of exhibitions as communication tools. A 'four levels' method to assess the qualitative aspects of exhibitions and shows is introduced as a technique to support decisions on location, space, staffing and design of the exhibition.

The chapter will help the reader plan, budget, execute and evaluate exhibitions and shows as result-oriented parts of a company's total communications programmes, not only for marketing purposes.

More than trade shows

Exhibitions, shows, displays and trade fairs represent a spectrum of communications techniques that have wide applications in industrial communications programmes. They are unique in many ways: they provide better opportunities for two-way contacts than most other communications methods, they can be adapted for large-scale impressive presentations or for highly specialized purposes, they can be vehicles for product selling or for corporate policy information and they can be geared to practically any of a company's various publics or, as we have called them, contact areas. And yet, in many industrial companies, exhibitions are still considered in a much too narrow perspective, used only for conventional communications needs, and sometimes not even included in the job description of the communications manager.

Here are a few examples to spark the creative thinking process:

- Companies have used exhibits, placed on the company premises, to inform their *employees* on new products, on new technology the company has introduced, on the reasons for an acquisition, on environmental measures the company has taken or is about to take or on organizational changes in the company.

- Companies have used and are using exhibits and shows as parts of their *local community* relations programmes. Placed in city centres, libraries, banks, sports arenas or on company grounds, such exhibits serve to illustrate the company's position and activities related to community goals, such as employment, taxes and other economic contributions, development plans, training programmes, environmental issues and other aspects.

- Companies use exhibitions and displays in connection with the annual general meetings with the *shareholders*, to give shareholders a clearer view of the company, its products and services, its markets and marketing work, its investment policies, its staff development programmes and its financial situation.

- Companies send travelling exhibits to *schools* and other educational institutions, explaining the technology it specializes in, or the workings and organization of an industrial company.

These examples show that exhibitions and shows can be used to establish or improve communications with many other categories than customers, for many other purposes than product selling.

Exhibitions and similar presentations thus form an important part of the range of communications tools available to a company, too important to be considered only as marketing support, which they obviously are, too!

Most of the comments and suggestions in this chapter apply generally to all possible uses of exhibition techniques, including but not limited to the usual trade fair participations. Examples and vocabulary are sometimes taken from this field, mainly because this may simplify comparisons between this presentation and traditional literature on the subject, which deals very much, or exclusively, with trade fair procedures. It is, however, essential that the reader takes the trouble to 'translate' ideas and reasoning to other communications tasks – only then can this chapter be fully productive and rewarding to the experienced communications manager as well as to the beginner or outsider.

'What's so special about exhibitions?'

Good exhibitions offer a range of benefits that are hard to combine in other forms of communications. Here are some of them.

Shows are not only shows

While, obviously, the main purpose of an exhibition is the opportunity it offers to exhibit your idea or product, to put it in the limelight, there is more to it than that.

'Show and tell' is a primary opportunity not only to show things, products and procedures statically, but to demonstrate them, let them move and act. Dramatization of reasons, backgrounds, origins, consequences, benefits and connections can be made more easily in exhibit form than with most other communications methods. In principle, all five senses can and should be considered in setting up an exhibit.

Exhibitions provide a two-way channel

Normally, we think of exhibitions as manned displays, thus creating great opportunities for immediate feedback, questions, comments, criticism, discussions (spontaneous or organized), and other forms of interplay between visitors and exhibit staff. Also unmanned shows (e.g., travelling school exhibitions) can easily be adapted for visitor feedback through contests, check cards, questionnaires, etc. They can also be designed to encourage visitor activity and involvement, such as taking part in the action, turning wheels, starting models or demonstrations, working multiple-choice buttons, etc. With proper follow-up, unmanned as well as manned exhibitions provide unique opportunities for two-way contacts.

Exhibitions can be anywhere on the audience scale

Exhibitions can be extremely general or highly selective. Placed at a general fair, in a community centre or at a World Fair, to take a few examples, your exhibit can be seen and visited by wide audiences. Sending your exhibit to technical schools, setting up a show on your company's premises or making a demonstration at a conference for nuclear physicists are examples of using the medium to reach very closely defined groups of people that your company may be interested in.

Exhibitions can stand alone or be integrated

Setting up an exhibition or participating in a fair can be the king-pin of a communications activity. Indeed, with supplementary material, it can be the main item in a communications programme. It can also – and more often – be a major or supporting part of a wide range of activities, integrated with space advertising, literature, press contacts, films, company visits and other communications efforts.

Defining the objectives

'Should you or shouldn't you?'

There are still few fields in the life of many companies where big money is spent with so little planning and follow-up as the communications area. And within this area, decisions on exhibition participation are often taken surprisingly lightly. Is there a way to sharpen the decision-making process to match the money and efforts involved in exhibitions?

'Media information' on trade shows is often inferior to that of trade publications. Worksheet 14.1 (p. 312) provides a guideline on what kinds of information a potential participant should request from an exhibit organizer before taking his decision to participate or not.

Requesting such information provides a base for a YES or NO decision, but the responsibility and most of the preparation work stays with the participating company.

As usual, the key question is *who* do you want to establish contacts with. Having defined that, the next task is to establish a benchmark. What do the specified groups of people know, feel and think now about your subject, your company or your product? What do you want them to know, feel, etc.? Is an exhibit a useful way to create such changes or contribute to them? What are the alternatives or what additional communications methods should we consider?

This process is worth more time and effort than is usually put into it. It puts the company in the driving seat, and it gives the communications specialist a better means to put his or her experience to work for the company's overall goals. The alternative, which is much too frequent, is that exhibit decisions are made on more conventional grounds, such as 'Which exhibitions did we take part in last year?' or 'Which exhibitions do our competitors use?' or, even worse, only in response to invitations from exhibit organizers.

Even if your company uses exhibitions mainly for market communications purposes, the process also encourages creative thinking of other applications of the exhibit technique, for other contact areas than various market segments. In principle and in practice, planning procedures, budgeting, evaluation methods, follow-up measures and other aspects of exhibition work apply to the medium as such, irrespective of what contact areas or communications purposes it is used for.

This is so much more true, as repeated surveys seem to indicate, that even in industrial trade shows, other aspects than direct selling/buying are listed as the primary reasons for participating in or visiting a trade fair. The reasons for participating in a trade fair are often given by the exhibiting companies in such terms as 'showing new products or applications', 'meeting new customers', 'preparing the market for future activities' or 'to get new distributors'. The reasons for visitors to go to trade shows given in similar surveys are often listed as 'learning about new products or applications', 'general information on "the state of the art" ', 'checking the competitors', 'getting new ideas for our production or product development'. It seems that even industrial trade fairs are judged more on their communications merits, both by exhibitors and visitors, than on their merits as a direct selling/buying opportunity.

If this is so, then it is fairly obvious that experience gained in planning and executing such exhibitions can, at least to a considerable extent, be used also for other applications of the exhibition medium.

Whom do you want to reach?

Defining the audience is the starting point in many communications projects, if not in all. In the planning process for an exhibition this process may follow a path like this:

- What is the typical 'profile' of the person you want to reach, in terms of:
    industry affiliation;
    position in his company or organization;
    educational background;
    age;
    sex;
    or other essential criteria?
- How many of these can you expect to come to the exhibit you are considering, and how many, specifically, could you attract to your part of the exhibition?
- What are your alternative methods to reach these people?

What is their background in relation to the presentation you may want to make?

- In other words, what do they know, think or feel about your company, about its products, about your technology, service network, software resources, etc.? Do you have any recent awareness or attitude surveys to work from? Would interviews with your field staff be helpful to establish reasonable benchmarks?
- If it is a new product or application you are going to present, what are the true customer benefits it offers? Higher productivity? Cost savings? A better product for your customer, in his market situation? Improved work conditions in his factory or office? Can those advantages be demonstrated, shown, felt, assimilated better in an exhibition situation than through alternative media?

What are the acceptable costs in relation to anticipated benefits?

Having established who you want to reach and basically what message you want to convey, how much would it be worth for you to reach that goal? What advantages would it give you in terms of awareness, good-will, competitive position, price acceptance, salesman's access, productivity of sales staff, penetration speed or other advantages? How much would that be worth over a given period of time? How much would it cost to gain the same advantages through alternative methods?

Encounters – of what kind? A look at some qualitative aspects.

What you get out of most exhibitions, especially manned exhibitions, is contacts. Obviously, you want to reach as many as possible in your target audience, but you also want the contacts to be at the right qualitative level. Defining your objectives in 'contact quality' terms can give valuable guidance in the whole exhibition planning process. Try the following classification of the benefits you aim for, in 'contact quality' terms:

General exposure/awareness
Your priority may be to give a certain number of relevant people an overall impression of what your company stands for, what business it is in, what range of products it offers, what its technology level is, how big it is, where its sales outlets are, what kind of a company it is, etc.

Positive interest/attitude change
It may be more important for you to get a number of relevant people to accept certain statements about your company and its products, technological leadership, reliability of products and company, value for money, availability, professional project assistance, worldwide service resources, higher precision, more sophisticated products or any number of value-related points.

Willingness to devote time
You may want a certain number of relevant people to take time fully to penetrate your message/your offer, to relate it to their own needs, immediately or in the future, to place your offer in the active parts of their minds, to place you in the range of 'preferred choices'.

Action towards acceptance
You may want a certain number of relevant people to take action of some kind – to sign a contract, to ask a salesman to call, to request more information, to engage in a serious discussion, to provide enough information about himself so that active follow-up can be meaningful.

Putting numbers to the process

The next step will be to quantify each one of those stages in terms of expected numbers of exhibit visitors who will:

1. At least *pass by* your exhibit stand to see the central company message.
2. *Walk through* your exhibit and give it enough time to get some details about the central messages.
3. *Take active part* in a demonstration (live or audiovisual), ask questions, follow a presentation of a process or a procedure, try your equipment, etc.
4. Engage in a *person-to-person conversation* with your staff, resulting in a request for follow-up action.

By all means, feel free to change the classification model to suit your own situation and needs (including such exhibitions which are not immediately market-oriented). Then continue your pre-evaluation process, by making reasonable assumptions about the numbers to aim for in each category. Work with the left column of the 'Contact opportunities' chart on p. 303.

Assumptions along these lines will make it possible for you to set specific objectives in measurable terms for your exhibit participation, taking both qualitative and quantitative factors into account.

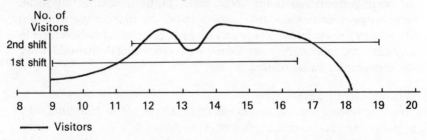

Figure 14.1 *Exhibition visitor attendance over a normal day*

Don't answer all questions on your own. Involve others concerned so that you get their active participation in the planning process from the start.

Don't fall for the temptation of setting unreasonable targets to justify a positive decision – but don't rig the figures the other way, either. Use the best available facts and your best judgement.

After working along this pattern in the planning process a couple of times, and having made the corresponding analysis after each show, your exhibition planning will gradually become more realistic and more reliable.

Guidelines for the total planning process

Setting your priorities and sorting them in qualitative and quantitative terms along the four categories indicated above are basic steps towards professional exhibition planning. It helps, not only in the cost calculation and 'value for money' analysis. It is also directly helpful in other aspects of the total planning and preparation process. Here are some examples:

1. If the main priority is to get people to take an active part in demonstrations, not only to create general exposure, the staffing requirements will be higher, in numbers of staff and in the quality of staff representatives. Training programmes for the exhibit staff will be more ambitious, demands on the exhibit organizers will be harsher (noise regulations, ventilation, power supply, etc.), and follow-up planning may be influenced.

2. If the main priority is to get visitors engaged in person-to-person conversations with the sales staff, then the stand will be designed in another way than if the aim is a big number of pass-through visitors. The design will include suitable seating arrangements, perhaps separate booths for talks in small groups, coffee, etc., will be served and the right documentation will be available. Selection and training of exhibit staff is made to suit the purpose, and follow-up is certainly planned very consciously.

Staffing

Over-, under- or 'just right'?

There are occasions when unmanned exhibitions can work well – say, a presentation of your local expansion plans in your community library. Even then, however, you might on some occasions invite special groups for discussions, and then, obviously, you would make sure that your own organization is well represented.

In most cases, one will want an exhibition to be permanently and adequately manned.

Some ocean-cruisers of the old school used to have a ratio of crew to passengers of two to one. I am not advocating a ratio of 2:1 between exhibit crew and visitors, but I would venture an opinion that the cost efficiency of exhibits has been wrecked more often because of under-staffing than because of over-staffing. And then I am not thinking in numbers only.

One reason why we go so deeply into a method of defining the objectives of exhibitions is that the defined objectives have far-reaching consequences on the staffing of an exhibit.

Exhibits are often 'expensive', in the sense that big money is involved. It is also true that qualified exhibit staff is expensive: in addition to their salaries, for which the normal work may not be produced, there are all the costs of travelling, hotel rooms, allowances, expenses, etc.

The balance between the investment in the physical stand itself and in the manning of the stand is therefore crucial to the result of the exhibit, and closely related to the objectives. It is obvious that if the objective is close personal contacts with good visitors there will be a need for more staff than if the objective is plain exposure. The 'mathematics' section on p. 307 will show that the difference is dramatic.

Staff quality – staff training

But the quality of the exhibit staff must be determined in relation to the objectives.

In most cases, there is a need for specific training for every new exhibition, even if high quality staff are selected, such as company employees with the right mix of technical background, sales

298

experience and personal qualifications.

The reasons why training is so important become very clear if one splits the total cost of the exhibit by the number of hours the exhibit is open. It becomes quite obvious that every minute of exhibit time counts and that no company can afford to waste any part of that investment through unprofessional attitudes or action by the exhibit staff.

The training programme may cover a few hours or it may cover a whole day. It may include advance material, on-the-spot instructions, formal training sessions and other aids.

Here are some items to be considered as part of a staff training programme:

1. The purpose and objectives of the exhibit participation, and its connection to overall company goals. High-level management involvement in this item can improve the return on the exhibit investment substantially, making it clear that the exhibition is not a 'gimmick' but part of a well-considered strategy.

2. Close definition of the kinds of visitors aimed for, if practical in the categories outlined above, including the quantitative goals. Breakdown per hour and per staff person.

3. Procedures for registration of visitors – importance of as complete registration as at all possible for the right follow-up.

4. Detailed information and background on the products, systems and issues to be featured.

5. Exercise in answering probable questions, preferably with video facilities for self-analysis. Pitfalls, limitations. How to handle competitor enquiries.

6. Organization of the exhibit. Who is responsible for what. Availability of telephones, telex, telefax, typing services, literature, etc. Who to ask for additional information.

7. Orientation on the total show, competitor's stands, public facilities, hours, etc.

8. Rules about duty hours, dressing, absence reporting, entertainment guidelines, etc.

9. Safety regulations and procedures in case of fire, accidents, etc.

Much of the need for good training derives from the specific situation every exhibit offers: every exhibit means a new environment for the staff. It is an unusual situation even for many experienced salesmen to have the customers come to see them, rather than the normal sales call situation. Psychologically, the difference is substantial. Also, while the environment is unusual to the exhibit staff, the visitor perceives it as the home territory of the host company. He therefore expects professional treatment – and should get it.

The importance of staff professionalism also indicates that the same personnel should stay on the stand throughout an exhibition period.

To sum up, make sure that good staff are recruited for the show, and that they are adequately trained, before the exhibit opens.

Location, space and design

The choice of location, the size of the stand and the general lay-out of an exhibit depend very much on the objectives: the types of visitor to attract, the numbers expected and the purpose of their visit to the show. Why not take a look at the table on p. 303?

Location by objectives

If the priority is general exposure to big numbers, the location of the stand should be at the mainstreams of traffic, at or near entrances, bars, restaurants or other public facilities.

If, on the other hand, in-depth contacts with more limited numbers are more important, the location can be chosen with other considerations. Special invitations, direct mail, advertising in the exhibition catalogue or in the appropriate trade press may then be more important to attract the right type and numbers of visitors than location as such.

Space by objectives

When it comes to the decisions on the size of the exhibit, it is useful to go back to the definition of objectives. Substantially more space per visitor is required for in-depth sales or technical talks than for more general exposure. Check the dramatic differences in the sample calculation in the 'mathematics' section on p. 309!

Design by objectives

There is plenty of literature available on exhibit design. What should be pointed out here is that the principles of exhibit design must be influenced by the same definitions of objectives as other elements in the exhibit planning, the types and numbers of visitor contact that are aimed for. If ambitions are for big numbers of visitors with high turnover rates but rather more limited impressions, awareness levels and attitude changes as communication results, then the designer and producer of the stand would get other directives than if the primary aim is for in-depth discussions with limited numbers of very important visitors.

In the first case, one would tend to stress easy access, fast flow, dramatic displays, intensive colours, simple but very clear slogans, a few concentrated messages and simple literature, maybe reprints of suitable advertisements.

In the other extreme, instructions to the stand producer would include comfortable seating arrangements, more detailed systems and process displays, more sophisticated captions, maybe facilities for some kind of drink and/or snack service. Literature and audiovisual displays would be more technical, light arrangements would be softer, the registration procedure would be more specific.

It is a useful exercise, well worth the time and effort, to try to clarify, in specific numbers, what the priorities are, before one gets in touch with the designer and producer of the stand, so that instructions to him are in line with priorities. It can save lots of disappointment at later stages, it will improve the overall efficiency of the exhibit investments and it contributes to the professional use of exhibitions as a result-oriented communications medium.

Budgeting

There are many lists of exhibit budgeting available. One example is given below, pp. 302–3.

Three requirements

Before choosing one list or the other, you should consider at least three things:

1. Itemize the budget in such a way that the items correspond with

your company's accounting system or take other measures to ensure that every cost item can be followed up against the budget.

2. Define the expected benefits of the show participation so that the real outcome can be registered during and after the exhibit in the same terms to make a comparison of results with objectives possible.

3. Establish a system, so that the budgeted costs can be evaluated against expected benefits of the exhibit project, number of contacts at specified levels, defined changes in awareness and attitudes in defined audiences, reactions in terms of questions, requests for tenders, demonstrations, or in sales, if that is your purpose.

Four comparisons

The budgeting system should enable you to compare:

- budgeted costs with anticipated benefits;
- budgeted costs with real costs, item by item;
- real benefits with anticipated benefits;
- real costs with real benefits.

This can be done in many ways. You may already have devised a system and got it to work satisfactorily. If not, here is one simple system that may be worth a try. It is based on two lists, one of budget items, before and after, and one of contact opportunities, listed before and after. (Cf. also Chapter 17.)

To give a more complete picture, add a budget figure for such investments in own staff time which are not translated into money charges, with appropriate follow-up.

Cost items

	Budgeted (before)	Real (after)
Rents Stand floor area Furnishings, carpets, etc. Water, electricity, telephone, etc. Other rentals		

con

cont

	Budgeted (before)	Real (after)
Stand costs Proposal, model and consulting Production or write-off Costs for building and dismantling Cleaning and miscellaneous		
Demonstration material Signs, blow-ups, models, etc. Audiovisual equipment Product samples Literature		
Staff costs Salaries Travelling costs Hotel costs Expenses Staff training		
Other items Transportation Insurance Publicity, press Entertainment Advertising Administration Invitations, tickets, etc. Result evaluation/Research Miscellaneous Allocation for unexpected costs		
Total Costs		

Contact opportunities at exhibition

	Projected/ target	Real outcome
Information from exhibit organizer: (Verified yes no) (Guaranteed yes no)		
Total number of visitors to the exhibition or fair		

Total number of visitors of interest to us (industry branch, geographically, position, education level, etc.)		
Information that we are responsible for: Total number of *'passers-by'* (approximately = exposure)		
Total number of *visitors* to our stand ('look-through')		
Number of *active* visitors to our stand (reacted, requested additional information, took part in demonstration, etc.)		
Number of visitors with whom our staff carried through *person-to-person* talks		
Direct *sales* at the stand		

A tool for improvements

Preparing the budget and quantifying the priorities and targets for the four categories of visitors this way makes it possible to see the weaknesses and the strong points of a suggested exhibit project. It signals which areas to improve to reach an acceptable cost/value factor.

In the calculation on whether or not to take part, and in setting appropriate targets, it should be quite clear that both the cost part of the equation and the value part of it can be influenced. If the cost/value figures do not seem to come out right, it might be easier to influence the value part of it than the cost part. One may even find that additions to the cost side provide a better overall cost/value factor.

If, for instance, a well-conceived promotion campaign can increase the number and quality of visitors to the stand, this may mean a considerable improvement in the value:cost ratio, since much of the costs may be fixed.

If, also, creative design and friendly, qualified staff can move some relevant passers-by actively to visit your exhibit, if good stand arrangements and staff can create opportunities for personal sales talks and if it is easy and attractive for the right type of people to request follow-up information, then the value:cost ratio improves.

This is why the pre-show objectives, as well as the post-show evaluation, should have a qualitative and a quantitative aspect.

The reasons for this become very clear if we draw realistic cost

304

consequences of the staffing and space calculations presented below. The costs – but hopefully also the value – of an encounter of the third and fourth kind, 'active visitor' and 'sales talk', are exponentially higher than the costs of an encounter of the first and second kind, 'passer-by' and 'look-through'. In fact, the cost ratio between a 'passer-by' and a 'sales talk' can be as high as 1:50 or more. Check the examples in the 'mathematics' section (p. 307), with your own experience. It may help in setting priorities between the four kinds of visitors.

Evaluation, follow-up

Proper evaluation of an exhibition project starts with the definitions of objectives. A realistic definition of objectives depends on good information from the exhibit organizer and on the pre-show analysis of opportunities and goals.

The exhibit organizer should be aware of his responsibilities. He does not sell space – he sells contact opportunities. It is his job to show – and prove – how many visitors of which categories are coming to the show. Based on that, you can judge how many of the visitors of interest to you that you can reasonably attract to your stand, and in what respects you can influence their awareness and attitudes, if not actions.

Working from the 'Contact opportunities . . .' sheet, your follow-up starts when you fill out the left column, the projected figures, and continues after the show, when you put in the real results in the same terms to the right.

Total number of visitors to the exhibition or fair

This figure should be verified by the organizer, through a procedure that the participating exhibitors can accept. An independent research organization of good standing should be retained by the exhibit organizer to ensure the quality of the counting procedure. In most industrial countries, the advertiser organizations, in cooperation with exhibit organizers, have set up such procedures. It is advisable never to participate in an exhibit which has not made satisfactory commitments to attendance reports.

Total numbers of visitors of interest

In most cases, the attendance registration or checks also takes basic visitor characteristics into consideration. Branch of industry or business, position in company, geographic basis, reason for visiting the fair and purchasing responsibility are examples of such characteristics, which are, again, the obvious responsibility of the exhibit organizer to provide, with proper guarantees for accuracy and impartiality. These two sets of information are in fact what the exhibit organizer sells. They are his 'product'.

Number of 'passers-by' (= exposure)
This figure can either be estimated by traffic counts at regular intervals during the fair, or it can be evaluated/checked through simple interviews with samples of visitors, when they leave the exhibition. Worksheet 14.2, in its simplest form, provides approximate answers to this item.

Number of visitors to your stand ('look-through')
Again, to verify this figure, use periodic traffic counts, either by exhibit staff or, better, through independent research staff. Alternatively, set up interviews at exhibit gates with visitors leaving the area.

Active visitors to your stand
Depending on your definition, make one or several of the following checks:

1. Count active participants in demonstrations and presentations on your exhibit stand.
2. Count requests for additional information, literature, follow-up visits.
3. Count registered contacts with your staff.

For 2 and 3 above, simple sheets or check-cards can be printed. They would be completed, preferably by your exhibit staff, and carry their signature or other identification. It should be made quite clear that it is one of the important responsibilities of your exhibit staff to produce good quality leads in adequate numbers and they should be given credit for doing so. Many exhibit organizers provide each visitor with an identity card of credit card type, which simplifies the processing of such contacts.

Person-to-person sales talks
This category, the most valuable contact form, is also the easiest form of contacts to register. If this is a high priority for you, make it a clear priority for the exhibit staff concerned to make detailed

reports of their sales talks, with specific recommendations for follow-up, and give due credit for such sales talks when reported.

Qualitative surveys

In addition to these routine checks, it is often appropriate to measure exhibit results in qualitative terms. Interviewing is the most frequent method.

Inquire, well before the exhibit, which plans for measurements and evaluations that the exhibit organizer is planning to carry through. The more you know in advance of his plans, the better are your chances to evaluate how you can use them. You may add one or two questions to his survey, you may save money by using the same interview staff for your own surveys and you find out what the exhibit organizer will not be able to provide.

Your qualitative surveys would probably concentrate on which impression your exhibit has made, possibly in relation to other companies you want to compare yourself with, and which of the basic messages you present that have been retained by the relevant groups of people.

If the exhibit organizers do not provide you with this kind of service, most industrial research companies can do it for you. In many cases, you can set up simple but adequate 'do-it-yourself surveys', using school or college students as interviewers.

To sum up: checking the budget items and verifying the costs against budget estimates is just one side of the follow-up. That side is usually taken care of. Equally important is to check the value you get from your exhibit participation, in terms of numbers of visitors of various categories to your exhibit, and in terms of changes in awareness and attitudes – possibly also action.

An exercise in exhibition mathematics

This exercise in 'exhibition mathematics' may seem theoretical to some readers but it is based very much on practical experience and it may lead to some very practical conclusions in deciding space and staff requirements. If adequate manning of an exhibit has ever been a problem for you, take five minutes to follow the reasoning and familiarize yourself with the principle. You may then choose to apply it to one of your own situations, or to use any other method you have used so far, including the rule of thumb.

Calculating staff needs

Start with specific and realistic objectives of the number of visitors you aim to serve. Since, obviously, you will want to spend more staff time per visitor of the more 'serious' categories, you will also have to go back to your qualitative objectives, the split-up between 'passers-by', 'look-through', 'active' participants and 'serious talk' type of visitors.

Here is a way to calculate, in which I have been bold enough to give specific figures. By all means, these figures are average numbers based on my experience. They may not apply to the exhibit situations you have in mind. Do adjust them according to your own experience and keep records so that you can gradually refine your own calculations. The method is the important thing, not the figures as such, even if the following figures may be good enough to use until you have formed your own set of numbers.

A 'passer-by' requires very little staff attention. The time he spends at the exhibit is also, by definition, short. One exhibit attendant is therefore capable of 'serving' big numbers of 'passersby'.

A visitor who 'looks through' your stand takes somewhat more time. He also expects and deserves somewhat more attention than a 'passer-by'.

An 'active visitor', who engages in demonstrations, who may ask questions, who looks in more detail at your displays, stays longer, by definition, and requires more time from the exhibit staff.

Finally, the visitor who is so interested that he engages in an individual sales conversation with the staff, stays longer in the booth and requires considerable staff time.

All this is obvious. But the consequences it leads to in staffing are maybe less so – and then we are only talking about the numbers, so far.

Take a look at this table, where the figures have been specified:

	Time spent at/in the exhibition stand	'Pass-through factor'	'Attention factor'	Handling capacity per staff man/hour	
				Theoretical	Practical
'Passer-by'	2 min	30	1/20	600	400
'Look-through'	5 min	12	1/10	120	80
'Active visitor'	10 min	6	1/5	30	20
'Sales talk'	20 min	3	1/2	6	4

Again, even if the specific figures in this table can be discussed, and for practical use should be adapted to various situations, the method shows the tremendous staffing consequences of the objectives set in terms of contact quality.

One of the factors I have eliminated, so as not to complicate the method unduly, is the size of the exhibit. The absolute size in square metres or square feet of the exhibit obviously influences the time per visitor at/in your exhibit and thus the pass-through factor.

The general interest your show manages to generate is another factor that influences the time per visitor and thus the pass-through factor. Just press the button and start an audiovisual show, and we know that visitors flock around the screen. In other words, you have managed to switch a number of visitors from a 'lower' category to a 'higher' one.

Calculating space requirements

Let us apply some of the same reasoning to help us estimate more closely our space needs. Again, the figures that I suggest below may deviate from your experience. If so, use yours for your applications. The important thing is the method to estimate space requirements.

The calculations are based on the fact that, in addition to space for products and other displays, both visitors and staff require some floor area. The factors that influence the need for floor space are the number of visitors, the pass-through speed, the attention each visitor should get from the exhibit staff and the comfort you want to offer the visitor.

The same values have been used for 'time spent', 'pass-through factors' and 'attention requirement factors' as in the staff calculation model above. I have been more generous in allocating space in the 'sales talk' category of visitors, 3 square metres per person, than to the other categories, as appears from the table below. Attending staff have been calculated to need the same space as visitors. This is how the table would look:

	Visitor	+ Attention factor	= Space required factor	× Time	× sq m	= (Comfort factor)
'Passers-by'	1	0.05	1.05	1/30	1.5	0.05
'Look-through'	1	0.1	1.1	1/12	2.0	0.2
'Active visitor'	1	0.2	1.2	1/6	2.5	0.5
'Sales talk'	1	0.5	1.5	1/3	3.0	1.5

In the above table, the last column indicates the theoretical space requirement per *visitor* per *hour*; and here is what an example could look like:

	Visitors per hour	Space required per visitor/hour	Total space requirement
'Passers-by'	200	0.05	10 sq m
'Look-through'	150	0.2	30 sq m
'Active visitor'	40	0.5	20 sq m
'Sales talk'	10	1.5	15 sq m

In this example you would need some 75 square metres of free exhibit area, excluding display, etc., to accommodate your visitors in a way that is consistent with your objectives.

Calculating contact costs

For calculation purposes, let us assume staff costs of $200 a day or $25 an hour and costs for exhibit space, design, production and all other costs together of $200 per square metre of exhibit space. If the exhibit is open for five days, eight hours a day, this means that non-staff costs amount to $5 per hour/square metre.

Your actual figures may obviously deviate very much, up or down, from these figures.

If we use the assumed figures, here is how the contact costs come out, by visitor category:

Visitor category	Handling capacity in practice, per staff/hour		Space required per visitor/hour cost		Total contact
		($)		($)	($)
I	1/300	0.08	0.08	0.40	0.48
II	1/75	0.33	0.22	1.10	1.43
III	1/15	1.67	0.63	3.15	4.82
IV	1/3	8.33	2.25	11.25	19.58

Can exhibitions be compared with other communications methods?

Exhibitions seldom work alone. Usually they are combined with other communications methods to form a total communications project. Due to their special features they are seldom completely replaceable. In other words, it may not always be possible to balance the cost/value figures of an exhibition activity with those of other communications programmes. Given these limitations, it may nevertheless be a useful exercise to see if your anticipated costs are 'in the same ballpark' as the costs of reaching similar communication goals by other methods, for example, space advertising. Here is how it can be done:

1. Take the per capita cost of exposure of a well-placed, well-sized advertisement in a magazine, geared to the same kind of audience as your exhibition, and compare it with your anticipated cost per relevant exhibit visitor, who will at least see your stand.

2. Take the projected cost per visitor who will look through your stand, and compare it with the cost per capita of a good advertisement, calculated by the 'seen' figure.

3. Similarly, compare the cost of an advertisement divided by the 'read most or all' figure with the per capita cost of a relevant active visitor to your stand.

4. Finally, compare the exhibit costs per request for further information with the costs per relevant coupon received in response to space advertising.

Also, why not compare the anticipated, and the real, cost of a substantial, registered sales conversation on your stand with the cost of a salesman's call to a potential customer?

If you wish to extend this method of estimating contact costs, you may gradually include other media, for example, direct mail. While the precision of such comparisons can always be debated, they may help to make approximations towards a more balanced communications programme. Certainly they may gradually help build up clearer links between costs and benefits of various communications media, thus making the choices more professional. If comparisons are imprecise, as they no doubt must be at the beginning, at least they make it easier to apply communications research more intelligently and to request data from media representatives in more usable forms.

___Worksheet 14.1   Should we participate?___

It helps if you have answers to most of the following questions before a decision is made to participate in a major show. The exhibition organizer should be able to provide you with the answers as part of his 'media information' responsibility. Remember, the exhibition 'space salesman' should not sell space. He should sell what you want to buy, that is, contact opportunities.

It may be easier to get the answers if you ask the questions before you have signed the contract, while you still have some clout.

1. Which organization/company is promoting the show and takes responsibility for its overall quality?

2. Is a conference, congress, etc., being combined with the show? (Ask for information on location, participants, etc.)

3. Is the show a one-off or a regular event?

4. If a regular event, how often?

5. When was it first held?

6. Information on the three latest shows:

Year	No. exhibitors	No. visitors	Paid space	
			Indoors	Outdoors

    How has this information been verified?

7. Expected data for the next show:

Year	No. exhibitors	No. visitors	Paid space	
			Indoors	Outdoors

    How will this information be verified?

8.1 What kinds of visitors have access to the show?
     Only qualified people
     The general public

Set times for each

8.2 How are 'qualified people' defined?

8.3 How is visitor quality controlled?
Special invitation
Proof of identity
Otherwise

If the show is labelled 'international':

9.1 Specify the percentage of *exhibitors* from each of the most important countries achieved last time
Country
Country
Country

How were these proportions verified?

Estimated share of *exhibitors* from each country at the forthcoming show?
Country
Country
Country

How will these proportions be verified?

9.2 Specify the percentage of *visitors* from each of the most important countries achieved last time
Country
Country
Country

How were these proportions verified?

Estimated share of *visitors* from each country at the forthcoming show?
Country
Country
Country

How will these proportions be verified?

Some service and support functions:

10. On what basis will exhibit space be allocated:
First-come, first-served
Priority for previous exhibitors
Priority for members of trade association, etc.
Other (please specify)

11.1 What is the exhibition organizer doing to attract qualified visitors?

11.2 What is the organizer doing to verify visitor quality (e.g., technical qualifications, purchasing influence, product interests, etc.)?

12. What promotional aids is the organizer making available for dissemination by individual exhibitors (invitation cards, promotional brochures, other)?

Worksheet 14.2 How did it work?

There are many ways to check the results of a show, provided that you have defined objectives to measure the show performance against. A simple survey may be one way to do it, for example, by interviewing visitors as they leave the show area. Here is an example of a simple survey form:

Are you in the .... business?

Which of the following companies did you notice at the fair?

Company A
        B
        C
        D
        E
        F

Which of them did you visit?

Company A
        B
        C
        D
        E
        F

Did you talk to the staff of any of these exhibitors?

Company A
           B
           C
           D
           E
           F

What were your main reasons for visiting this exhibition?

What company (or industry) do you work in?

What is your position in your company?

15

'Face-to-face':
Meetings, conferences, speeches

In this chapter the reader will find a presentation of the characteristics of meetings and other forms of face-to-face communication with different priority groups.

It will help the reader plan, budget, execute and evaluate meetings, conferences and other face-to-face contacts as results-oriented parts of a company's total communications process.

'Face-to-face' is something special!

If it is true that all communications between business and its various contact groups are contacts between people, then it must be important to make these contacts human, as much as possible. Indeed, all other contact methods can be considered only as substitutes for person-to-person contacts. Advertisements in the press or in broadcast media, leaflets, direct mail, editorial work and all other multi-communications media are used only or mainly because they increase the reach and reduce the cost of what should, ideally, have been face-to-face contacts, the unbeatable method to create real two-way communication.

Meet your contact groups

We cannot always afford to use direct face-to-face contact. That does not mean that we should exclude it. Rather, it should always be a goal to create as much immediate, personal contact as at all possible. This implies a strong effort to:

1. Use all opportunities offered to us to reach out, to meet our contact groups in person, at meetings, conferences and gatherings arranged by those groups or by clubs, associations or unions to which they belong.

2. Specifically create such opportunities by inviting to such meetings, 'open house' and similar events, establishing advisory panels or just informal meetings, company visits or other forms of get-together.

3. Train and develop the ability and motivation of company representatives actively to use such opportunities to listen and tell the company's story.

4. Adopt the personal touch as the natural approach to most communication tasks, even when, for different reasons, other methods have to be used as carriers in the contact process.

The advantages of face-to-face meetings are obvious: no other method can beat face-to-face on such scores as penetration, acceptance, credibility and human touch. But there are also obvious disadvantages. They can be summed up in two words: time and costs. These drawbacks force us to plan our face-to-face contacts

318

with great care and to make sure that we use the face-to-face method for such parts of our total communications programme where it can give maximum return. How many communications managers allow as much time and effort for the planning of contact meetings and sessions with various priority groups as they do for advertising campaigns or for editorial contact work?

Facing your contact groups

A good way to start is to go through the priority contact areas, one by one. Consider the suggestions in Chapters 2–8! In this chapter we shall review specifically how face-to-face meetings with big or small segments of each contact area can contribute to the organization's long-term communications goals.

Meet the employees

Is there anything that should be changed in your company? It would be surprising if there wasn't.

Do the employees as a whole, or specific categories of them, have anything to do with what should be changed? It would be surprising if the answer were no.

Would an open exchange of views, face to face, with those concerned be a useful ingredient in a recipe for change? Again, it would be surprising if the answer were no.

Western industrial managers have begun to find that Japanese companies give more consideration to the opinions of the workers than American or European companies have traditionally done. Japanese workers are thoroughly briefed, not only on facts and conditions of immediate importance for the specific operations they are engaged in, but also on background, company policies, corporate aims and problems, etc., and they are encouraged to ask questions and provide their own input to the management process.

'Inefficient'? 'A waste of time'? Who can say Japanese industries are not at least as efficient as their European or American counterparts?

'It won't work here', 'Our workers are not interested'! Who knows before one has tried – wholeheartedly?

In a small company, management, staff and workers know each other naturally. They know the company's goals and problems.

They come up with ideas and suggestions jointly, often to the extent that no one really knows on which side of the desk a good idea came up. The fact that such meetings occur spontaneously does not mean that there is no need for planned informal meetings, perhaps outside the normal work environment, between managers and employees of small companies too.

But as a company grows bigger, the contact lines stretch out and sometimes become so thin that they are unable to serve as communication carriers. Then the time may have come for actively planned get-together activities.

Start this planning process, as any other communications programme, by an analysis of whom to meet and what to change.

Are there frictions between various groups of employees, staff–workers, young–old, head office staff–branch office staff, design engineers–production engineers, marketing–finance, men–women, or any other subdivisions or segments?

Are there segments of employees that management does not have satisfactory contacts with, employees that could share valuable thoughts, comments, suggestions or grievances (yes, grievances can also be valuable!)?

Take an example: assume that one of your company's main problems is the fat balance-sheet. If your supply and delivery function could speed up the handling of bulk orders, this would contribute a great deal towards slimming down the item 'products in transit'. Has anyone taken the time – beside the normal hierarchy – to sit down and talk and listen to the people in the shipping department who do the job? Not only on a very narrow item-by-item agenda basis, but on a human level, with time for free comments from those involved, and in an atmosphere that encourages an open, spontaneous exchange of views?

Some of the problems of motivation, capital utilization, working conditions, product quality deficiencies, delivery time delays and other plagues of Western industrial development could be improved or solved, if those on the floor were given a fair chance to voice their views. They would be able to contribute even more if the broad aims and problems of the company were explained to them in person-to-person meetings, where problems can be brought up in explainable terms, with time for amplification, background, examples, questions and suggestions.

So, what are you waiting for?

Meet the shareholders

Of course, you meet your shareholders. Once a year, at least, they are invited to the annual general meeting. Fortunately, not all of them come. One company I know has some 40,000 shareholders. They are invited to the annual general meeting in a hall that can take, at most, 400. It is seldom, if ever, crowded.

So what if they don't come, as long as they are invited! Should the fact that they *don't* come be taken as an *in blanco* vote of confidence in the board and management of their company? Or are there other reasons?

1. Has anything been done to get them to come, to attract them, to make the invitation compete with all other claims on a busy man's (or woman's – most shareholders in big companies happen to be women) time?

2. What day did you invite them to attend – a day in the middle of the week, when most people are supposed to attend to their work duties? Did you ever experiment to check out whether one weekday would be more attractive than any other, or did you choose a day that happened to suit your chairman's schedule?

3. What time of the day did you decide? Have you ever tried the end of the day to allow your shareholders a chance to attend after their main working hours? Or would you, as a manager, representing the interests of efficiency, profits, good working habits, really want those of your shareholders who hold regular, paid jobs to be absent from those jobs to attend a shareholders' meeting?

4. What place did you choose? Did you consider transportation facilities, timetables and other practical aspects of attending the meeting? What services did you offer those who come from other locations?

5. And – perhaps more important than any of these questions – what kind of meeting did you offer those who came, despite all the odds against? The same dreary old routine as all other companies offer? Or did you take the opportunity to give your shareholders a feeling that they are *shareholders*, that they have a *share* in your company, in the problems and difficulties their company has experienced, in the satisfactions and successes the company has scored, in the new products that have been launched, in the new facilities that the company has acquired,

in the new working methods that have been tried, in the moves up or down the competition scorecard that every company finds itself in?

6. Did you show not only what your sales figures were, but how they came out in relation to the industry in general, or your two or three closest competitors? Did the sales figures include any significant contracts that you landed? Were there any important chunks of business that you failed to get?

7. How did your company's profit performance look in comparison with competitors, with business in general, with other similar companies?

8. How did inflation, wage costs, protectionism, government measures, new EC initiatives, environmental regulations affect your company, for bad – or good?

9. Did you give your shareholders a chance to feel what your company, its products and services, accomplish in your own community, in the Third World, in your customers' industries, in the economy, to the *people* who work with them, use them or consume them?

10. How were your products and services produced, stored, distributed, designed, marketed?

11. Did you facilitate two-way communications? Did you actively encourage shareholders to send in questions before the meeting – not only offer the legally required opportunities, but really encourage questions – and did you provide the right expertise to give adequate answers? As an alternative to loading the meeting itself, did you ever consider a follow-up meeting, immediately after the legal annual general meeting, where a knowledgeable panel could be available to answer impromptu questions or questions sent in in advance?

Many companies have tried these and other methods to create meaningful exchange between the shareholders and the board and management. Others still have a lot to do. It is hard to understand how a company management can expect the public to invest their savings in a company and then give them very little of real shareholding except the dividend and a glossy annual report. Is this one of the reasons why direct private shareholding has dropped in many countries and been replaced by indirect, less personal shareholding through insurance companies, pension funds and other institutions?

The opportunity to meet the shareholders face-to-face should be so highly valued that no board or management would miss making the most of it as an important communications method with one of the most important contact areas of a company – its owners.

Even if the annual general meeting is one of the great events in a company's shareholder relations programme, it is, of course, not the only way. No matter how well you plan and prepare it, it can seldom attract a majority of the shareholders in big companies. There are also other opportunities to meet shareholders face-to-face.

Geographic distance is one factor that prevents shareholders in big companies from attending. If shareholders are spread nationwide – or worldwide – invite them to meetings with the management on a regional basis. A planned programme of regional shareholder meetings, to which other guests in that region, such as bankers and financial editors, can be invited, may help strengthen the position of your company.

Meet community leaders

The local community leaders and the citizens in general learn about a company in many ways. They read about it in the local newspapers, they hear about it from employees, they see, themselves, some of the effects it has on the community. All these impressions help form opinions, both positive and negative, about the company and what it does.

Most companies would benefit from a planned programme of local community relations. Many communications methods can be used to stay in close contact with local opinions and attitudes, but face-to-face meetings should be an important part of any such planned programme. Visits to the company, company participation in public or private meetings, staff membership in associations and political parties, create opportunities for person-to-person contacts. They take time, often management time, and should thus be planned as all other company activities, to give maximum return. The office of communications and public affairs is the normal centre of responsibility for planning, coordinating, executing and supervising such programmes, although they are not part of traditional 'advertising' or even 'public relations' departments.

Any suggestions given here can only be starters for the reader's own thinking, since the local communities are so different, ranging from big capitals to small country towns, and since companies are so different. In fact, if the company is spread nationwide, or worldwide, individual programmes may have to be initiated for a number of very different locations, where it has factories, service centres, laboratories or other facilities.

What is required is a listing of local authorities, clubs, associations, councils and other groups that you may want to develop a face-to-face relationship to, or that may want a relationship with you. Here are some examples of groups that may appear on such a list (for an in-depth discussion, see also Chapter 4).

- The local town or city council, with its elected members and the professional staff that work closely with them, preparing and executing the decisions made by the council.
- The mayor, alderman, chairman, council president or other top man – or woman – who is the spokesman and leader of community affairs, as well as the staff around that person.
- Specialized local committees and offices, dealing with such issues as employment, business development, environment regulation, roads and transportation, education, long range planning, real estate regulation, taxation, etc.
- Local schools and other educational institutions.
- Service clubs, such as Rotary, Lions, Zontas and similar organizations.
- Local sports and hobby clubs, if they have a relation with the company and its work.
- Special interest organizations, such as local environmentalist groups, 'women's rights' groups, etc.
- Political parties, especially those with strong views for or against companies of your type.
- Groups or associations of any kind, in which your employees, customers, bankers or suppliers are strongly represented.

From a gross listing, specifying these various categories, it is easy to make up a 'short-list' of high-priority groups, with a closer definition of the issues that are of concern for each group, their present position or opinions on these issues, and your possibilities to contribute.

And then the time has come to make a time-table, to select the company spokesmen who are best suited for each of these contact tasks, to brief them, to run a programme, and to create continuous follow-up of results. In this work, don't forget the two-way nature of a good communications programme. That means that relevant opinions and attitudes among the priority groups should be transmitted to decision-makers in the company. Meeting interested parties in the local community is one ingredient in this awareness-building process.

Meet the government

The same consideration given to local community contacts applies also to regional and national government bodies, politicians and special interest groups. They may be different in that distances are usually longer and the contact persons in your company are normally on a higher level. Consequently, opportunities for face-to-face meetings have to be nurtured, planned and prepared more carefully.

A physical listing of priorities – important in all planned contact work – is essential in government contacts. It ensures that none of the really significant contact points is overlooked, that the right issues are analysed and documented properly, that the best contact persons for the company are selected and properly briefed and that the follow-up work is adequate. The follow-up work includes reporting back to others in the company the findings and results of meetings with government staff, with a listing of appropriate action to be taken in various line functions.

Meet the educators

As with other contact areas, personal contacts with key groups in the educational field are important parts of a planned contact programme. Take opportunities offered or created to appear before teachers' meetings, conferences and courses, get involved in school boards, invite teachers to visit the company and offer teachers and other educational staff openings for practice work in the company.

Consider also, in your inventory of educators, such institutes or schools where future teachers are being trained. As a long-range investment, it might give an even better return than working with those who are already in the midst of their career.

Teaching is a big profession, ranging from junior stages to the highest academic ranks. Be sure to make priorities, based on the company's situation. Geographic location, special technical and business interests, stages from which you recruit are among the criteria you will use. In addition, consider long-range 'political' issues of concern to your company and to business in general. It may well be those considerations that are given top ranking when investing in various forms of personal contacts, rather than other communication methods. Personal contact may have maximum impact in situations where 'politics' in a wider sense plays an important part. Is there any better way to convey a message to a group of teachers or students, whose only knowledge of the business world comes from political writers who misunderstand or misinterpret business, than through a sympathetic and committed businessman, who can add real life experience, emotion and belief to the pure facts of how business works?

Meet the customers

Obviously, your sales staff meets customers every day. In fact, most of traditional market communications has as its main purpose to make the personal sales work more productive, more efficient and more profitable. There is no doubt that most companies regard personal customer contacts very important, with non-personal customer contacts as a support to the personal selling process.

However, there are other forms of face-to-face contacts with the market than the immediate selling process. Such forms can be developed and refined to serve the company in its broad marketing aims, but also for still wider purposes. This is especially true, if the 'market' is defined to include not only the direct purchasing influences, but also other categories, such as the financial, technical, marketing and general management of customer industries, and, furthermore, other commercial contacts that contribute to your success in the market-place, such as suppliers of raw material, products and services.

Industrial and business organizations and Chambers of Commerce provide excellent platforms for such face-to-face contacts. What does your score card look like in such contact work:

1. Who in your company keeps tabs on your company's representation in such contexts?
2. Who are registered as members or contact persons?
3. How active have they been lately?
4. Have they volunteered to serve in central functions where their voice will be heard and their opinions considered?
5. Have they made presentations, led study groups, taken part in

committee work or contributed papers or studies on important issues?

6. Have they invited the organizations, local chapters or special groups from them to visit your facilities and get to know your industry?

Some branch organizations come very close to real customer categories. A company in the construction equipment business certainly wants to play a role in builders' associations. A company selling paper wants to keep in touch with printers' associations. In the 1980s and 1990s it may also be useful to consider the spread of influence that has originated in countries like Germany, France and the Scandinavian countries, where trade unions and other forms of worker representation are playing a part in policy and day-to-day decisions. A company in the office equipment business will not necessarily focus all its efforts on the office managers but also on office workers and their trade unions. A company that makes hand tools which are less noisy than competing brands would like to make its message known to the factory workers and their unions. Good personal contacts and personal presentations at meetings and conferences should be part of that communications process.

A form of face-to-face contacts with customers that some companies have tried is setting up advisory panels, on a permanent basis or for limited projects. Those who *have* tried this are mostly in consumer fields, while companies, selling to business and industry, often claim that they have excellent contacts with their customer companies through the sales staff. Creating such contact channels may be helpful in a company's long-range planning, for example, in planning the research efforts, in planning geographic priorities for new plant or service facilities, in planning sales methods, delivery methods, service plans, credit and payment programmes as well as the general 'positioning' of the company in the market-place.

A planned communication process

No matter which contact area you want to communicate with through face-to-face methods, a common feature is that, in general, such contacts require more planning and preparation than they usually get. Higher return on the time and effort put into personal contacts is a result of setting the right priorities, selecting the best contact persons, giving them appropriate training and support and preparing meetings and conferences professionally.

Setting the right priorities

The planning work is certainly part of the communication manager's responsibility.

The first step in that planning process is selecting the priority contact groups, from the range of contact areas discussed above, in this chapter and elsewhere in this book, in cooperation with top management and functional managers. This will guide much of the planning that follows.

For each of the priority groups, there are 'critical issues' that 'they' are likely to bring up or that 'we' want to discuss. Selecting and evaluating those critical issues can give very important indications to company policy and strategy development.

Selecting the best contact persons

The analysis of contact groups and critical issues will almost automatically bring to mind staff in the company who will be good spokespersons for the company. In some cases top management will be the first category to be considered. Top management has the authority and the wide outlook that will be indispensable in many cases. Yet, it is not – and should not be – the only source for recruiting company spokespersons in an active person-to-person communications programme. The simplest reason is availability. Everybody knows that the bottle-neck is at the top of the bottle. If management is seen as the only staff resource in building person-to-person communications programmes, the programmes are bound to fail for bottle-neck reasons.

There are other reasons as well for widening the circle of staff representing the company. Depending on the contact group, those reasons can be age, sex, educational level, professional background and expertise or decision-making responsibilities.

Once the right people have been selected and trained, make a list of those who are willing and able to appear in contact roles. Let it be known that the company is prepared to accept invitations for speaking assignments and other forms of face-to-face meetings. One way to do this is to establish a 'speaker's bureau', listing staff members prepared to make presentations to various contact groups. Other ways are to invite relevant contact groups to the company. Set up advisory panels, with categories of employees, customers, shareholders or other groups. Set up appointments to meet people of importance, either in groups or on an individual basis.

Giving them appropriate training and support

The importance of each meeting they are going to run, the time invested and the benefits/damages that a good or bad meeting could result in means that the selected spokespersons should get good *training* in advance. A minimum requirement is that the communications manager is confident that they have the personality, the knowledge and the presentation skills that will make them good 'ambassadors' for the company in the groups they will meet.

Many managers are reasonably good at person-to-person communications; it is after all one of the important factors in selecting and promoting somebody to a managerial position. Still, even experienced managers will benefit from *training* in personal communications skills. Many companies have good experience from engaging outside consultants, specializing in personal appearance, presentations, voice-training, speech-writing, body language, or any other specialities which together make up the art of person-to-person communication. Managers and other company staff who get the benefit of such training are likely to be able to make more of their other skills than those who do not.

In addition to personal training, the selected spokespersons will require the right kind of *support material* to be really effective. The subjects will be chosen depending on the company's special situation, for example, environmental issues, free trade versus protectionism, dividend policies, the reason for company profits, the impact of automation (computerization, robots, etc.) on employment, product responsibility policies, trade with and industrialization of developing countries, worker protection, social responsibility, the role of productivity, consumerism, taxation or any other issue that is seen as important, by the company or by 'the other side'.

They will need prepared 'position papers', explaining the company's opinion, viewpoints and reasons on such 'critical issues' as those listed above. Try to limit each paper to one page, using short sentences and key words, rather than elaborate 'legalese'. Add concrete examples, case stories and references!

Such position papers will require the endorsement of top corporate staff and may, incidentally, have positive side effects, in addition to making face-to-face communications easier and safer.

Those 'position papers' that you expect to get most attention and to be most widely used can be converted into draft speeches, or fully prepared speeches with appropriate slides or overhead illustrations.

Make an inventory of printed matter to match those issues and, if required, produce additional material. Screen the films available and consider, if necessary, the production of new films or other audiovisual aids.

Preparing meetings and conferences professionally

If the value of the time of those attending is taken into account, meetings are expensive. Sending an invitation to a meeting is therefore quite a responsibility. On the other hand, a well-run meeting can produce more significant results than almost any other communications method.

Organizing effective meetings and conferences is an art in itself that requires a high degree of professionalism. For big or especially important conferences it is advisable to find and use specialized professional expertise from outside consultants, if the company does not have it available inside.

There are, however, some important checkpoints that could be helpful to consider, either in organizing conferences of a more mundane kind or in briefing an outside specialist before a meeting.

What are the objectives of the meeting?
As other forms of communication, a meeting is usually intended to create change, in levels of awareness and understanding, in attitudes or in behaviour/action patterns. Defining the objective as closely as possible in terms that fit the reference frames of all those attending is the first and compulsory step to take. It is a useful discipline to put it in writing in the invitation: 'The objective of this meeting is to . . .' or 'This meeting will be considered successful, if . . .'.

Who will participate?
How many do you expect? What categories in terms of age, sex, professional, personal and educational background will be represented among the participants? Do they know each other before the meeting or not? What mood will they be in? What common interests will they have in relation to the subject – and in what regards will they have different or even opposing views? How can we prepare the participants, before the meeting: advance material, questionnaire, challenges . . .?

Who will chair the meeting?
One of 'us' or one of 'them'? What do we know about him/her? Need for pre-meeting preparation?

What is the environment?
Will it match the meeting style we want? Will the meeting be on 'our' home ground or on 'theirs', or on 'neutral' ground? How formal or informal is the setting? How can the environment, room layout, seating, lectern or not, lights, ventilation, microphones, etc., be influenced to suit the purpose of the meeting? Food, drink, other 'ambience factors'?

What are the time factors?
At what time of day will the meeting take place? What will the participants have done before the meeting? What are they typically planning to do after the meeting? How long will it take? Is the meeting a one-off or is it one in a series? What were the subjects/experiences/locations of earlier meetings? What do you know about future meetings?

What presentation method will be most appropriate?
How much audience involvement do you want? Questions? Comments? Discussion? Controversy? On that basis, choose between formal lecture, symposium style, question/answer model, panel, group work, 'witnesses', open forum, dramatization, role play, combinations?

What presentation aids should be used?
Film, video, slides, overheads, blackboard, flip-chart, documentation, handouts, models, real examples? Note-pads? Check that all equipment is available and in order.

Arrangements around the meeting?
Promotion, transportation, security, stand-by for key speakers, entertainment, refreshments, photography, press/radio/television, VIP guests, souvenirs, gifts?

How to evaluate the results
Evaluation should close the loop between objectives and results, so the evaluation forms, etc. should be linked to the expressed pre-meeting objectives. What changes in awareness, attitudes, preferences, action patterns, have been achieved? Can it be assessed through feedback from the participants? From others involved? Direct at the meeting? After the meeting? Surveys, competitions, quizzes, audits, evaluation forms?

What's next?
A meeting is seldom an island unto itself. Most meetings have a pre-history and practically all meetings should be followed up one way or another. Put participants on a mailing list, appropriately coded for segmented follow-up mailings of press articles, research reports, additional documentation, new material on the subject. With all mailings, enclose response cards, questionnaires or other instruments to create a dialogue.

Evaluation of face-to-face communications

Evaluating more closely the results of the total programme and of individual parts of it is, as always, a function of the objectives you have defined. With well-defined objectives, results can be measured against the objectives in person-to-person communications as in other communications work.

Overall programmes and priorities can be evaluated with the help of categorized awareness and opinion surveys, repeated at intervals before, during and after the programme period.

Individual items can be tested with very simple methods that will gradually help refine the presentations and programmes. To test the efficiency of prepared speeches, you can prepare a questionnaire – perhaps 'disguised' as a competition with prizes – with multiple-choice questions on some of the key issues or items included in the speech. A less exact, but hopefully satisfying, result of your programme will be the demand for participation that your company will experience from groups that you have an interest in. Register the requests from various categories and check the figures periodically with past performance and with your priorities, as they are adapted to new situations for the company as a whole.

A well-coordinated programme of this kind, in combination with other communication methods, will probably do your company a lot of good. It will, above all, contribute to give your company an image of being human, personal and responsible. Furthermore, it will create opportunities for feedback of attitudes and opinions, which will have an impact on future policies and help guide the company's future development towards its business goals.

16

'The synergy of an orchestra':

Combining the instruments

In this chapter the reader will find advice and thoughts on how to combine various communications methods into 'campaigns' and other forms of coordinated programmes.

It will help the reader plan, budget, execute and evaluate total result-oriented programmes using a full range of 'tools' from the 'communications tool-box'.

The medium and the message

Did Marshall McLuhan really mean that 'the medium is the message'? As I see it he wanted to call our attention to the fact that different media have different qualities, qualities that make them suitable in varying degrees for certain communications tasks. Perhaps more than that: the medium as such influences the users, senders as well as recipients, and colours the information or communication process in such terms as emotional value, credibility, suitability to convey facts, capacity to 'trigger action' and several other factors.

To some extent, the medium *becomes* the message.

'Reach' and 'time' as factors in media selection

While all these aspects influence the media choice and media balance of the practitioner in business communications, there are two that may be even more important in the day-to-day work, that is:

- the 'reach' of various media, and
- the 'time lag'.

The desirable reach can range from one key person to millions. It can be concentrated to a limited geographic area or cover the world. It can be geared to highly specialized and closely-defined target audiences in terms of their profession, age, sex, income level, educational background, industrial field, employment position or other factors, or it can be very broad and general.

By the same token, the time factor may vary, from the kind of rush communications needs where 'yesterday!' is the only adequate answer, to, say, anniversaries or factory inaugurations, where you may have years for the communications planning. Figure 16.1 illustrates the *time* versus *reach* aspect for some frequently used communications media.

The exact location, horizontally or vertically, of all media can be discussed. Some media are missing and some of those indicated are of limited use in some situations. The reader should feel free to take the idea and adapt it so that it suits individual needs more closely,

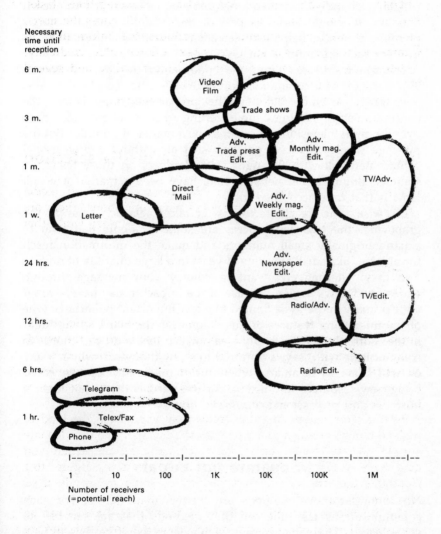

Figure 16.1 *Time/reach diagram of various media*

for example, by extending the time axis to cover not only the time lag from conception to reception but also the 'duration' of various communication methods. As an example, a leaflet may last for years, and a catalogue usually does, while a radio or television message flashes by and is gone in a moment – although, of course, its effects may be long-lasting.

After such individual reworkings and adaptations of the time/reach diagram, it should serve as part of the reader's communications planning tool-box, helping to establish an optimum overall 'media mix' for each communication task.

The time from conception to reception is not the only time factor. The duration of a communication effort *after* the reception stage is one thing. Another factor is the preparation time before the conception stage. As an example, getting an editorial message across over the right television stations may be a matter of minutes. But the message would not have got across at all without a professional contact network with the right staff members on those television stations. Building that network may have been a matter of years. How is that time accounted for?

Likewise, the reach factor is certainly elastic. Gossip, the grapevine, the two-step process are some elements that tend to expand originally small numbers and make the information reach formidable, like small amounts of yeast in a large quantity of dough. You may, alternatively, want to convey your message through widespread news media, because of the impact it may have, even if your primary audience is limited to a few important politicians. One of the interesting features of this diagram is the blank space. Right in the centre there is an empty area – which media do you choose to communicate with, say, a hundred to a few thousand, within a day or two? This may be an area where future media development could bring new resources into action, for the need is there, not least in business and professional communications.

Separate but equal

No communications methods are 'better' than others. For each communications task one can find methods that are suitable, to some extent. The communications manager, therefore, has to be a generalist in communication methods, knowing enough of each method to be able to estimate and choose the best method, or combination of methods, for each task he is facing.

This is no small requirement, since the range of communications methods is wide – and growing. It means that the communications manager should have basic knowledge in graphic principles, printing methods and printing techniques (even new developments), in press and broadcast journalism, in advertising planning and mechanics, in media planning and selection, in direct mail and similar techniques, in audiovisual techniques, in exhibition planning, in preparing and running meetings and conferences and in communications measurement and research. Since pictures enter as an element in – or in themselves are – important communications methods, evaluating photographic and artwork is a useful ability. Spoken and written languages always play a part – so it is important to be able to handle them properly.

If 'media management' is not one of his strong sides, he should have somebody very close to him to assist in that selection process, which has to be made again and again. Creativity and accountability in selecting and combining communications methods are as useful and vital as in other forms of human relations.

United we stand

To do his job well, the orchestra conductor does not have to be able to play every instrument as a maestro, but he should know them well to distinguish the role of each one of them in the total performance. In the same way, the communications manager should know enough about the various media alternatives to give each of them a proper role.

In addition to the general knowledge of each of the instruments, the conductor needs the ability to coordinate the whole orchestra, all the instruments, into one entity, where the sum total of the contributions from each instrument is bigger than all the individual parts, one by one.

Real professionalism in communications consists in no small measure on the ability to combine media into a synergetic system for individual communications jobs, and for overall communications programmes.

In such exercises it comes out clearly how useful it is to separate, mentally and organizationally, the two aspects of all communications projects, the analysis and definition of contact areas and the application of various media techniques. If, say, the method of media advertising is regarded as a sales tool, rather than as a communications method, it may very well be under-utilized for other communications tasks than sales promotion. If editorial work is considered as part of an esoteric 'public relations' concept, then it may be used more or less exclusively for government, community or financial relations, depending on the inclination of the public relations officer.

Let us take a few cases and discuss possible media combinations to show how useful it is to think creatively across the whole media register. The media combinations suggested here may not always be ideal for your taste. The point is, for each communications task one should be prepared to consider *all* the instruments at your disposal, then, when the score has been analysed, one engages the instruments selected, at the time that fits the purpose.

Communications task 1 – attracting youth labour

Objective: To increase your company's attractiveness in the youth labour market.

The specific goal: to receive 200 applications from eligible candidates for industrial jobs.

You have analysed the opinions of the group, you know how they feel about your company and as a consequence some changes, among them in the hiring and training procedures, have been initiated. The message has been carefully discussed and finally agreed on. Other preparations have been made. The discussion is now focusing on the 'media mix'. What media should be considered in that discussion? Consider some of the following:

1. *Printed matter*: A leaflet giving the background of the company and a summary of employment conditions, training and career opportunities may be the backbone of the whole programme. Distribution in combination with other steps indicated below. Printed career orientation material to teachers, leaders in youth organizations and employment agency staff.

2. *Editorial work*: You will certainly want to contact the editors of the youth pages of the newspapers and the local youth radio channels or editors concerned. You will consider inviting the editors of the school papers to see your plant, as well as the editors of the more popular, specialist youth magazines. Maybe you will set up a contest or competition jointly sponsored by

338

you and some of these media. Articles to appear in staff magazine, inviting employees' children to consider employment.

3. *Media advertising*: Radio advertising, if available, in combination with popular youth programmes, is a possibility. Listeners invited to request leaflet (and poster). Space advertising in attractive youth magazines and in connection with youth-oriented editorial material in the newspapers.

4. *Direct mail*: Checking availability of addresses on a cross-referenced age/education basis for a creative response-oriented direct approach campaign.

5. *Pictures/visual media*: Cinema advertising, where available. A non-stop video film, as part of the exhibition below, and posters with high-fashion artwork.

6. *Exhibitions*: A travelling exhibit, with light display units and a video programme, distributed to schools and employment agencies. Accompanied by leaflets and by special career orientation material for teachers and employment counsellors.

7. *Face-to-face*: Company staff offer to make vocational training presentations in schools, in combination with exhibit, leaflets and teacher programmes. Students in appropriate categories invited to visit your plant.

8. *Coordination/synergy*: Messages and visual identity, where applicable, coordinated throughout the media range. Leaflet and poster referred to in other media.

Communications task 2 – handling an environment protest

Objective: Your company has been attacked – unfairly, in the company's opinion – by an environment protection group, who claim that you regularly pump unauthorized quantities of harmful chemicals into the local river. The communications task is to make your emission standards, procedures and control system known to those concerned. The various contact groups have been defined and their positions have been clarified through sample interviews.

What would the media considerations include? Perhaps something like this:

1. *Printed matter*: Copies of authentic internal instructions and verified test results to be reproduced and distributed to all

members of the environmentalist group, to community leaders and to others concerned.

2. *Editorial work*: Editors from local newspapers and radio stations invited to check your internal procedures and systems. Dramatized measurement operation. Article in your staff magazine to ensure your own staff are informed of the situation. National environmentalist magazine provided with complete fact material and offered personal interview with company spokesman.

3. *Media advertising*: Advertising in local newspapers to ensure that your message comes across in the correct way, with all facts and figures exactly right.

4. *Direct mail*: Hard data as described above, sent by mail to environmentalist group, to local and regional community leaders, to local and regional press, to teachers in local schools and others concerned.

5. *Pictures/visual media*: Photographer commissioned to take extensive series of photos from river area, for use in exhibit, for press releases and in slide presentation.

6. *Exhibitions*: Screen exhibit for city library and staff canteen, later to be used as bank window display.

7. *Face-to-face*: Speech with slides on environmental protection in the chemical industry, for presentation in environmental groups, schools and local service clubs.

8. *Coordination/synergy*: Unified message, 'The Chemical Industry Cares' in all media. All visual material coordinated.

Communications task 3 – new factory start-up

Objective: Your company is going to start a new factory in Middletown. The communications objective is to get the new factory accepted and integrated into town life at an early stage. Attitude measurements have been made and you know the basic pattern of positive and negative reactions that can be expected. As a communications manager, you have got the negative reactions considered in the planning of the new factory: fears of excessive road traffic have been alleviated through an improved traffic and loading system, fears of too heavy water demands from the river have been considered, and a more water-efficient production process has been introduced. The factory is in the build-up stage, and production will start eight to ten months from now.

Which media will you consider in the 'launching' of the new factory?

1. *Printed matter*: A basic eight-page leaflet will be produced, showing the location of the factory, explaining the production process and the products and giving details about employment and training opportunities it will create.

2. *Editorial work*: Initial presentation to the editors of the local newspapers and radio stations. During building and start-up they are to receive continuous progress reports, as the building work proceeds. Information on hiring procedures and progress. Background information and invitations to visit the building site at suitable stages. Increased production resources featured in customer and internal house magazine.

3. *Media advertising*: Ads in local media: a backgrounder, a progress report ad and an inauguration ad. Inauguration ad also in international trade press.

4. *Direct mail*: Progress reports, with cover letter signed by the new manager to all members of city council and to key citizen groups.

5. *Pictures/visual media*: Architect's sketches reproduced, photos taken during building process, combined into a slide presentation, and for use in press releases and inauguration material.

6. *Exhibitions*: Pictures from factory construction progress integrated into all regular trade fairs in which company takes part. Local exhibition in library or bank?

7. *Face-to-face*: Personal presentation of the new factory, by the manager or other staff, offered to local service clubs, Chamber of Commerce and industry association, with or without site visits, as well as to national specialist groups and 'concerned citizens' groups'.

8. *Coordination/synergy*: Safe production process, employment opportunities and the new manager are consistent themes. Illustrations/photos give synergy effects.

I have purposely omitted any sales-oriented cases, since they are described in many other books and articles.

What is interesting to note is that the media mix and imagination is much the same, whether the objectives are 'sales-oriented' or 'PR-oriented'. It is, in other words, the same type of challenges that meets a communications manager in his media selection job, irrespective of whether he is on the sales promotion side or if he works more with different aspects of community, staff, government or other contact area relations. The tools are very much the same, since they are communications tools, which, in themselves, can be used very much for very different messages, and for different types of contact work. The communications manager needs to know them all, to make the right selection and to make the appropriate coordination between the media categories he puts into gear.

Budgeting and evaluating media performance

In the communicator's work situation, media have no value as such. There are no 'good' or 'bad' media. Their only value lies in how well they perform the communications job they are expected to do in the given situation.

The first part of this chapter indicated some factors to be considered in selecting an appropriate mix of media and methods. We have then reviewed some possible media combinations for different communications tasks. This section will sum up and try to give cost/value factors to consider in the process.

Reach

How well do we know and how well can we define the audience we want to establish contacts with? How many are they? What are their characteristics and how can they be used for media selection?

If we want to reach a big number – or even a small number – of people whom we do not know very well, advertising or editorial publicity may be cost-effective methods. Obviously, within the advertising/editorial publicity methods group there is a wide variety in reach, from network television to closely defined trade publications.

The more closely one can home in on audience characteristics, the more cost-effective can the media selection process become – provided there are media that match your audience profile. Various forms of printed matter can come in as parts of the communications methods chosen. If the target audience can be narrowed down to small, closely-defined categories, or even to specific individuals, the media choice would tend to be direct mail or face-to-face meetings. Exhibitions could come in almost anywhere on the 'reach' scale, as would audiovisual presentations.

Time factors

How quickly do we have to get our message across and how long do we want the information process to work?

Radio and television editorial contacts provide the fastest communications, but requires that the content is suitable for it and has editorial value. Press editorial material and radio commercials can be produced rapidly and can be published or broadcast at short notice.

Four-colour printed material may take a long time to produce, but there are many forms of printed matter that are very responsive to tight schedules. Direct mail can be timed fairly precisely, as can many kinds of space advertising.

At the other end of the time range are advertising in monthly magazines, where four-colour creation and production may take months, to which must be added one or two months in booking and press time. On the other hand, one can expect the impact period to be longer using the 'slow' media than from the 'fast' media, so it all depends on what you want to achieve.

Anticipated results

Certain media are more suitable than others for the kinds of result that you may be looking for in a specific situation.

For broad exposure, aiming at changes in general *awareness*, few methods beat advertising in the daily press or in broadcast media. Advertising and editorial publicity can create similar awareness results in more targeted audiences, using specialized press.

To reach a higher interest level, aiming at changes in *attitudes* or opinions, advertising is also a useful method, if the impact can be high, through frequency, creativity, colour, size, or if advertising can be combined with other methods, such as direct mail, editorial work and exhibitions.

If changes in action patterns, in terms of response, is the result aimed for, again high-impact advertising can be used, either alone or in combination with any of the other methods available.

Emotional values

In addition to the 'rational' reach-, time- and result-related considerations, there are emotional factors that influence the choice of communications methods. Television advertising can create an

343

emotional impact that cannot be generated in a trade magazine, even if the 'rational' factors are there. An exhibition that engages hearing, smell, touch and other senses or a three-dimensional piece of direct mail can be more emotional than a catalogue or a brochure, which, in turn, can give additional impact by appearing to be factual.

'Other things being equal . . .'

Many experts maintain that, 'other things being equal', editorial press relations, followed by direct mail, are the most cost-effective methods and that product and company brochures, films, exhibitions and advertising are less cost-effective. But 'other things' are seldom equal, so one can never really escape from painstaking calculation before each project, followed by an evaluation process. Unless, of course, as seems to be the case in many communications projects, 'money is no object'.

Part III

Measuring communications results

This part will help the reader define objectives, measure results and improve the return on investment in communications.

17

'It can't be done':
But it must

In this chapter the reader will find a thorough discussion of one of the classic problems in business-to-business communications, that of measuring the results of communications projects and programmes. The need for setting specific objectives is emphasized and techniques for doing so are outlined.

The chapter will help the reader identify communications needs, establish benchmarks, set specific targets (quantitative and qualitative) and select appropriate measurement methods to make communications result-oriented in the same sense as any other company function.

'If you don't know where you're going . . .'

It is not true, as they say on some of those little cards you may have seen:

> 'If you don't know where you're going, any road will take you there.'

There is another variation, that may be slightly, but only slightly, better:

> 'If you don't know where you're going, you're likely to end up somewhere else.'

The truth is, of course, that if you don't know where you're going, you will never know if you got there or not. You will not even know if you ended up somewhere else.

Can communications results be measured?

There are managers in other fields, and even communications professionals, who maintain that it is impossible to measure the results of communications work, especially in business-to-business communications. Considering all the money, talent and effort that go into business communications, it would be sad, indeed, if this were true.

Whether communications results can be measured is not a matter of communications measurement methods, opinion polls and their reliability, ad coupon responses and their value, media surveys, exhibition traffic or direct mail reach. Neither is it a question of in-depth – or superficial – psychology, perceptions research, psycho-analysis, charts or diagrams. It is not a matter of technique. It is not even a matter of money or budgets. At least not primarily.

The main problem in measuring the results of communications work is not measuring results. It is in defining *in advance* what you want to achieve and defining those objectives and targets in terms that make them clear, understandable, operational and measurable.

The important step in creating accountability is not seeing if you succeeded. It is deciding where you are going. It is a process that requires professionalism, experience, know-how and one more factor that seems to be even less frequent among many of those who are involved in a company's communications process. We shall return to that factor later. In this chapter the reader is invited to go through a step-by-step process, including suggestions on how to:

- Define communications objectives.
- Evaluate some of the main components of a communications project (audience, message, 'sender', form).
- Analyse methods and media channels.
- Use formal research.

After reading the chapter, the reader will not necessarily know everything about communications research, but he or she will feel more comfortable in making target definitions and evaluation a natural part of professional communications work.

How to define communications objectives

A big plus

Let us look at this process from a positive background – working from a big plus (+) sign.

The + sign in this case divides the planning and accountability process into four fields:

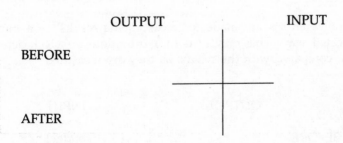

Communications managers, consultants, agencies, media staff and others involved are usually well acquainted with the field at the bottom right corner, the INPUT/AFTER field:

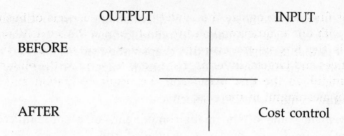

This is the field in which accountants and others check all the invoices that have come in after an event or a campaign, to see whether the sum total of all costs fitted within the budget, the amount in the INPUT/BEFORE field.

Comparisons between the INPUT/BEFORE and INPUT/AFTER fields are made as a matter of routine, at least for all major events, programmes, projects or activities:

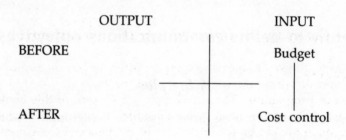

Everybody feels at home in this process – although not always at ease.

Sometimes efforts are made to 'measure the results' in a more sophisticated way. This may lead to a procedure in which actual costs are compared with the results as they are measured:

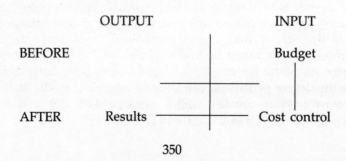

This is fine: we recognize the model from other aspects of business life – with one main exception: the empty box in the top left corner. This is the box where everything should have started, defining objectives and targets, in terms that would have made the budgeting meaningful, in the first place, and the result evaluation and cost control meaningful in the end:

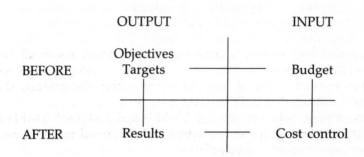

Get everyone involved – in the top left box!

Obviously, the key to measuring results afterwards is an appropriate definition of what you wanted to achieve when you started your project or programme. That is why in each section of this book we have emphasized the need to set appropriate targets. It is an area where there should be complete agreement between the communications manager, other company managers involved (the personnel manager in a staff communications project, the marketing/sales manager in a market communications project, the local plant manager in a local government communications project) and consultants and others who are supposed to contribute to the success of the whole project – and who should be held accountable for their contributions to the results! This is also the area, where the higher echelons of management should be actively engaged – more so the more sensitive, significant or simply expensive the project is.

Chances are that the more input, background and information that can be collected from everyone involved, in the early stages of the process, in the target definition phase, in the 'top left corner', the more successful the project will be. And you have a standard by which the degree of success can be measured afterwards. You will know where you're going.

Who says it is easy?

Defining the objectives is not always an easy task. For many smaller day-to-day jobs one may even say it is hardly worth the effort. You will trust your experience and that of your colleagues concerned. But for major projects and programmes, such a *laissez-faire* attitude is certainly not professional and should not be accepted.

Where is the borderline between simple routine tasks, where decisions are made on a hunch, and major or unusual tasks, where a professional decision process is a must? There may be different criteria to consider. One of them is bound to be the amount of money and work involved.

Most companies set a strict limit, in money terms, for the authority to make investment decisions at different levels of the company hierarchy. Whether communications projects are to be seen as investments or not can be debated. There are pros and cons for both opinions. It might still be practical to use the same limit as a guideline for when a communications project should be subject to a formal planning process. This would mean, in most cases, that a large brochure, a house magazine, a major exhibition project, a video or film production, a conference, and certainly most space advertising programmes, will fall in the category where careful analysis and definition of objectives and targets will have to be made.

The result should be something that can be measured, preferably in a way that is agreed between all parties concerned, before the go-ahead is given.

Tedious? Boring? Expensive? Time-consuming? Kills creativity? It may seem so to many who think communications should remain the playground at the rear of the company.

Others will see this as a very natural way to work. A planning process of this kind is certainly commonplace for most managers in functions other than communications. A plant manager will have to submit to it before he gets an appropriation for new machinery; an office manager, before he is authorized to buy a new computer system; and a production manager before he can expand his factory. Why should it be a strange procedure for a communications project?

'Whose head on the block? – not mine!'

Some may accept it in principle, but find it hard in practice. Indeed, many executives do not seem to demand the same accountability for their communications money as they do for other allocations of company resources. And quite a few consultants, advertising agencies and media salesmen are not prepared to put their heads on the block by committing themselves, in advance, to specific, quantifiable results.

This may have been understandable, and even acceptable, some years ago, when both management thinking and methodology in communications were less developed than they are today. Today we have systems – including user-friendly computer software – and techniques that can take communications planning to a higher level. There is no reason today to accept poor planning of communications projects.

'What seems to be the problem?'
Identifying the needs for communications

Some executives do not have enough confidence in what can be achieved through professional communications. It is equally true that there are occasions when executives seem to believe that a communications effort can work miracles. Neither approach is realistic or business-like.

If a company's personnel policies are ill-conceived, no staff publication, however good it is, can make the employees happy, ambitious and eager to do a good job. If a company pollutes the environment, the local government will not be fooled by a pretty four-colour brochure. If a company's product is unreliable, or if its service is bad, no advertising campaign can help it or cover it up.

In such cases, the role of the communications function is to ensure that the opinions of those groups who are affected get conveyed with satisfactory impact to the decision-makers in company management, so that basic facts are in order, before active communications money is spent.

It is as simple as this: communications efforts can be used to improve situations where an essential part of the problem is lack of appropriate communication, awareness, knowledge, understanding, contact. This is why it is important to make an evaluation of the audience in terms of awareness, attitudes or opinions before a communications project is launched, so that we do not administer the wrong medicine to an ailing patient.

Communications problems do, indeed, exist often enough. There are few management problems where lack of appropriate communication, one way or the other, is *not* a significant part of the problem.

Bad management is often linked to poor communications and good management often starts with good communications.

'This project will be considered successful, if . . .' *A practical way to formulate specific targets*

It may be desirable to work with quantitative or qualitative targets, or a combination of the two. The targets should probably also be linked to a time-frame. The following examples show a simple pattern that can be modified and applied to various situations:

'This government relations project will be considered successful if we get 1,500 orders for our new water quality checklist after the third mailing.'

'This advertising project will be considered successful if we get a coupon response from 4 per cent of our target audience after five insertions.'

'This customer magazine project will be considered successful if 50 per cent of the circulation audience confirm, after the fourth issue, that they want to remain on the mailing list.'

'This corporate advertising project will be considered successful if our new theme is recognized by 60 per cent of our target audience after one year.'

'This trade show participation will be considered successful if we get at least one hundred serious customer visits to our stand.'

'This issue campaign will be considered successful if the share of our target audience who agree to our key statement increases from 18 to 35 per cent, within the first six months.'

'This catalogue will be considered successful if 80 per cent of our distributors order additional copies within five weeks of the first mailing.'

'This press project will be considered successful if two-thirds of the journalists invited to the press trip accept our invitation and if a majority of them use material from our press kit within three months of the event.'

How to evaluate the main components

'What is there to measure?'
The two measurement aspects

Once it has been decided that a fair amount of accountability should be built into the communications work, two different measurement aspects come into play. Keeping those two aspects in mind makes it easier to stay on the track through all varieties and specialities in measurement approach, techniques and methods. One deals with where to go, the other with how to get there. Or, as the same problem is defined in other management literature, one is doing the right things, the other is doing things right.

The first aspect requires audience-related knowledge, measurement and research to find answers to the questions: 'Where to go?' or 'What to do?'

Audience-related measurement and research techniques deal with doing the right things – to the right people. They help answer questions like: 'Who are they really?' and 'What do they think, feel, know and do about us and the subject we want to bring up?' and 'What are their interests, in relation to mine?'

Based on answers to such questions, we can define targets, main message platforms and approaches before we start a project. When the project is running, or has run, progress and results can be measured, in the same terms.

The research jargon for the same thing is measurement of communications needs, attitudes, preferences, awareness levels, knowledge and behaviour patterns of priority audiences or special segments of those audiences.

This category includes demographic studies ('Who are they really?') and, perhaps, in special cases, psychographic studies ('What are they like?'), of the audiences one wants to improve communications with. It may include:

- Benchmark measurements before a programme is planned or at least started.

- Possibly measurements *en route*, if you are working on a project of long duration.

- Finally, similar measurements after an activity.

The second main aspect of communications research is methods and media-related measurement and research. This kind of research helps answer the question: 'What is the best way to get there?' It deals with doing things correctly.

Methods-related knowledge, measurement and research help answer questions like: 'What is the reach of these media, in relation to our target audience?' 'What impact are these methods and media likely to have on my audience?' 'What reactions can we expect to generate through these media?' and 'How do I design and present my message to get it across?'

The techniques are intended to help us assess how useful the various tools are for the communications jobs on the programme, and indicates what we can do to sharpen them. They include research comparing main communications channels, such as exhibitions, seminars, space advertising, editorial work, direct mail, etc., to help us make more intelligent choices between them and evaluations of individual media within these categories. Research and evaluations of the creative approach and variables, such as layout, artwork and copy, are also part of this category.

In the end, what is required is a synthesis of audience-related and media-related questions and answers, so that realistic targets can be formulated before the project, and measurements can be made afterwards, on how well we reached them.

'Who are they, really?' Evaluating the audience – in relation to our communications task

Audience-related research includes worldwide opinion polls as well as small focus groups, surveys on attitudes to big business among college students as well as purchasing patterns in the industrial tools industry. Corporate image surveys come in this category. So does an internal attitude survey on new work schedules and a customer awareness study on new materials in rock-drilling tools.

What can audience-related research be used for?
Audience-related measurement and research techniques are used to establish benchmarks, set realistic targets and measure progress and results, in terms of audience awareness, attitudes or action patterns.

They also serve as input to formulate relevant messages, in a 'copy platform', and for the creative approach that will 'move' that audience, i.e., create the change we aim for, in that specific audience, at that specific time.

They provide information on how wide the gap is between the

situation as it is and the situation we want to achieve. In that sense, they will give an indication of the impact that will be required to reach the goals, frequency, intensity, volume, size and other factors that will influence the budget. Obviously, we have to put in more effort to make a jump over a wide rift than a narrow one.

'We know our audience – we don't need any research!'

If this is the case, fine! Research in business-to-business communications has no value in itself, only to help do a better job, reduce costs or improve results.

Before the statement is accepted at face value, however, it may be useful to ask a few simple questions, including:

1. How many are they – the whole group?
2. How many of them do we want to reach and influence?
3. Where are they?
4. Men/women?
5. Age distribution?
6. Typical educational features?
7. Typical professional characteristics?
8. Typical personal features/interests?
9. Earlier contacts with or experience of our company?
10. Earlier contacts with or experience of this product/service/idea/issue?
11. Their position now in relation to this product/service/idea/issue?
12. Their position now in relation to our company?
13. What position do we want them to take?

If consistent and satisfactory answers to these and other similar questions can be obtained from reliable sources, it may be enough as a basis for the project. If not, or if the project is large-scale and important, it may be worthwhile to proceed with more formal research.

A final function of audience-related research is to test our own concepts and thoughts about our audiences. Are they real and realistic, are they based on wishful thinking – or the opposite?

Start with the hard facts. This process is often fairly simple, and can sometimes be done as 'desk research'.

'Who are they?'
Make the answer specific. Put a label on the group you want to communicate with: 'Hourly paid employees in the Singleton plant', 'All members of the Green Party in Fairfield', 'Business school teachers, teaching international business', 'Foremen and engineers in automotive assembly shops'.

'How many are they?'
An obvious question, often overlooked, but necessary in order to set quantifiable targets, to choose a combination of media and for many other purposes.

'Where are they?'
Widely scattered over a wide area, all over the country – even worldwide – or in a limited location?

'Other hard facts?'
Find and register other common characteristics, such as educational background, typical age-clusters, men or women, national or regional common denominators, or others.

Then go into soft facts. Desk research may go a long way if the group is well known from earlier contacts, but more or less formal research may be needed to find unbiased answers to questions like:

'What do they know about this – and about us?'
Is the subject familiar to them, or is it a new subject, a new approach? Do they know us well from earlier contacts (how?) or are we new to them?

'What do they think about this – and about us?'
Do they have more or less fixed opinions (what are they and are they correct, fair or wrong in our own opinion?) on this mattter? How were they established (own experience, 'competitor' information, other sources)? Or can they be assumed to have no opinions at all in this matter?

'What do they feel about this – and about us?'
Are there any special emotional 'charges' that need to be considered? Do they have any special feelings regarding us as communicators? Are we considered acceptable, trustworthy, for example, on this issue?

'What position do we want them to take?'
What benefits would they get in accepting our message? Again, try to be as specific as you can – and as honest as you can possibly be! Is our (so far tentative) message relevant to this group? Is it believable and acceptable? How will it benefit them if they 'go for it'?

'Where do we start from?'
Establishing communication benchmarks

After an analysis of communications needs, at whatever level of sophistication, with or without outside help, it should be much easier to establish specific communications benchmarks, to state where you are now in relation to your planned project. For example:

> 'Our target audience is 1,570 teachers in business schools. Most of them are in the 35-45 years age category, have a BA or an MA (28 per cent) in Business Administration. They are scattered over the country but with a majority in the capital area. Eighty-five per cent of them have little or no practical experience of international business, although they teach it. They feel it is of growing importance. The educational material they use is not up-to-date. They have a high opinion of us as an international company, but with some scepticism of us as 'big business'. They would definitely benefit from our planned three-day seminar, with practical sessions, and the educational package considered. It would improve their ability to make their teaching more interesting.'

A benchmark statement of this kind – or more detailed, if necessary – with relevant quantitative and qualitative factors specified, built on adequate research, provides a platform for everyone involved in a communications project of any kind. It defines the customer group, the segment of a local community, the staff or employee group, or any other category of target audience. It serves as a starting point in formulating the message, maybe even the 'product', the creative approach and the media strategy. It also offers a true benchmark against which targets can be specified and agreed on, before the project, and against which the results can be measured, after the project.

'What do you want to get across?'
Evaluating the contents, the message

With the benchmark study as a background, and with other input on the audience, their background, their interests and their earlier relations with the company, you can tentatively formulate a message, based on the common denominators between the interests of the audience and the company's interests. Some advertising agencies call it the 'copy platform'.

At this stage, don't bother about the form. Don't try to create slogans, headlines or special phrases. Be direct and to the point and keep the interests of the audience in focus. There are few methods better, in fact, than the General Electric 'Focus' concept (see p. 225). Test the basic message, the 'copy platform', in advance, if at all possible, on a segment of the right target audience. Is it relevant, does it feel right, is it in the interest of the audience, is it clear and understandable? Does it create the right feeling, the right reactions?

'What do you want them to know, think or feel?'
Measuring results in awareness and attitudes

There are cases when a company is not prepared to accept the response challenge, or when a company for other reasons aims for communications results in terms of attitude or awareness changes 'only'. Such activities and programmes are more difficult to specify in targets before the campaign, and in measurement of the results after the activity.

With appropriate benchmark research, focusing on existing attitudes and awareness levels before the campaign, and a commitment to make similar studies on the same pattern afterwards, it is, however, perfectly feasible to make such projects equally disciplined and measurable as response-oriented projects.

The same instruments as usual, i.e. questionnaire surveys, in-depth research methods or focus groups, are available. What about costs? The costs of establishing benchmarks and measuring results should not be a problem. It is usually quite possible to create adequate research at costs that are less than a few percentage points of the total cost of the communications programme.

360

'What do you want them to do?' Measuring results in action

In the end, in practically all cases, the communications projects should result in a change of action pattern. We want a reasonable share, as big as possible, of our target audience to start doing something in a different way from what they did before our activity, to buy a new product, ask for more information, read material we have prepared, vote differently, make decisions in a new way. As a consequence, we want, as far as possible, to set the targets of our communications activities in action terms, rather than in terms of attitudes or awareness levels. And there is no better way of doing this than in creating communications programmes that generate response.

This is obviously true about marketing communications programmes that are ultimately designed to generate buying action, direct or in the form of measurable steps towards buying. But it is equally true about most other communications programmes, geared to other audiences than customers. Feedback, response, reactions or comments are certain signs that the message has got across, has reached the other party effectively. The main ambition should always be to define targets for communications programmes in response terms. Other forms should be accepted only when all possibilities of defining targets in response terms have been tested and discarded.

The forms for response can be different, depending on media and campaign theme. At conferences and meetings, one can set up electronic or questionnaire-based systems for audience feedback. In direct mail campaigns one provides challenging response cards or telephone alternatives. In advertising campaigns, creative coupons entice the reader to respond. At trade shows, quizzes can be a useful form. In trade press articles, 'bingo cards' and other services from the publisher can be utilized.

The response challenge does not necessarily mean that the goal is to provide big numbers. Indeed, sometimes, in recruitment ads, for example, a very small number of high-quality responses is what you really want.

Responses to the first communications round can often serve, and should often be designed, as the first step in a dialogue, elevating one-way communication to a two-way process. This, combined with the 'funnel' principle, can make a communications programme really professional, perhaps leading to person-to-person contacts when the time is right.

Designing communications programmes for active response has the advantage of making the results relatively easy to measure. They do, however, put a responsibility on the communicator's shoulders. If communications programmes are designed to invite responses, they also imply a promise to handle those responses as they come in. The inevitable partner to a response-oriented communications programme, therefore, is a well-tailored and well-manned response management programme.

There are computerized, easy-to-handle software systems available for such programmes. However, even computerized programmes require a clear management commitment to the time and effort that has to be devoted to serving them.

Most of these systems are basically built up for market-oriented communications and are sold as sales lead management programmes. Several of them can be adapted to support other communications activities as well.

'Who says?'
The credibility or acceptability of the 'sender'

What you do in a communications programme is to invite the audience to join you on a trip into partly unknown territory. You want the readers, viewers, visitors or listeners to spend some of their valuable time with you and on your proposal. You expect them to open their minds to new thoughts and concepts. You want them to shed some opinions and beliefs that they have carried with them for some time and replace them with yours. Finally, you hope that they will sacrifice time, money and other assets, perhaps their own reputation in their environment, by accepting what you suggest and committing themselves to it.

Would you join somebody on a trip like this without a basic feeling of trust and confidence in him?

The degree of confidence that a 'receiver' of messages has in the 'sender' impacts on the whole communications process more than any other isolated factor. Building a platform of confidence in the 'sender' is, or should be, the stated objective of most corporate communications efforts. With a strong platform of confidence, the impact of all separate message and the productivity of other communications investments improves substantially. Without it, even the best efforts will fail.

The practical research implications of this statement in day-to-day communications work are worth considering. Do you know the credibility value of your company as a spokesman, a 'sender', to different audiences and on different topics? If IBM makes statements on computers in business situations, they have a well-deserved credibility base, at least in business audiences. If they make statements on other issues, or to other audiences, the situation may well be completely different.

Before taking off on a communications venture, especially if it has new aspects, test your company's credibility in the intended audience and on the topics you will cover. Such tests can be made with a 'profile' survey method, at costs that can be calculated accurately in advance by most professional opinion research consultants. (Cf. Figure 17.1.)

And, of course, every time an audience is invited to take a trip, make sure that the trip with you takes them to places they will like. If not, it is not likely that they will ever go on another trip with you again.

'How do we break the ice?'
Evaluating the form, the presentation

Going back to the profile of your audience, looking at such factors as age, sex, educational background, geographic location, industry category, personal position, etc., and matching it with the environment you plan to provide for your message is the starting point. Here are some key questions:

'What would their reason be:
    to read that magazine – and to select my article or my ad,
    to visit that show – and to look for my booth,
    to read that brochure – and do something about it,
    to open that letter, accept my message and respond to it,
    to see that video – and start thinking differently?'

What are they looking for? What would they expect to get out of it, professionally or personally?

Will your presentation match their expectations? How does it fit the frame of mind of typical members of your target audience in that environment? Are the illustrations appropriate? Is the language right? Does it weaken or reinforce your credibility, your message, your impact?

Testing creative approaches can be quite a sophisticated task. The techniques for formal pretesting of creative alternatives exist, but the

363

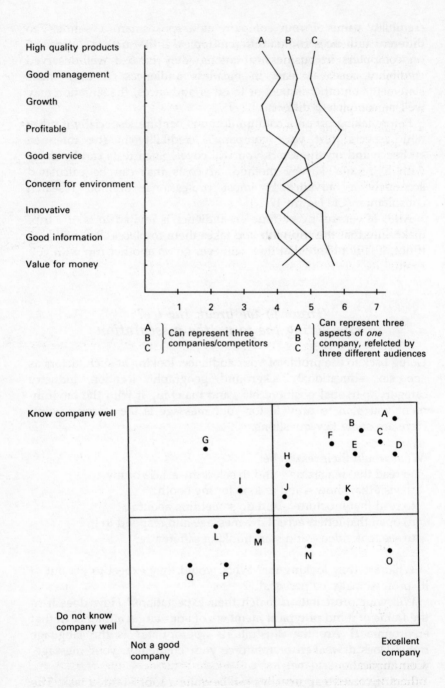

Figure 17.1 *Two basic ways of presenting corporate image profiles*

procedure can be expensive and time-consuming to an extent that prevents it in many business-to-business situations.

Fortunately, there are useful guidelines, especially for space advertising. 'Copy Chasers' in the American magazine *Business Marketing* list ten criteria, reproduced as Figure 11.2 on p. 228.

While the criteria have been designed primarily for advertising in the business-to-business context, they contain ideas and experience, appropriate to other communications methods as well. They deserve consideration whenever you face an important communications task. They provide an excellent base for 'do-it-yourself testing' and can be applied also in more formal tests of creative approach.

If your activity is a major one in which you plan to invest substantial sums, make draft copy versions and have them professionally copy tested. Ask questions in terms and with words that make it possible for you to duplicate them when you check acceptance of the message, after the campaign.

If it is not possible to go for a full-scale copy testing, it may at least be worth the trouble to make simple readability tests, checking the length and complication level of words and sentences. 'No word more than three syllables, no sentence more than five words' was a rule a newspaper editor used to give his new journalists. You may not want to take that rule literally, but understanding a text is seldom hampered by simple words and simple grammatical structures.

How to analyse media

'I don't believe in trade shows.'
Evaluating communication channels, methods and media

The responsibility stops with the buck
All the tools in a carpenter's tool-box may be very good. Yet he would not dream of using a hammer to cut a piece of wood to the right shape; and even for the simple task of hitting a nail, one hammer may be better than another.

A communications manager has a wide range of tools in his tool-box. Each group, each communications channel, may be excellent for its purpose. As we have discussed earlier, trade shows have their specific advantages over customer magazines, conferences and meetings over staff publications, direct mail over telemarketing and the trade press. Even within a category, each individual tool has its specific applications, based on its unique characteristics. Not all publications are alike, neither are all trade shows equally useful for all purposes.

The selection of channels is a big responsibility. There are few areas where the communications professional can contribute as much to the productivity of the communications process as in evaluating and selecting the best channels and media for each task. Conversely, mistakes in the channel and media selection process can never be compensated for by exemplary messages and excellent creative artwork. If the message is sent in the wrong way, it will never do the job.

Media are neither good nor bad

There are no 'good media' or 'bad media' as such. There are only media that are good for the purpose or not good for the purpose.

It is realistic to start with the assumption that there is no such thing as a perfect media match. There will always be segments and individuals in the target audience that will not be reached by the media combination you have chosen, and there will always be an overspill, i.e., the media selected will reach some who are not part of the primary target audience. The trick is to reduce those two factors to a minimum and to make cost/value comparisons based on how good the potential productive coverage really is.

The media selection process starts 'at home', in defining the target audience as closely as possible. Any information on media and channels is useless, unless it can be correlated with clearly specified information on whom you want to reach. The benchmark studies discussed above are the starting point in finding out or specifying who 'they' are, in relevant quantitative and qualitative terms. And, as part of that, how do they 'take in' information of the kind you are about to serve?

With a clear profile of the target audience, one can start matching it with channels and media available. As in defining the target audience, there are quantitative and qualitative aspects on the choice of channels and media.

Quantitative aspects

Quantitative aspects are easier to handle and they are getting even easier through new computerized media evaluation systems. Even so, there are channels where even quantitative aspects create problems.

The process of quantitative 'media match' can be as follows – each step to be verified by formal or informal research, as the need appears:

1. Describing the target audience in usable terms, such as geographic spread, industry code, position in companies, age, sex, educational background, reading or viewing habits, etc.
2. Deciding total verified 'reach', i.e., readership, including verified 'pass-along', of a publication (your own in-house or an external publication), (calculated number of) visitors to a trade show, addresses in the mailing list, participants in a conference or meeting, etc.
3. Breaking down these figures in categories that can be matched with the target audience specification.
4. Estimating the quantitative 'media match', i.e., the coverage of primary interest to you.
5. Calculating the theoretical cost of exposing the message to individuals of interest.

Remember, quantitative media research provides only a theoretical exposure cost figure. Even so, it is valuable, since it shows minimum potential contact costs.

Qualitative aspects
Qualitative media research may create bigger headaches. Different media have different impacts on their audience and on segments of their audience. Not every visitor will spend the same amount of time at a trade show, not every reader will read a magazine, an annual report, a sales leaflet or a staff newsletter the same way. Not everyone in the target audience will be equally impressed by the media of your choice. The number of people reached is always lower than the exposure and contact costs consequently higher than what appears from the space salesman's chart, for example. The degree of success in closing the gap between 'exposure' and 'reach' is dependent on many factors.

Some of these factors relate to the relevance and creativity of a presentation, others are linked to the media. To what extent do 'the right people' appreciate that magazine, respect that show, open such a mailshot, etc., and what impact are various media likely to make on the target audience?

One way of looking at this is to study the intensity or 'contact quality' of different media categories, in such terms as:

1. Selectivity/exposure factors.
2. Understanding/cognitive factors.
3. Credibility/acceptance factors.
4. Interaction/involvement factors.
5. Action factors.

Choosing a few of these factors as an example, some traditional media can be placed in the contact intensity diagram (Figure 17.2) (feel free to disagree with the placement of the media – individual experience in relation to target audiences may be entirely different, so go ahead and modify the diagram!).

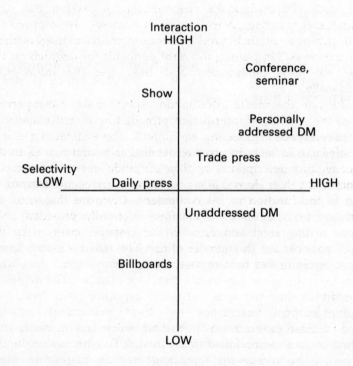

Figure 17.2 *Contact intensity diagram*

Your responsibility – but the media can help
The balancing act between exposure and media impact is an exciting part of every communications project, an act where measurement techniques and available research should be used for support.

The media and their organizations, publishers, exhibit organizers, suppliers of data-bases for mailings and other media suppliers, do more and more to improve their accountability and support the decision-making process. However, most media do this only to the extent that their customers, the advertisers and other users of the media put clear demands for information on them. The responsibility rests with the communicators to make their demands heard. They will not get the answers if they don't ask the questions. Some find it difficult to make good use of the information that is actually available. Others will have to put on the right sunglasses when they look at the information to reduce some of the glare that accompanies facts and figures that media supply about themselves.

The media buyer has the responsibility of asking the right questions and insisting on well-founded answers. To improve the cost-effectiveness of their work, communications managers must improve their skill in putting the right demands for research on the media, not least publications and then use the information professionally.

To illustrate the media information aspect, make a comparison between the amount of information provided by a media salesman and a salesman of engineering equipment. The engineering equipment salesman is likely to provide detailed facts and figures in the form of product descriptions, application guidelines and statements on functional value. He will also provide guarantees and warranties related to the function of his equipment. Compare that with the information and 'functional warranties' normally provided by a salesman selling exhibition or advertising space, even when the contract amounts are in a similar range! The old rule *caveat emptor* seems to apply in this field more than in many others.

Press media
Good newspapers, magazines and trade publications provide audited, verified research on their distribution, reach, readership and reaction-creating performance. Although this information sometimes has to be taken with a pinch of salt, or be read 'wearing sunglasses', it is a good platform for media effectiveness evaluation.

In addition to their standard data, they can often, on request, supply tailor-made information, based on your definition of a specific target audience. Ask the publisher for more than quantitative data.

Ask for relevant qualitative audience research on:

- Awareness and preference studies.
- Business, company and reader profile studies.
- Editorial research on reading frequency.
- Reader traffic and habits.
- Studies on recall and response ('bingo cards' and other forms) related to advertising and editorial material.
- Follow-up studies of inquiries.
- Reader loyalty, expressed as average duration of subscriptions and other kinds of publications-related research.

Start collecting examples of what magazines and other publications in your field offer in terms of research. Then make comparisons as part of improving the media evaluation process and as part of your own professional development. Don't hesitate to 'challenge' the publishers who offer less than you require.

Find the right ambition level and apply similar standards to publications under the company's own control, staff publications, customer magazines, shareholder newsletters, etc.

Incidentally, don't see media research as simply an advertising tool. Much of it is equally useful in planning a company's editorial relations work.

Direct mail
Direct mail and similar communications methods have outstanding potential in research and measurement terms. With appropriate definition of targets, we get result evaluation as a built-in factor.

Mailing lists have gained substantial credibility and offer great opportunities for tailor-made reach data to match your pre-project specifications for direct mail projects. Still, most list suppliers have a long way to go before they offer research-based data on qualitative characteristics of their audiences and the impact that mailings on their lists can create.

Response data, case stories and breakdown possibilities that match your needs are ways for list suppliers to help improve the effectiveness of their medium and at the same time reduce the 'communications pollution'.

Exhibitions and shows
Good exhibition organizers are improving fast in providing useful

media documentation and research. The span between the good ones and the not-so-good ones is very wide though. Most trade shows still provide relatively poor advance information on such media factors as demographics, traffic, reach, message absorption, impact and action/response.

The lower ambition level among most exhibition and trade show organizers in providing relevant media data reflects a frequent lack of professionalism from exhibitors and potential exhibitors in demanding and using such information from the suppliers. It is understandable that the organizers do not provide reliable quantitative or qualitative data to visitors to trade shows if there is no expressed demand.

The questionnaire on p. 312, based on a form developed by the author for the Swedish Advertisers' Association, offers suggestions on questions that a potential exhibitor should ask of an exhibition or trade show organizer, before a decision is taken to participate in an event.

To be reliable, answers should be based on adequate research. The potential exhibitor should be given access to this research. Qualitative and quantitative data on expected attendance should also be supported by guarantees, so that the exhibitor can feel comfortable in making his decisions or recommendations.

Other media

Cost/value analyses on the reach and impact of other media, such as printed matter, conferences and audiovisual presentations may seem to be more difficult to make. Certainly, less support is provided by the suppliers.

However, it is still necessary and worthwhile to go through the exercise and establish check-points for the actual utilization of a brochure, a film or a video presentation and the results expected. Even if exact numbers and other impact factors are hard to state in advance, in the budgeting process or before a production decision is taken, making reasonable assumptions at least provides a benchmark against which to evaluate progress.

In these and other media categories, what can be considered after the homework has been made, at least for major activities, is limited test-runs of the planned project. This, however, is often too expensive and time-consuming for anything but really big projects.

How to use formal research

'Do-it-yourself' or ... using outside research services

Yours for the asking

The most difficult question in communications research and measurement is knowing what one needs to know. Once you have learnt to ask the right questions, you will find, perhaps to your surprise, that many of the answers are easily available.

Much information is published or can be provided on demand from business organizations, government agencies, publishers, trade show organizers or other sources. 'Desk research' using such material can be inexpensive and fast. Answers to many questions may already exist. To find them, good advertising agencies or PR consultants can often be helpful.

But when that is not enough, find help

Alternatively, they can conduct the studies required or suggest good specialized research services.

Using professional outside services probably has more advantages in communications research than in any other field. It is beyond the competence of most companies to keep methods and standards on a high professional level in a field that is as specialized and develops as fast as research. After all, very few companies run communications research projects every day! Furthermore, the outside supplier is more likely to keep objectivity on a high level. And even the suspicion that awareness, attitude or similar surveys are 'rigged' is enough to make them useless.

Choosing a research supplier, check with colleagues, agencies and your business organization for information on potential alternatives.

Inquire about their professionalism and their business practices. Check their professional level through such questions as:

- Do they have their own field staff and their own full time office staff?
- What staff resources do they have available for your project?
- Are they experienced in the specific research methods considered, such as psychological techniques and in statistical methods?
- What resources do they have in data processing?

- What standing does their staff have in general research ethics and planning?
- Can you rely on their integrity and independence?

Check their business practices through the following questions:

- Are they prepared to give you a firm quotation, with price and delivery time, as soon as you have agreed on the scope of the research project?
- What are their payment terms? It is normal that the payment should be made in three instalments: (1) at the commissioning, (2) when the field work is completed, and (3) after the final report has been delivered.
- What are their principles as to the rights to use and publish the material?

Make a short-list, then ask the companies you consider for references and don't hesitate to check those references!

Test the resources in close relation to the specific project you are considering, not to just any kind of research. It is no use getting a research agency specializing in eye movements (oh yes, there are such research services!), if you want an attitude survey among your new employees.

Don't ask for more than you can swallow!
At least in the first efforts in this field, don't try to be too sophisticated. One must obviously insist on reliability of the research results, but remember that communications research in business situations is a way for the company to create practical results and make the communications process more effective. The project is not an academic research project. More communications research in business has probably been aborted because of over-ambition than for any other reason.

Make sure that the research you commission will be relevant to your communications work. If your task is communications, in terms of changing awareness, attitudes or behaviour, don't treat it as a market survey.

Include only those questions that will affect the communications project in mind. For each question in the planned survey, check its value by asking:

1. How will it affect this communications project? What will I do differently, if the answers come out this way or that?

373

2. If I repeat this question after my communications project, what difference can I expect?

Try to resist the temptation to clutter the survey by asking for too much information. One of the dangerous – and expensive – expressions to watch out for in this phase is: 'Since we are doing the survey anyway, why not ask about X, Y, or Z at the same time?' More often than not, such 'tag-on' questions will make the project less useful and more expensive.

'Once is not enough'
General Electric kept its public issues survey QICR running for more than fifteen years – and on a quarterly basis!

An internal communications survey made among the staff in one engineering company has been repeated every fifth year since 1971. Each time the results become more reliable and more useful. Changes in attitude among various groups of employees are studied and conclusions drawn for the company staff magazine and other communications tasks.

At the very outset of most, if not all, communications research projects, it is a good idea to decide on a repeat study after a given time, be it two months, one year or five years. With many of the methods used in practical communications research, a one-time reading can often be debated or questioned. Repeating the research project, duplicating the method, audience, questions, as closely as possible will narrow the margin of error. Many research projects provide really useful conclusions only when they have been repeated once or several times. Only then will they show a direction, a trend, that will serve as a basis for supportive or corrective measures.

'It's got to be good'.
Research methods and standards

Methods in communications research
The variety of research methods in business-to-business communications is almost unlimited, ranging from advanced experiments, based on academic psychology and sociology, to simple mail surveys. In-depth specialized literature is available on the subject; here we can only touch on some areas of frequent interest to a practitioner, mainly on focus groups and surveys.

Focus groups

Focus groups are a practical and useful technique in getting access to certain types of qualitative data.

A focus group typically consists of between six and twelve participants representing a significant target audience. The selection process is critical – while the group is supposed to represent one category or sector, it is of course necessary to try to reflect the variety that is assumed to exist within that audience.

For this reason, one single focus group on one subject is not advisable. Two or three groups should be a minimum.

The group moderator should be a professional in the focus group technique, well briefed on the subject to be reviewed but not necessarily an expert. Subjects suitable for focus group techniques can include pretests of communications concepts, reviews of editorial/advertising strategies, product (existing or planned) and corporate positioning problems, political or semi-political issues (e.g., in preparing public affairs positioning), target audience thinking and feeling, preparation for larger-scale surveys, trends and changes in audience perceptions or specific problems that are not suited for quantitative surveys.

Surveys

The most frequent method in communications research is surveys, by mail, telephone or personal interviews.

The three kinds are different in applications and are used for different purposes. Neither of them is 'better' or 'worse' as a method.

In choosing the right method for a specific task, it is advisable to let the research specialists or consultants have their say. In general terms, a mail survey is sufficient for a job where it is important to get a great number of responses, and where the questions are not very probing, preferably questions that can be answered by a YES or NO, by simple choices, ranking or marks on a scale (using scales of the 1–5, 'Very much–not at all' or 'Agree–disagree' types). A telephone survey can do much the same as a mail survey, but can also provide more in-depth answers. Telephone surveys normally offer higher response rates than mail surveys, but at a somewhat higher cost per interview. Personal interviews are more expensive, but can provide more detailed information, of a more qualitative nature and with high response rates.

The questionnaire

Many public opinion polls are biased from the start, because of the questionnaire. In politics and similar situations this may be acceptable – the poll in such cases is often a propaganda exercise more than an effort to get real information. In business communications research, a biased survey is useless – or worse than that – as a basis for decisions. Designing the questionnaire is consequently best left to the (supposedly unbiased!) research specialist. Even so, it is usually advisable to pretest the questionnaire on a small group from the same audience as the final survey.

The sample
Start with an assessment of the size of the total audience and make your sample on that basis. In most cases a sample of less than 500–1,000 is not advisable for mail or telephone surveys. Any breakdowns from a smaller sample will be of limited value or of no value at all.

The response rate
The American-based Advertising Research Foundation recommends that every effort be made to reach a response rate of no less than 60 per cent for a mail or telephone survey and it should be around 70 per cent to be any good. Lower response rates leave too much to the risk of non-respondents being significantly different from respondents. Consequently, there is the possibility that the information obtained is worthless. To achieve these response rates, the design of the questionnaire and the ease of responding are the prime factors, but there is also a wide range of experience on how to build incentives of different kinds into the project.

The recommendation
When commissioning a survey, consider requesting a recommendation for action as part of the research company's task. It will force the research company to stick to the purpose, not only to do research for its own sake, and it will help everyone involved to make the research project action-oriented.

And now – what about 'the missing factor'?

This chapter has dealt with various aspects of measuring communications results. Hopefully, the reader has seen that it is, indeed, possible to measure the results of communications work, at least in most cases. So, at the end of the chapter, there is one question that may be worth reflecting on: why is it so often neglected, when it can be done?

At the beginning of this chapter we talked about a mystic factor that is sometimes missing. Until we come to grips with this factor it will be difficult to bring the communications profession to the same level of accountability and acceptance as many other corporate functions.

The missing factor, more often than professional knowledge, is professional courage.

The communications profession will be taken seriously when this challenge is accepted:

1. When anticipated results of proposed projects and programmes are *predicted*, after careful analysis and with appropriate reservations and limitations.
2. When results are regularly *measured*, afterwards, to check to what extent the targets were reached.

Part IV

Organizing the communications function

This part will help the reader organize the communications function in a company in relation to company needs and priorities. Special consideration is given to aspects on international communications work.

18

'Structure out of chaos'

In this chapter the reader will find a discussion on the strategic role of communications and on setting up a communications function based on accountability.

It will help the reader establish a communications function with clear direction, with a structure in line with the company's needs and with an appropriate balance between 'do-it-yourself' and using outside resources.

Communication – a management tool

Communication is an important management instrument. Indeed, there are those in academia and business who maintain that management *is* communications.

If communication is important as a management tool and a company function, how do we define it, structure it and make it manageable? Much of this book has discussed this issue and practical solutions have been suggested, from the viewpoint of contact areas in Part I, communication methods in Part II, and result orientation throughout, but especially in Part III.

In this chapter we offer some suggestions on the role and structure of a company communications function. Most of the suggestions can be applied irrespective of the size of the company or of the communications department.

The semantic mess

Try this experiment when you are with a group of management colleagues who would like to play a little game. Ask each one of them to define on paper, without consulting the others, the following terms: 'Public Relations', 'Advertising', 'Publicity', 'Sales Promotion', and 'Communications'. Then add some others for comparison, such as: 'Engineering', 'Accounting', 'Production', 'Research' and 'Finance'. They will probably produce widely different definitions, perhaps for all the functions. Chances are, however, that they will be somewhat more consistent on the second group than on the first one.

There are, indeed, accepted definitions of all these words, some officially approved and sanctioned by the associations in the business. This does not prevent what we could call a 'semantic mess' among non-specialists and, for that matter, even among professionals.

Does it matter? Perhaps not. 'A rose by any other name would smell as sweet . . .' But the semantic mess is often reflected in a similar mess in defining responsibilities and priorities. Important issues can be left unattended, mismanaged or fall between stools in the corporate structure. Money, manpower and other resources are wasted. Strategic and operational thinking in a company gets confused.

This chapter will use a consistent terminology, the same as that used in the rest of the book, and will apply it to help create a clearer purpose and structure in 'getting the job done'.

'Identity' and 'image' – the strategic role of communications

The working material of the communications function is the strategy of the company, including its identity, the image it wants to project, and what the company should do to live up to that image. The role of communications is – or should be – a strategic function in corporate management, based on the *what* of the company.

If the identity of a company is 'what it really is', and the image of the company is what others think or believe it is, then the communications job is relatively easy: to bring the two together. But 'identity' and 'image' are complex concepts, both as they apply to people and to companies or organizations.

A person is not an absolute self, identical in all situations. His or her identity is also a function of the opinions, expectations and attitudes of others – family, friends, bosses, colleagues, etc. Some features are consistent and stay the same over time – the core personality, if you wish. Other features vary with the environment, with the other players, with the role one is expected to play and with time.

A company has a 'personality', whether it knows it or not. Indeed, a company *is* a personality. That personality is a combination of identity and image, what the company 'really' is and what others think of it.

The communications function should support top management in the strategy process and make sure that it:

1. Establishes satisfactory strategies for the company, including definitions of the 'identity' of the company.
2. Is aware of what the relevant contact groups within the company and outside think of it, what its 'image' in different key groups is.
3. Knows how this 'image' affects the success and development of the company.

The strategy development process is sometimes initiated by the communications manager, sometimes by other functions in company management. Whoever takes the initiative, the whole process must be driven by a strong will from top management.

The communications management of the company has two distinct roles to play in the process. In the strategy development phase, the communications management should ensure that the strategy is developed in full awareness of existing opinions and attitudes relating to the company. Once the strategy has been established, it is the communications manager's responsibility to ensure that it penetrates and is accepted inside the company and among its various external contact groups.

Organizing operations for responsibility and accountability

The communications manager is, to the same extent as other managers, responsible for the planning and follow-up, and account-able in measurable result terms for his or her work. This concern for accountability applies to each project and to the overall work of the function. Techniques that will achieve a higher degree of account-ability in communications were discussed, from a project or programme perspective, in Part III. In Part IV, accountability is seen from the perspective of organization and structure.

The operations of the communications department deal with the who and the how.

Who?

The demand for communication as a management instrument is widening. Old and new groups expect or request to be heard and to learn more about the business world in general and about individual companies. Who are the groups that should take prioritity?

How?

Person-to-person communications is the ideal form, but is not always feasible for time and money reasons. Other methods are available and ready to be utilized, each one in situations and for purposes where it does a good job. Which methods do we choose in each situation?

Selecting the priority audiences to communicate with, both to listen to and to address, then choosing the best way to get the messages across, are the two main operational tasks of a communications function.

If the operational concept of 'Who' and 'How' is adopted, it can help give clearer purpose and firmer structure to the communications function in most companies and other organizations, irrespective of whether the function is a one-person operation or a big department. Budgets can be discussed, set and checked appropriately. Relations to other functions in the company can be explained. Outside services can get their tasks and responsibilities spelled out. Accountability can be developed.

Under this concept, a big department would have some of its staff allocated to the defined priority audiences or 'contact areas'. They would closely follow trends and issues in those audiences, together with personnel management, marketing management, local plant management and other functions concerned, and they would be prepared to recommend and guide communications work geared to those audiences.

Others in a large department would specialize in methods and media. Some of them would perhaps be audiovisual specialists, others would be knowledgeable in the production, use and handling of printed matter, or they would be exhibition specialists, advertising specialists or experts in editorial work and editorial relations.

In both small and large departments, the budgets would be built up along the same lines, with 'contact areas' or audiences as the primary structure, and 'methods' as the secondary. The focus will be on the objectives, related to changes in the contact areas, rather than on methods, the means to an end.

Adopting this principle of communications by objectives can lead to new thinking, new structures and a higher level of accountability in many companies.

Organization by contact areas

An organizational structure oriented towards the main 'contact areas' or audiences, such as staff, market, local community, the financial community, etc., and budgeting made accordingly, will be easier to focus on purpose, objectives and results. Somebody is responsible for keeping the relations with each of these groups active, smooth and positive. Somebody follows development trends in each one of those groups and sees to it that they are being conveyed to the right levels of company management.

In an organization of this kind, the communications staff controls the work in an audience-related spirit. It is easier to establish fruitful links with other departments or functions in the company who share the interest, and sometimes the responsibility, for certain contact areas with the communications staff, such as the personnel department on internal communications, the financial department on owner/shareholder communications, etc.

Accountability and performance are linked to objectives rather than to methods. Communications services are seen as less important and may well be purchased from external suppliers. Budgeting is goal-oriented rather than methods-oriented.

Organization by communications methods

Other companies with a big communications function organize it by methods, with departments or specialists for printed matter, audiovisual work, exhibitions, advertising and perhaps direct mail and telemarketing. Press relations may be combined with advertising, handled by a separate group within the function or be a separate department altogether.

Typically, a communications function of this kind has its origins in an 'advertising' department which at some stage was given a wider brief, perhaps to produce the staff newsletter or the annual report. With the right staff, there is no reason why this increased responsibility should not provide effective services and do a good job.

Specialized knowledge in the various media and methods to be used in communications is certainly useful and necessary. Dynamic changes in printing techniques, electronic communication, advertising and editorial media, audiovisual techniques, direct mail techniques, telemarketing (not only as a 'marketing' tool) and trade show practices have emphasized that need. Intelligent selection and use of media categories and vehicles can contribute substantially to the profitability and productivity of a company's communications programmes.

There are, however, certain risks involved in running a communications function with media/methods as the only or primary structural base. The focus tends to be on the tools, the methods, rather than on the audiences and objectives. Budgeting tends to be on certain amounts for printed matter, exhibitions and advertising, rather than on messages and audiences. Results tend to be measured in brochures produced and exhibitions built, rather than in changes in audience attitudes, awareness levels and action.

'How does it look in practice?'

An example of a combined organization

The example below is an expression, in instruction terms, of an organizational structure, where the two aspects above have been relatively clearly defined. The example is from an international engineering equipment company, with a central communications department of some thirty employees, and with an annual budget in the range of $7–8 million.

The responsibilities of the Contact Areas departments and the Communication Methods departments are:

Contact Areas:

Each Contact Area department is responsible for establishing and developing two-way communications between XYZ and the priority contact area it is in charge of. Its responsibilities include:

Budgeting – Our communications budgeting should be made by contact groups, after considering questions like: How much can we invest in improving our staff relations next year? How important are our relations with the shareholders? What are the broad customer groups that have got too little/too much attention lately? What are the new political/social trends we have to be aware of?

Planning – Short range, by defining desired goals and results, as closely as is practical, and long range, by reviewing and revising our objectives from time to time, and checking progress in the same terms.

Executing continuous and special programmes to establish and improve smooth, friendly and active communications.

Taking the pulse of its respective contact area to ensure that opinions, attitudes and knowledge are at desirable levels.

Creating feedback to make sure that relevant attitudes and trends in that contact area are known by corporate management.

Communications Methods:

The Communications Methods departments are responsible for maintaining high standards of creativity, production efficiency and corporate identity in the various media categories that are normal to the company.*

Their work is geared to serve the Contact Area departments of Headquarters as well as other functions in HQ, the divisions and sales companies. The work is basically of three different kinds:

1. to coordinate and give necessary guidance to the communications work of divisions and sales companies

2. to provide services in the respective areas groupwide

3. to produce corporate communications material and campaigns.

* The six departments within Communications Methods in this company were graphic design and production, space advertising, audiovisual presentations (with film and photo), exhibitions, editorial work and communications research.

Communications and corporate management

Resources generated through active communications work, such as positioning and good-will in the various contact areas of importance to the company are strategic assets, to be compared with financial strength, top-level products and a qualified staff. Indeed, those assets will to some degree be a result of professional communications work.

Close and frequent relations

Seeing communications as a management function means that corporate management will expect close and frequent relations with the communications function. This should be reflected in an organization, where communications reports directly to corporate management. Corporate management will give broad direction to the management of the communications function, as it will to all other central functions. Similarly, the communications function has a duty to give continuous input to corporate management.

Responsible and responsive communications programmes begin with the role of the communications function in keeping top management, and management at other levels, informed of awareness levels, attitudes and opinions towards the company among important groups inside and outside the company. It is important that the two-way nature of the relationship between these functions is spelled out clearly and recognized by both parties, as it is, for example, in the following quote from an internal instruction:

> The basic communications objectives of the XYZ Company are to establish and continuously improve two-way channels between the company and all relevant groups and segments of society, in order to:
> – ensure that opinions, attitudes and development trends are communicated from such groups to decision-makers in various functions within the company and are given due consideration in the decision-making process
> – gain respect and understanding among such groups for the company, its policies, its products and its contribution to the societies where it works.

It is worth noting that in this example the 'inward', 'listening' function is described in the first paragraph, and the 'outward', 'spokesman' function in the second paragraph.

A company cannot always please all groups, but if a company is hit by negative reactions to its decisions without being prepared for such reactions in advance, then the communications function has not done its job properly, or it has not been involved in the decision-making process as it should.

The communications function must be informed

In some companies it happens that the communications manager is only informed about plans for a merger, a plant closure, a reorganization, a new product, an important staff appointment or other major events when the whole thing is a *fait accompli*.

In a company where this is normal practice, the communications manager should bring the matter up for serious discussions with management so that his role and responsibilities are reviewed and clarified. If he is only considered as a producer of press releases and a postman, then he should seriously ask himself, if that is a role he is prepared to continue with. A communications manager worth his salt should be able to contribute more than that.

Management has a lot to gain by involving the communications manager at an early stage in deliberations on important matters. The more delicate an issue is, the more problems it usually involves of a sensitive opinion/attitude nature, and the more important should the input from the communications manager be.

One of the benefits is an additional 'neutral' review function. The communications manager should professionally be familiar with evaluating attitude and opinion factors from many sides.

The communications manager can also offer additional thoughts on who should be consulted or informed in the decision-making process, in what sequence and by whom.

Finally, with more advance notice the communications manager can better prepare the technicalities of the announcement itself, such as the choice of channels, media, spokesmen and timing.

Top management must have confidence in the communications manager

The above attitudes must be based on complete confidence in the communications manager's ability and loyalty. In fact, in my experience I have never yet learnt of a situation where leaks have come from a communications function. Information is the communications manager's working material. He is more familiar with the dynamite power of information than any others. Like an experienced miner, the communications manager can be expected to handle his 'dynamite' with care.

At the risk of oversimplifying: if I were a company chairman, I would rather share sensitive material with the communications manager than with any other functional manager in the company.

Top management must be prepared to listen

The third requirement is a clear understanding from top management that other considerations than financial and legal should play a part in making significant decisions. Assessing relations with employees, local communities and other important contact groups, goodwill gains and losses, political risks and opportunities are parts of the decision-making process, and the communications manager should by profession be an accepted and respected channel for such input.

He or she should be able to offer warnings on opinion risks that management may not be aware of and suggestions on how to avoid them. This may lead to reconsideration of the whole project, to a change in timing or procedures, or to a different tack in explaining the project. At the very least, it means that management may be more acutely aware of opinion factors, negative or positive, and consequently avoid what management never likes – surprises!

Obviously, a company sometimes has to make decisions that are unpopular. In fact, most decisions are unpopular in some quarters. The point is not that management should avoid unpopular decisions at any cost. Rather, that this aspect should be regarded as a natural element in the decision-making process, so that management is aware of opinion consequences of major decisions. No surprises!

Communications and other management functions

The communications manager has to develop and maintain a close network of contacts, inside and outside the company. One part of the network is relations with colleagues in management, for support, operational work and as an adviser. In addition to top management, the network of frequent contacts includes:

1. The personnel manager – for staff relations and educational relations work.
2. The local company and plant managers – for community relations.
3. The financial manager – for shareholder and other financial relations work.
4. The marketing and sales managers – for marketing communications.

The list could be much longer. In fact, since there are few areas of a company's life that do not have communications aspects, the list could go from accounting to waste management – or beyond.

In some of these areas, the communications function can make a bigger contribution than in others. Its role certainly changes, depending on the company, the organization, the staffing and the resources allotted to communications and to other functions.

In some cases, communications has a directly operational role, in others its role is more of a consultative or guiding nature. Both can work well. The alternative chosen is directly related to company culture, strategy, traditions and the personalities involved.

Catalyst or traitor?

A characteristic feature, which comes back in many cases, is the 'catalyst' function. Typically, the communications person, staff or consultant is used to looking at things 'from the other side'. He tries to 'walk in the other person's shoes', before he makes a recommendation. Taking a seat on the other side of the negotiating table to try to see and feel as 'they' do it is standard procedure for a communications professional.

Sometimes this leads other managers to question the dedication or loyalty of a communications person. He can appear to be a 'traitor', when he questions the wisdom of the company's position, taken or considered. The wise executive realizes that this enquiring attitude is one of the essential contributions a communications manager can make to a process and a condition for professional handling of any communications problem.

The communications department and outside agencies and consultants

Few companies, large or small, have communications departments capable of handling all aspects of communications in-house. Some companies make a point of having only minimum communications staff and rely instead to a great extent on outside help, temporarily or for long-lasting tasks. Other companies, with more resources of their own, buy outside services only for very specialized or *ad hoc* jobs. Whatever policy a company adopts, buying outside services is a job the communications manager should be able to handle.

A buying process like any other?

A PR consultant, an advertising agency and other outside suppliers of communication services can be regarded and selected just like any other supplier a company uses.

Many of the regular criteria that a qualified purchasing manager applies to a potential supplier of steel plate, machinery, office equipment or transportation services are equally important when considering, evaluating and finally choosing a communications service company. Earlier performance record, financial stability and reasonable pricing are parts of those aspects.

But selecting a communications consultant has additional implications. The consultant is likely to get access to company strategy, guidelines and other information of a secret nature. Confidence is a necessity.

Experience and background from similar companies and projects are valuable – up to a point. In some situations the important contribution from outside consultants is the ability to provide new input, a different viewpoint, other experiences than the traditional ones.

When the consultant's 'product' is his own person, there has to be a foundation for good relations, both professionally and personally. The proverbial 'chemistry' must work.

Some thoughts before shopping

Some aspects of buying outside communications services are worth consideration. The following questions may be helpful when you go shopping for outside help.

1. Are the agencies you are considering interested in the planning and follow-up process, or only in the creative?

2. Can they show results from clients with similar demands, problems, products and services as yours?

3. Is the team from the agency qualified, from a cultural, technical and marketing viewpoint, to handle an account such as yours?

4. Can they show results from all or most of the various channels you may be interested in, such as trade press, trade shows, direct mail, editorial relations, graphic production and others?

5. Are they willing and able to transfer to the client the usage rights of copy, artwork, photographs and other material produced on behalf of the client?

6. What are their principles for giving price estimates in advance?

7. How do they charge agency work, expenses, purchases from outside suppliers, media space, etc. (commissions, flat fee, hourly charges/how much for the various staff categories?/, other?).

Before making the final selection and signing a contract with a new consultant or agency, talk with two or three of the past and present clients of the candidate agency. Also, get contract examples and advice from the advertiser association of the country in question and compare the agency's proposal with their recommendations.

The communications department as an in-house agency

Some companies have chosen to set up their own communications department, more or less formally, as an in-house agency. Still others have toyed with the idea without reaching a decision.

It would be presumptuous to try to find 'an all-encompassing answer' to the question of whether an in-house agency or a more traditional arrangement with outside agencies is the best solution. The volume and complexity of the communications work, the resources available, earlier experience, company policies, organization and structure of the company are different from company to company and would favour one or the other solution. What might be worthwhile is listing some factors usually considered in the decision-making process.

Commissions

The first factor might be the question of agency commissions and agency mark-up on charges from media and other suppliers. However, in most countries today the old rigid commission system has been considerably softened, if not completely abolished. One of the consequences of the new trends is that the commission question has been largely defused.

If a company chooses to stay with an agency, it can normally negotiate a compensation system that is 'commission-neutral', i.e., a system under which the agency pays back all or most of its commissions from media and other suppliers, printers, graphic shops, research companies, exhibition contractors and others. By the same token, a company that chooses an in-house agency arrangement can normally negotiate with its suppliers to get the same discounts as an outside agency would get.

Creativity

Can you expect more creativity from an outside agency than from an in-house team? It depends on the people involved, of course, but in general, it is reasonable to expect that the creative staff of an outside agency, working with many different accounts, get more varied input; and if an outside agency does not work to the client's satisfaction, it is easier for the client to call for new talent on the account or go to a new agency.

On the other hand, even an in-house agency does not necessarily have to do everything with its own resources. An in-house agency may, for many reasons, want to buy in some services, including creative, from specialized outside shops, and may thus get fresh new looks and competition for its own staff.

Continuity

The other side of that coin is the question of continuity. Advertising agencies are traditionally a business where people move fast. A client has only limited possibilities to influence the situation, when an account executive, art director or other important member of the agency team is promoted, moves to another account or leaves the agency. No company is immune to changes of that kind in its own staff, but when you have a good team working in your own company, you have more resources to hand, financial and others, to keep the team together.

Continuity is also promoted in-house through the more frequent flow of information on orders, new products, staff appointments, restructuring and other events within the company.

Control

Cost control should be easier to maintain, at least on the surface, with an external supplier. Agencies must work with good traffic systems, job numbers, progress reports, time recording, cost accounting and other administrative support systems to be able to serve the customer, bill him fairly and know if it makes enough profit on the account. An in-house agency must do the same to survive, but it will take a certain amount of discipline, previous agency experience and management will power to install such systems and keep them running. The discipline will be needed also to ensure that hidden costs are brought to light, so that all costs are really included in the comparisons.

Credibility

'No one is a prophet in his own country'
Does the in-house agency have the same credibility as an outside agency, when it makes unconventional or uncomfortable, maybe even revolutionary recommendations? Or does it even tend not to make such recommendations, being steeped too deeply in the company tradition?

Executives may find it easier to accept bold recommendations from an outside team: 'After all, that is what we pay them for!' The in-house department might have a credibility problem and could even be faced with the question: 'If you think this is such a bright idea, how come you haven't thought of it before?' On the other hand, the in-house agency with its presumably closer contact with what is going on in the company, should be able to make more realistic recommendations. On that basis its credibility could even be higher.

Consulting

The independence of an outside consultant is one of his assets. He brings input from his other clients to the party and should consequently be able to offer independent advice. While this is true of many good consultants, including outside agencies, it also happens that consultants, in an effort to keep a good client, easily comply with expressed or implied wishes from the client. Professional integrity is a quality a good client wants and actively encourages in a consultant. If the client does that, integrity can be fostered and found in-house as well as in an outside consultant or agency. Likewise, if the customer only wants to get his own opinions confirmed, he can find consultants who are prepared to give him such 'advice' anywhere.

Capacity

Communication work seldom runs in an even flow through the year. Even with good planning, there are big projects, sudden emergencies, major events and short deadlines that have to be dealt with.

Using an outside agency, one puts the problems of meeting these ups and downs in the agency's hands and expects it to be capable of handling the problems. After all, that is what you have an agency for.

Your own staff are always limited. And just when the workload peaks . . . somebody falls ill or becomes pregnant, or resigns.

An in-house agency can never work entirely with its own resources. It has to build up a sub-supplier network, just like an outside agency does. With such a network, one may still run into capacity problems, but they should not be much more difficult to handle than with an outside agency. But, of course, there is no one to blame if things do not work as they should.

Client know-how

A good communications programme normally stands on three legs: the agency account executive, the project manager from the communications department and the specialist – the marketing manager concerned for a product marketing project, the personnel manager for a staff relations project, the financial manager for a financial communications project, and so forth. With an in-house agency arrangement the three parties may be reduced to two.

This may be a cost-saving measure. On the other hand, it reduces the input to the process. The outside account executive may be able to see the forest better because he is not so close to the trees, he can steer away from in-house bickering and power struggles and he has the added weight of being an outsider.

Copyright

Copyright issues may be a detail, but they seem to become increasingly difficult to handle in many agency–client relationships. There is no reason why copyright problems should force a company to go for in-house agency arrangements, but they may well be a contributing factor.

Culture

Corporate culture could be the strongest factor in deciding whether to go for an in-house or an external agency set-up. Some companies have strict working practices in not hiring their own staff but using external suppliers as a principle, whether or not there are logical reasons pointing in the other direction. Other companies prefer the comfort and feeling of security that in-house resources tend to vouch for.

In real life there is no such thing as a full-blown solution in one direction or the other. A company must at least have the communications management function – and it certainly has the responsibility, even if outside agencies, consultancies and other suppliers have a major role to play. And a company that decides to base its communications work on in-house resources will find that it will require a good supplier network from outside, to get its inside group to function really well.

Coordinating international operations

Is business local or global?

David Collier, Vice President of General Motors, was quoted in *The New Yorker* a few years ago to have said: 'There's no such thing as a domestic industry. There's no such thing as a domestic market. There's an international market and an international set of manufacturers.' This may be a natural statement from a leader in one of the world's top industrial companies. But it could have been said, with equal conviction, by thousands of smaller manufacturers and businessmen from countries like Taiwan, Japan, Holland, Mexico, Italy, Sweden, Great Britain and the United States.

Big and small industries realize today that the world is one market – with some exceptions for products that are protected for special reasons, such as agricultural products and defence products, or because they don't ship easily, such as industrial gases; and 'the world as one market' is not a concept limited to products and services. It applies to trends and ideas as well, political opinions that influence business, management concepts and fashions, ideas about accounting, policies in management–staff relations, trends in education and research, all part of the ever-changing climate in which business lives and works.

The case for global coordination

What about the cultural differences – have they gone? Certainly not. Differences between people and cultures, based on national origins, legal differences, languages and other factors are likely to stay with us for a long time, even in a shrinking world. And, as a private human being one would be tempted to say: 'Vive la différence!'

In most business-to-business contexts, however, the differences should not be exaggerated. There is a lot to be gained from recognizing the opportunities in globally coordinated communications – with local input in the planning and creative process. Here are just a few reasons:

1. If the thinking and creative process is centrally coordinated, after tapping a variety of sources, the communications 'products' – advertisements, press releases, brochures, audiovisuals and other forms of presentation material – are likely to become better than if everybody has to do his own homework in isolation.

2. Time and money can be saved – sometimes substantial amounts – through coordinated planning and production. Alternatively, for the same budget one can get better quality, higher frequency, wider reach, adding up to more impact.

3. The company identity is maintained – not only the graphic identity but also the 'ideological' identity. The same key messages are used consistently. Central and local company staff get in the habit of basing their work on the same expressions and the same thinking.

4. Coordinated management of the communications work helps to expand the influence and reach of central management in other business aspects and makes better use of management resources.

And the audiences, what about them? Addressing people in business, we shall find that most of them, in their professional roles, share important values and priorities. They will certainly retain national and regional characteristics, related to culture, religion, language and other distinctive features. But there are also equalizing factors. Most businessmen have been exposed to educational programmes, to a management training process and to corporate cultures that are becoming more and more similar, from one country to another. For their business decisions, they will need much the same information and they will be influenced by much the same reasoning.

Global/local – can the twain be made to meet?

In practical terms, it is seldom a matter of 'either-or', *either* a total 'steamroller' cross-national communications management style, *or* complete independence from country to country.

What is reasonable in many companies is a 'spectrum' approach: such an approach would go from coherence to independence along the route from strategy to execution.

Strategy would be worldwide, global, with the obvious limitations that market opportunities, competition and the company's own resources would impose. The strategic concepts also include such items as corporate graphic identity.

Methods in communications planning and follow-up can be conveyed and applied globally, with limited needs for national variance.

Message platform would be centrally coordinated, but with room for variation, depending on national cultures, preferences and needs, sometimes even legislation.

Creative execution of communications programmes would be 'cross-national' if possible, but wherever a national or even regional approach is better, it would be chosen, on a case-to-case basis.

In practice, the degree of cross-national coordination depends to a considerable extent on the person-to-person contacts between central communications resources (staff and agency) and the national communications managers and agencies.

What has shown to be a practical approach in many cases is joint planning sessions in the early stages of a programme or project. If the 'centre' invites the five to ten most important national companies to planning sessions, shows a serious will to listen to suggestions and advice coming from those countries, and spends enough time on such brainstorming sessions, it is often possible to create a high degree of coordination. The real differences are not swept under the carpet through this approach. They may remain, as they, indeed, should do. But the psychological problems in coordination – the 'not invented here' syndromes – are easier to handle, if honest opportunities for input are provided at early stages in the development process.

Agencies – part of the solution, or . . .?

Working with agencies on international communications projects certainly puts demands on the agency as well as on the client. In many cases, the client may feel that difficulties in creating cross-national communications programmes rest more in the agencies involved than in the client company itself.

To avoid such a situation, the following points may be worth considering in looking for agencies in international projects, in addition to the general thoughts on agency cooperation above:

1. *Planning and follow-up* functions are much more difficult to handle in cross-national than in national projects. Check the planning/follow-up 'philosophy' and resources of the agencies concerned. Are they actively interested in the planning and follow-up aspects, or are they merely creative-oriented? Do they have established planning systems, preferably computerized, that can work in an international context? Can they show records of cross-national campaigns and programmes, demonstrating their planning and follow-up capacity, not only nice creative work?

2. It is hard to work with an agency on an international project if the agency does not have cross-national experience. A degree of listening ability is necessary if a cross-national programme is to be successful. It may be worthwhile to check, and perhaps demand, that the agency should have creative and administrative staff who have worked in at least one foreign country.

3. The big international media are relatively easy to handle, whether considered for advertising or for editorial relations. Their readership statistics are usually good and their editorial direction is fairly clear. In many business-to-business programmes it is not enough to work with these media. To reach their real target audiences, many programmes require that local, perhaps specialized trade media are considered. Check the agencies you are considering on their ability to get the right information on such national, less glorious media and to work constructively with them.

4. The media selection problems get even more difficult if methods other than space advertising and editorial relations are considered. To what extent do you want the agency to support you in the production and distribution of printed material, in direct mail or similar programmes, in trade shows or exhibitions, in audio-visual material and presentations? What is their track record on international projects of such kinds?

5. Cross-national communications work often forces you to face unexpected problems of a legal nature, such as local media

restrictions, product liability questions and copyright problems. Are the agencies you are considering capable of handling such issues?

6. Ability to handle multi-lingual work is, of course, a minimum requirement. Are the agencies you are choosing between familiar with the subject-matter of your programme, the technology, the market situation and the jargon prevalent in your target audiences, in your home country and in at least one or two other priority countries?

7. Traditionally, companies have worked with international campaigns through chains of agencies, established or suggested by the agencies, rather than through client-based agency groupings. Making a cross-national programme work in many countries may be somewhat easier if the client's existing local agency relations are maintained and respected, especially if those local agencies are involved from the planning stages. Check the attitudes of your agency(ies) to such cooperation models.

The Olympics of business-to-business communications

Working with international communications programmes is, indeed, entering the Olympics of business-to-business communications. The difficulties, costs and time required should never be underestimated in the planning process.

Given the rapid multinational development trends of practically all kinds of business, it is in this environment that more and more of us will be expected to work.

At the time of writing, the European Community is taking big steps towards 1992 and a practically borderless Europe. The United States and Canada are planning to open up trade and investments on the North American continent. Other countries that have isolated themselves for decades behind iron or bamboo curtains are looking for new openings, with new opportunities for international business contacts. Japan and other countries in Asia have become leaders in productivity development and make that their launch-pad into the international business community. Yet other regions are looking for opportunities to become partners in this historically unique process of cross-national exchange. Companies with ambitions to succeed outside their own home countries have more opportunities than ever. But then, those companies will also meet more formidable competition than they ever met in the relative calm of their traditional home market.

The stakes are high, as in the Olympics. A company that expects to win in the international arena must be professional in everything it does. One of the elements that can make the difference between success and failure is the company's ability to communicate professionally.

Postscript
Let's get going!

Sir Winston Churchill's famous words during World War II apply here: 'This is not the end. It is not even the beginning of the end. It may possibly be the end of the beginning.' No book on the subject of professional business communications could possibly cover the subject fully and for all time. The author has tried to describe the field of professional business communications in an all-encompassing perspective. This does not mean that every aspect of the subject has been covered. That would be impossible, one reason being that the field is limited only by the imagination and work situation of the readers themselves.

There are contact areas that are essential to some readers, and yet may not have been discussed in Part I. There are new and old communications methods that could and perhaps should have been discussed in Part II and yet have not been included. The planning, evaluation, follow-up and research area could have filled a book on its own, rather than only Part III of this book. The questions of organizational structure and use of external services are important and could well have deserved more coverage than was given to them in Part IV. International aspects are increasingly important.

All this indicates that this book, despite its overall communications perspective, should be seen only as a beginning. Readers who are new to the field will, in their practical work, find situations not covered here and will have to make their own experience. Readers with an extensive background in professional business communications will have met views in the book that they disagree with or would want to add to. In both cases they may find that the field is wider than they had previously imagined.

It would be a great help and stimulation to the author if the readers would take the trouble to share their comments, advice, criticism or suggestions with him. Any real-life stories of direct or indirect reader applications of ideas and material from the book would be welcome, too! Address them to the publishers, Prentice Hall, who will be pleased to pass them on to me. Such feedback could help improve future editions, and it would demonstrate to me the value of two-way communications, one of the central themes of this book.

If we want to influence the world – and allow ourselves to be influenced – there is no other way than through active, two-way communication. When this happens on a personal level, we change ourselves and others around us change too. Whenever it is done professionally, our organizations and companies, and their environment, will change, hopefully for the better. And we shall all be enriched in the process.

What are we waiting for? Let's get going!

Checklists

Many of the chapters in this book contain practical guidelines that can help make communications work easier and more professional. Those guidelines are listed below to make it easier to find them when needed.

Part I: The primary contact areas

407

Additional reading

The wide field of communications has produced many excellent books and is bound to produce more. The following list is a small selection of the many books available on various aspects of communications work. The books are listed according to the concept and structure of this book. I hope the reader will find this useful, even when the books listed do not fully match the concept.

1. A network of human relations

Northcote Parkinson, C. and Nigel Rowe, *Communicate. Parkinson's Formula for Business Survival*. Prentice Hall, London, 1977.

Hart, Norman A., *Effective Corporate Relations: Applying Public Relations in Business and Industry*. McGraw-Hill, Maidenhead, 1988.

2. 'It's all in the family': Staff communications

Hodgetts, Richard M., *Modern Human Relations at Work*, Holt, Rinehart & Winston, Eastbourne, 1987.

Vandamme, Jacques, *Employee Consultation and Information in Multinational Corporations*, Routledge, Chapman & Hall, New York, 1985.

3. 'Whose is it, anyway?': Communicating with shareholders and financial groups

Bowman, Pat, *Handbook of Financial Public Relations*, Heinemann, London, 1988.

4. 'There goes the neighbourhood': Communicating with the local community

5. 'Here, there, everywhere': Government relations

Lusterman, Seymor, *Managing Business–State Government Relations*, The Conference Board, New York, 1983.

Ellis, Nigel, *Parliamentary Lobbying: Putting the Business Case to Government*, Heinemann, London, 1988.

6. 'I know, teacher!': Communicating with the educational world

Education for Life. A European Strategy, Butterworths, Borough Green, Sevenoaks, Kent, 1988. (A report on initiatives for better contacts between business and the European educational system.)

7. 'Where the buck starts': Market communications

Coulson-Thomas, Colin J., *Marketing Communications*, Heinemann, London, 1983.

8. 'Broadside': Communications across the board

Cutlip, Scott M. and Allen H. Center, *Effective Public Relations*, Prentice Hall, Englewood Cliffs, NJ, 6th edition, 1987.
Howard, Wilfred (ed.), *The Practice of Public Relations*, 3rd edition, Heinemann, London, 1988.

9. 'Gutenberg – and then?': The printed media

Stock, Raymond F., *Sales Literature for Industry*. McGraw-Hill, Maidenhead, 1976.

11. 'Let's put an ad in!': Media advertising

Wilmshurst, John, *The Fundamentals of Advertising*, Heinemann, London, 1985.
Hart, Norman and James O'Connor, *The Practice of Advertising*, 2nd edition, Heinemann, London, 1983.

12. 'The direct approach': Direct mail and similar methods

Baier, Martin, *Elements of Direct Marketing*, McGraw-Hill, Maidenhead, 1983.

14. 'Show and tell!': Exhibitions, fairs and shows

Powell, John and Patrick Quinn, *The Secrets of Successful Low-Budget Exhibitions*, Heinemann, London, 1988.

15. 'Face-to-face': Meetings, conferences, speeches

Huseman, Richard, Michael Galvin and David Prescott, *Business Communication, Strategies and Skills*. Harcourt, Brace, Jovanovich, Australia, 1988.

16. **'The synergy of an orchestra':** Combining the instruments

Hart, Norman, *Business To Business Advertising*, 3rd edition, Associated Business Press, London (re-titled and rewritten, 1984; first published, 1971).

17. **'It can't be done':** But it must

Churchill, Gilbert A., *Basic Marketing Research*, Holt, Rinehart & Winston, Eastbourne, 1987.

18. **'Structure out of chaos'**

Johnsson, Hans, *Mass Communication and Productivity in International Industrial Marketing*, Anderson & Lembke, Stockholm, 1979.

Lusterman, Seymor, *The Organization & Staffing of Corporate Public Affairs*, The Conference Board, New York, 1987.

Michell, Paul, *Advertising Agency–Client Relationships. Increasing their Effectiveness*. Routledge, Chapman & Hall, New York, 1988.

Pebbles, Dean M. and John K. Ryans Jr, *Management of International Advertising: A Marketing Approach*. Allyn & Bacon, Boston, 1984.

Roth, Robert F., *International Marketing Communications*, Crain Books, Chicago, 1982.

Index

Index

415

Index